Until recently, early recordings were regarded as little more than old-fashioned curiosities by musicians. Scholars and musicians are now beginning to realise their importance as historical documents which preserve the performances of Elgar, Rachmaninoff, Stravinsky and other composers, and of the musicians with whom they worked. In a more general way, recordings reveal the detailed performance practice of the early twentieth century and illustrate how styles have changed over the years. Early recordings also shed new light on nineteenth-century performance, but at the same time they highlight the limitations of our attempts to recreate the styles of the period before the development of recording.

In this fascinating and detailed study, Robert Philip argues that recordings of the early twentieth century provide an important, and hitherto neglected, resource in the history of musical performance. The book concentrates on aspects of performance which underwent the greatest change in the early twentieth century: rhythm, including flexibility of tempo, rubato and the treatment of rhythmic detail; the use of vibrato; and the employment of portamento by string players. The final chapters explore some of the implications of these changes, both for the study of earlier periods and for the understanding of our own attitudes to the music of the past.

The book contains informative tables, music examples and a discography and will be of interest to scholars and students of music history and performance practice as well as to musicians and collectors of historical recordings.

D1605363

Early recordings and musical style

Early recordings and musical style
Changing tastes in instrumental performance, 1900–1950

ROBERT PHILIP

CAMBRIDGE
UNIVERSITY PRESS

PUBLISHED BY THE PRESS SYNDICATE OF THE UNIVERSITY OF CAMBRIDGE
The Pitt Building, Trumpington Street, Cambridge, United Kingdom

CAMBRIDGE UNIVERSITY PRESS
The Edinburgh Building, Cambridge CB2 2RU, UK
40 West 20th Street, New York NY 10011–4211, USA
477 Williamstown Road, Port Melbourne, VIC 3207, Australia
Ruiz de Alarcón 13, 28014 Madrid, Spain
Dock House, The Waterfront, Cape Town 8001, South Africa

http://www.cambridge.org

First published 1992
Reprinted 1994
First paperback edition 2004

A catalogue record for this book is available from the British Library

Library of Congress cataloguing in publication data
Philip, Robert.
Early recordings and musical style: changing tastes in instrumental performance,
1900-1950 / Robert Philip.
p.   cm.
Includes bibliographical references.
Includes discography.
ISBN 0 521 23528 6 (hardback)
1. Performance practice (Music) – 20th century. 2. Style, Musical.
3. Sound recordings in musicology.
I. Title
ML457.P5 1992
784′.026′6 – dc20   91-30814 CIP

ISBN 0 521 23528 6 hardback
ISBN 0 521 60744 2 paperback

CONTENTS

Acknowledgments

My work on early recordings (that is, records of the 78 rpm period) dates back to an afternoon in Cambridge in 1968, when I was trying to find a research topic for a Ph.D. dissertation. I had formed a vague idea that the history of recording was an important subject which nobody was taking seriously, and I walked into the Music Faculty library to ask the advice of the ever-helpful curator, the late Charles Cudworth, who was then the only person in Cambridge who knew much about recordings. He led me into an inner room, gestured towards shelves of dusty 78 rpm records (many of them uncatalogued), and suggested that I work on those. That conversation led to a Ph.D. dissertation on changing orchestral style, which in turn supplied me with material for my first broadcasts on Radio 3, produced by Robert Layton. John Lade, head of the Gramophone Department at the BBC, then gave me many opportunities to appear on the Saturday morning 'Record Review' programme, and offered me my first series, 'The Long-Playing Era'. This, and other series which followed on Radio 3 and the World Service, were produced by Patrick Lambert, whose infectious enthusiasm for recordings has helped me in my work over the years. Other BBC producers with whom I have worked happily include Arthur Johnson, Christine Hardwick, Andrew Lyle, Anthony Cheevers and Nick Morgan. All of them have indirectly contributed to this book, because most of these broadcasts have been about recordings, old and new. This material has enabled me to develop that first vague idea, with which I embarked on my Ph.D., into a conviction that old recordings provide a vital key to our understanding of past and present performance practice.

My ideas on the relationship between early recordings and the more distant past, which form an important part of this book, were sparked off by Richard Abram, who had the provocative idea of inviting me to write an article for *Early Music* on Elgar's recordings. This was followed by an invitation from Stanley Sadie to write a chapter on early twentieth-century performance for the New Grove handbook, *Performance Practice*, and it was the preparation of this chapter which developed my interest in the written documents of the period. In a more general way, my colleagues in the Open University (where I work as a BBC producer) have enlightened me over the years about the nature of historical evidence and our understanding of it. This is what the book is fundamentally about, and I could not have written it without this broader perspective.

Acknowledgement is due to EMI for the photograph on the jacket, which shows the orchestra assembled for Elgar's first recording session in 1914 (contrary to what has been written elsewhere, it clearly does not show the musicians in their playing positions; they have been crammed into the field of view of the camera, with most of the music stands removed). The source of all other copyright material is given in the text and notes.

I had no idea when I first started writing this book how complex the subject would prove to be, and it has taken, on and off, fifteen years to write it. I must therefore thank not just one editor, but a succession of editors at Cambridge University Press: principally Penny Souster and her colleagues who saw the finished book through the press, but also her predecessors Rosemary Dooley and Claire Davies-Jones, who, often to my surprise, continued to think the book was worth waiting for. I hope they were right. My wife, Maria Lukianowicz, also bears considerable responsibility for its completion. I particularly remember a point about five years ago when I had finally decided that I had neither the material nor the competence to write it, and she persuaded me otherwise. Again, I hope she was right. Finally, I also hope that my daughters, Charlotte and Lara, will in the end see the point of what they have had to put up with for the last eleven and five years respectively, and in that hope I dedicate the book to them.

Introduction

Twenty years ago, music historians paid virtually no attention to early twentieth-century recordings. At best they were thought to have a period charm, but they certainly had nothing to teach the sophisticated modern musician about the history of performance. They were old enough to be old-fashioned, but too recent to be historical. Even now, the performing habits of the early twentieth century are, on the whole, habits which musicians would like to think they have outgrown. Scholars in the field of nineteenth-century performance have recently begun to take early recordings seriously, but study of them is in its infancy.

The reasons for examining early twentieth-century performance are compelling. In the first place, it is the earliest period from which the primary source material has survived. For earlier periods we have documents and instruments, but no performances (except as played by a few mechanical instruments, such as barrel organs). For the early twentieth century we have the performances themselves, often recorded by the composers or by musicians of whom they approved. We do not have to conjecture about how Elgar or Rachmaninoff or Stravinsky or Bartók performed their own works in the 1920s on the basis of documentary evidence; we *know* how they performed them, at least in the recording studio.

But the importance of early twentieth-century recordings extends far beyond composers' own performances. The recordings have preserved the general performance practice of the period in great detail, and the detail includes habits which are scarcely mentioned, if at all, in written documents. The recordings therefore shed light on the limitations of documentary evidence in any period, not just in the early twentieth century.

Early twentieth-century recordings have a particular relevance to the study of performance practice in the nineteenth century. Many of the musicians heard on early recordings were brought up in the late, or in some cases mid, nineteenth century, and their performing styles can be seen as remnants of nineteenth-century style.

Recordings also show how performance has gradually changed from the early twentieth century to our own time. They demonstrate how the practices of the late twentieth century, including those which we take entirely for granted, have evolved. The greatest value of this is that it forces us to question unspoken assumptions about modern taste, and about the ways in which we use it to justify our interpretation of earlier performance practice.

In the history of performance, the early twentieth century has an importance which has never applied to any period before it, and which will never occur again. It stands at the end of the era, stretching back over the centuries, in which knowledge of performance practice was imperfectly preserved in written documents, and at the beginning of the modern era, in which performance practice is (with minor limitations) preserved on recordings. The recordings of the early twentieth century are the link between these two eras, and they provide a valuable key to understanding both the development of modern performance practice, and the practices of earlier centuries.

This book therefore looks at aspects of early twentieth-century performance, as described in documents and preserved on records, and explores some of their implications. The potential scope is enormous, and the book makes no claim to cover the field. It is restricted to instrumental performance, apart from a few comparisons with singing, and it concentrates on the features of performance which have undergone the greatest change during the century – or to put it another way, the habits which make the performances on early recordings sound most old-fashioned to a modern listener.

The book is divided into four parts. The first three parts cover the three main topics:

 I Rhythm, which is divided into chapters on flexibility of tempo, tempo rubato, and the treatment of patterns of long and short notes (notably dotted rhythms);
 II Vibrato, divided into chapters on strings and woodwind;
III Portamento, both solo and orchestral.

Each chapter begins with the documentary evidence of the period: what did musicians recommend or claim, and how did their views change over the period? Then recordings are discussed, to show what musicians really did in practice. One of the themes running through the book is that musicians do not necessarily do what they say, or follow the advice of teachers or contemporary writers, and that in many cases it would be impossible to deduce everyday features of performance without the recordings. The importance of this for students of earlier periods is obvious.

Part IV explores some of the implications of these early twentieth-century habits and their evolution. Chapter 8 asks to what extent early twentieth-century recordings can be used to shed light on nineteenth-century practice. It may seem strange to put a chapter on the nineteenth century at the end of a book on the twentieth, rather than at the beginning, but the point is to show that we can only begin to get a realistic impression of nineteenth-century style if we start from a knowledge of early twentieth-century recordings and work backwards. The final chapter looks at some of the broader implications of the recordings. What sort of evidence are they? What do they tell us about the evolution of modern style, and about our ability to recreate the styles of the past? The conclusions will not satisfy those who like neat and tidy answers to questions of performance practice. But the whole point about early recordings is that they present us with real history, not history as we would like it to be.

PART I

RHYTHM

Introduction

The three chapters in Part I are about the most fundamental aspect of musical performance, rhythm, from the basic tempo, and the extent to which it changes within a movement, to the detailed relationship between one note and another.

Rhythmic habits have changed very greatly over the twentieth century. To a late twentieth-century listener, recordings from the early part of the century at first sound rhythmically strange in a number of ways. They seem hasty, slapdash and uncontrolled, in a manner which now sounds incompetent. But this impression is to do with style as well as competence. The impression of haste is caused partly by fast tempos, partly by a tendency to underemphasise rhythmic detail compared with modern performance. A slapdash impression is given by a more casual approach to note lengths and a more relaxed relationship between a melody and its accompaniment. Lack of control is suggested by flexibility of tempo, particularly a tendency to hurry in loud or energetic passages. All of these habits are generally avoided in modern performance, and rhythmic competence is now measured by the extent to which they have been successfully controlled.

Improving discipline has played some part in these changes. Orchestras, in particular, were often a great deal less rehearsed in the early years of the century than they are now, and the general level of rhythmic precision and unanimity was therefore lower. But when we find that the leading soloists and chamber groups also shared many of the rhythmic characteristics which now seem hasty, slapdash and uncontrolled, then it becomes clear that we are dealing with changes in style, not just in competence.

This section divides the most obvious characteristics of early twentieth-century rhythm into three different topics: first, the overall flexibility of tempo; then different kinds of tempo rubato, including detailed changes of pace, the use of tenutos, and the dislocation of a melody from its accompaniment ('melodic rubato'); and finally a flexible attitude to the relationship between long and short notes, particularly dotted rhythms.

1

Flexibility of tempo

Many writers from the end of the nineteenth century and the early years of the twentieth century recommend flexibility of tempo, and reject the idea that a piece of music should be played at a constant pace. Hugo Riemann (1897), writing on expression, advises,

First of all, in the matter of small changes of *tempo*, it may be remarked that hurrying implies intensification, and drawing back, the reverse; hence, as a rule, a slight urging, pressing forward is in place when the musical development becomes more intense, when it is positive; and, on the other hand, a tarrying, when it approaches the close. These changes must naturally be exceedingly minute in detached musical phrases, but can already become more important in a theme of a certain length; while for whole movements they are of such extent as to be seldom ignored in the notation.[1]

The singer David Ffrangcon-Davies (1906), in a book prefaced by Elgar, writes: 'An inelastic time-measurer, can never give us characteristic Bach or Beethoven, Mozart or Wagner. Metronome marks are never more than approximate at best.'[2] Arnold Dolmetsch (1916) argues that alterations of time are 'as old as music itself', and states, 'It is obvious that emotional feeling, if there be any, will cause the player to linger on particularly expressive notes and to hurry exciting passages.'[3]

Some writers are more cautious in their recommendation of tempo flexibility, and a number of them suggest that it is more appropriate in Romantic than in Classical music. The pianist Alfred Johnstone ([1910]) allows slight changes of tempo in Beethoven's compositions 'for the purpose of making clear the varied expressions of soul depicted in the music'. But it is only in modern music, from Chopin and Schumann onwards, that the varying of tempo has its full play: 'Capriciousness, then, is a characteristic of this modern emotional style; moods vary capriciously, and constant variations in the *tempo* is [sic] one of the means adopted to interpret these capricious moods.'[4] Similarly, the violinist Hans Wessely (1913), while cautioning against excessive freedom in Classical works, allows that 'More recent (French) compositions demand greater freedom of phrasing and time changes.'[5]

Some writers urge more general caution. Giovanni Clerici (1906), though allowing singers slight variations in pulse 'for the purposes of expression', objects to artists who 'interrupt the rhythm at any point they please', and writes that 'as a whole, the pulsation goes throughout a movement at a given rate'.[6] Sterling Mackinlay (1910) advises singers that changes in tempo 'must be made with the utmost discretion. To launch out into making perpetual little alterations in time throughout the piece, quickening here, slowing up there, without rhyme or reason, is the sign of a poor singer. The great artist is a great timist, and is found to interfere but little with the *tempo* of a piece. Consequently, when he does so, he produces a marked effect . . . '[7]

Despite these words of caution, there was a general acceptance in the early twentieth century of the need for flexibility of tempo. The ideas of Wagner and Bülow, who had advocated great flexibility, were still influential, and Wagner's essay *On Conducting* had been recently translated into English. Wagner states, 'We may consider it established that in classical music written in the later style *modification* of tempo is a *sine qua non*.'[8] By 'classical music in the later style' Wagner means music from Beethoven onwards, including his own.

In the early years of the twentieth century, the leading advocate of Wagner and Bülow's kind of flexibility was Mahler. He is reported by Natalie Bauer-Lechner to have said,

All the most important things – the tempo, the total conception and structuring of a work – are almost impossible to pin down. For here we are concerned with something living and flowing that can never be the same even twice in succession. That is why metronome markings are inadequate and almost worthless; for unless the work is vulgarly ground out in barrel-organ style, the tempo will already have changed by the end of the second bar.'[9]

Bauer-Lechner heard Mahler demonstrate at the piano the importance of tempo fluctuation, giving among other examples the beginning of the variations in the last movement of Beethoven's 'Eroica' Symphony (bar 12ff, pizzicato):

Mahler sang the passage as the bad conductors perform it, and said: 'They mistake this for the theme . . . and consequently take it far too quickly, instead of realizing its true meaning. Beethoven is trying it out meditatively – then playfully – he is learning to walk – he gets into his stride gradually. That's why the latter part of it – like an answer – should follow rather more quickly.'[10]

Mahler went rather beyond most of his contemporaries in his flexibility of tempo, as some of the remarks of hostile critics show. In Beethoven's Overture *Leonora* No. 3, Mahler habitually started the Allegro slowly, only reaching the main tempo at the forte repetition of the theme, and he accelerated in a similar way at the beginning of the presto coda. Mahler wrote from London, 'Apropos my performance of Fidelio – especially the *Leonora* overture was violently attacked and condemned by half the critics here.'[11] By contrast, one critic found this interpretation 'an accomplished masterpiece',[12] and it also met with the approval of Dukas. Hanslick praised Mahler's interpretation of the 'Eroica' Symphony,[13] and his performances of Wagner, which some critics found full of 'arbitrary nuances', others praised for 'the natural and measured changes of tempo'.[14] When Richard Strauss visited Mahler in Leipzig for a performance of his Symphony in F minor, he remarked that Mahler 'seemed to me a remarkably intelligent musician and conductor, one of the few modern conductors to understand "modifications of tempo". On every subject he expressed excellent points of view, especially concerning Wagnerian tempos (unlike some of the accredited Wagner conductors of today).'[15]

Mahler's tempo modifications included not only slowing down for passages of great significance, but also speeding up to pass over passages requiring less emphasis. Bauer–Lechner writes,

The most extraordinary thing ... is that, although Mahler has every *cantilena* passage very *sostenuto*, never rushing like other conductors, his performances are usually shorter than theirs. (In a Wagner opera, this can sometimes make as much as half an hour's difference!) 'That', Mahler told me, 'is because most conductors don't understand how to distinguish what is unimportant from what is important. They put the same emphasis on everything, instead of passing lightly over what is less significant.[16]

Mahler also seems to have expected more fluctuation of tempo in his own music than is made explicit in his scores. The published score of his Second Symphony (1897) contains a number of indications of changing mood, some of which suggest a change of tempo. But metronome markings are given only for the beginning of the first movement, in a note to the conductor. Here the basic tempo for the movement is given as ♩ = 84–92, apart from the opening figure on cellos and basses which is to be played ♩ = 144. Mahler's autograph score gives additional metronome markings later in the symphony, of which some add substantially to the indications in the published score, and others actually contradict them. For example at figure 2 of the first movement, where there is no marking in the published score, the autograph gives a rise in tempo to ♩ = 100. The third movement begins in the autograph at ♩. = 52, and rises to ♩. = 58 at bar 14. In the published score this is contradicted by 'sehr gemächlich, nicht eilen' (very leisurely, do not hurry).[17]

Contemporary comment on Mahler's conducting is unusually detailed, which is fortunate because he did not survive into the period of orchestral recordings. Comments on the conducting of Richard Strauss and Elgar, who did record their own works, are much less detailed than comments on Mahler, though, as examples from records will show, both conductors often used much more tempo fluctuation than is indicated in their own or other composers' scores. Strauss's approval of Mahler's tempo fluctuations has already been quoted. Leo Wurmser remembers a passage in *Der Rosenkavalier* where he first heard Strauss in the early 1930s suddenly change tempo (Act III, at the climax after the end of the trio, 4/4 D flat major):

Here Strauss, who had considerably broadened the end of the trio according to the metronome marks, suddenly dashed ahead in a big *stringendo* from the second bar onwards; then he remained in the quicker tempo, and slowed down again with the diminuendo, so as to be back in the broad tempo when the tonic is regained and the oboe starts its solo phrase. He invariably did this, although there is no indication of it in the score; yet I have never heard anyone else do it, not even Clemens Krauss.'[18]

On the other hand, Wurmser remembers rehearsals for the first performance of *Arabella*, in which Krauss had inserted many flexibilities of tempo for dramatic effect. When Strauss took over the rehearsals he removed most of these additions, often commenting 'Simply. In time.'[19]

Elgar is reported to have complained about performances of his music: 'Beethoven and Brahms ... wrote practically nothing but *allegro* and *andante*, and there seems to be no difficulty. I've done all I can to help players, but my efforts appear only to confuse them.'[20] The principal source of his dissatisfaction seems to have been inflexibility of tempo, judging from the following comment: 'I only know that my things are performed – when they go as *I* like – elastically and mystically people grumble – when they are conducted squarely and sound like a wooden box these people are pleased to say it's better.'[21] But Elgar's comments about performance are contradictory. Ernest Newman remembers, 'More than once he protested to me that all his music required was to be left alone to say what it had to say in its own way: the expression was *in* the music and it was not only unnecessary but harmful for the conductor to add to it an expression of his own.'[22] Without recordings it would be difficult to know what to make of these contradictions. Elgar's scores, though full of detailed expression marks, contain few specific indications of tempo changes, and it is only when we turn to his own performances that we discover the full extent of his tempo flexibility.

The scores of Sibelius's symphonies do not contain metronome markings, but Sibelius's own metronome indications were published in a Finnish journal during World War II.[23] They reveal the full extent of tempo changes which Sibelius had in mind, but only partly indicated in the scores. Notable among these are gradual accelerandos in the Fifth and Seventh Symphonies. In the first movement of the Fifth Symphony (1915, rev. 1916, 1919), four tempo indications are printed in the score between pages 30 and 66 (the end of the movement), beginning with the instruction, 'Allegro moderato (*ma poco a poco stretto*)' (see table 1). What is not clear from the score is how long the instruction 'poco a poco stretto' is to be applied. Is it to extend only over a few pages, with the subsequent instructions causing sudden increases in tempo later on, or does it apply to the whole of the rest of the movement, with the subsequent instructions simply marking stages in the accelerando? Sibelius's metronome markings show that he intends a continuous acceleration throughout, and he asks for a gradual change between each of the tempos. At the time the score was published, Sibelius did not regard it as necessary to indicate this accelerando in detail. The instruction 'poco a poco stretto', with occasional reminders later, was clear enough to any conductor brought up in

Table 1. *Sibelius, Symphony No. 5, first movement*

Cue	Indication in score	Metronome marking
p. 30 (5th bar of N)	allegro moderato (*ma poco a poco stretto*)	𝅗𝅥. = 80
p. 39 (D)		𝅗𝅥. = 96
p. 49 (K)	vivace molto	𝅗𝅥. = 104
p. 52 (M)		𝅗𝅥. = 112
p. 54 (N)		𝅗𝅥. = 126
p. 60 (5th bar of Q)	presto	𝅗𝅥. = 138
p. 64 (16 bars before S)	più presto	—

the performance practice of the time. What is striking to a late twentieth-century musician is the extent of the accelerando. 𝅗𝅥. = 138 is extremely fast for the final Presto by modern standards. (Sibelius gives no marking for the più presto on p. 64, which he presumably intends to be even faster.) Even Sibelius's collaborator Kajanus, in his 1932 recording, adopts a more moderate pace for the final section. The Seventh Symphony (1924) contains similar examples where a gradual accelerando is intended by Sibelius, but not indicated unambiguously in the score. Recordings of these two symphonies, and Sibelius's markings in No. 7, are discussed later in this chapter.

After the first performance of *The Planets* in 1918, Holst wrote to the conductor Adrian Boult about 'Mars': 'You made it wonderfully clear – in fact *everything* came out clearly that wonderful morning. Now could you make more row? And work up more sense of climax? Perhaps hurry certain bits?'[24]

Marguerite Long reports that one of Fauré's favourite maxims, which he repeated often, was 'Nuance is the thing ... not a change of movement.'[25] However, one of the words which she uses most frequently when trying to convey Fauré's requirements is 'suppleness'. Writing on the metronome she says, 'There should be sufficient suppleness in the fluctuation of the phrasing, a thing which wavers, that it is impossible to advise inexorable rigidity throughout a piece by marking the time ... '[26] On the other hand, in her notes on the fourth Nocturne, Long writes: 'Fauré was very sparing with the expression "appassionato" so as not to give it its full range. One should play here [bar 52] "full steam ahead" but not brutally.'[27] About the Ballade, bar 94, she writes, 'do not trust the introduction of the marking "un poco più mosso", since the music here should correspond with the passage which precedes it'.[28] It is difficult to know how much faith to put in such comments, since it is impossible to separate Fauré's own views from those of Long herself. She does clearly suggest, however, that Fauré allowed more 'interpretation' of his music than Debussy or Ravel. Long quotes Ravel as saying 'I do not ask for my music to be interpreted, but only for it to be played', and she observes that in their markings in the text 'Debussy and Ravel are imperiously exacting, while Fauré is just as vague.'[29] Subtlety of expression is required, rather than obvious tempo changes. Writing about the second movement of Ravel's Sonatine, Long observes, 'As in the preceding pages one notes the frequency of the indication *rallentando*. With Ravel this seldom means a sense of flagging: the effect of *rallentando* must come from nuance and from sonority rather than from a real change of speed.'[30]

Klemperer, remembering the 'energy and lightness' of Bartók's piano playing, writes, 'He played with great freedom, that was what was so wonderful.'[31] This description alone does not explain what sort of freedom was involved, but Bartók's liking for flexibility in others is suggested by a comment on the Czech conductor Václav Tálich in 1920, in a programme of Smetana, Suk and Dvořák: 'the conductor, V. Talich, recreated the compositions with wonderful plasticity, understanding and orchestral mastery'.[32]

Schoenberg's comments on tempo and flexibility are, like Elgar's, contradictory. In an essay 'About metronome markings' (1926) Schoenberg asks conductors to respect them, adding,

Anyone who has learned at his own expense what a conductor of genius is capable of, once he has his own idea of a work, will no longer favour giving him the slightest scrap more freedom. For instance, if such a man has got into his mind a 'powerful build-up', which means he has found a place where he can begin too slowly and another where he can finish too fast, then nothing can hinder him any longer in giving rein to his temperament.[33]

This sounds like thorough condemnation of the flexibility practised by Wagner, Von Bülow, Mahler and others. And yet, twenty years later, when the prevailing fashion had changed, Schoenberg expressed longing for the old days when musicians understood the essential flexibility of tempo, and he attributed the modern stiffness to 'the style of playing primitive dance music'.[34]

Two members of string quartets confirm that most contemporary composers accepted tempo fluctuations. Egon Kornstein of the Hungarian Quartet writes (1922) of his experience of playing works to their composers – Bartók, Kodály, Dohnányi, Leo Weiner, Debussy, Ravel and Rachmaninoff – 'each to whom we have played has been contented with the principal *tempo* when the principal theme was rightly phrased; consequently also with the changes of time within the movement demanded by the phrasing of a transition motive, repetition, or a moment of increased emotion. *Footnote*: We have always found that the metronome indications can only be treated as hints, and to stick to them rigidly is tantamount to killing the composition.'[35] Adolfo Betti, leader of the Flonzaley Quartet, states (1923): 'I don't believe an author can assign an absolutely exact pace to his work', and, like Kornstein, Betti writes of the limitations of a composer's expressive instructions: 'How often ... after having tried every possible other way, one is obliged to do exactly the reverse of the literal indications of *tempo* or dynamics in order to get the effect the author actually wants!'[36]

Ravel's view, that he did not want his music to be 'interpreted', has already been quoted. The most famous attack on the freedom of the interpreter was made by Stravinsky in his *Autobiography* (1936), writing about the first performance of *Petrushka* in 1911 under Pierre Monteux:

He knew his job thoroughly and was able to achieve a very clean and finished execution of my score. I ask no more of a conductor, for any other attitude on his part immediately turns into *interpretation*, a thing I have a horror of. The *interpreter* of necessity can think of nothing but *interpretation*, and thus takes on the garb of a translator, *tranduttore-traditore*; this is an absurdity in music, and for the interpreter it is a source of vanity inevitably leading to the most ridiculous megalomania.[37]

The correct observation of his metronome markings was very important to Stravinsky. When other conductors were to perform his works in the 1930s, Stravinsky urged them to attend to his metronome markings, and to check them with his own recordings.[38]

Stravinsky's scores contain traces of the battle against conductors who took liberties with his tempos. The works which were most often performed (and recorded) during the 1920s and 1930s were the ballet scores of 1910–11, *The Firebird* and *Petrushka*. Both scores were revised by Stravinsky in the 1940s, and as well as changes in instrumentation, the revised scores contain changes in expressive and tempo markings which seem designed to limit the freedom to which Stravinsky had objected in early twentieth-century conductors. There are a large number of these changes in *Petrushka*, some relating to details, others to broad tempo changes (see table 2). Similar examples can be found in the revisions of *The Firebird* and *The Rite of Spring*. However, as later examples will show, Stravinsky's recordings from the 1920s and 1930s reveal that he was in practice not quite as rigorous in his control of tempo at this period as his scores and comments would suggest.

Among conductors, the leading pioneers against the tradition of flexible tempo were Weingartner and Toscanini. Already in 1895, Weingartner attacked the followers of Bülow as 'tempo-rubato conductors' with their 'continual alterations and dislocations of the tempo ... in no way justified by any marks of the composer'.[39] Toscanini's ideas on control of tempo were influential on conductors later in the century. George Szell wrote that Toscanini 'wiped out the arbitrariness of the post-romantic interpreters. He did away with the meretricious tricks and the thick incrustation of the interpretive nuances that had been piling up for decades.'[40] As examples later in this chapter will demonstrate, neither Weingartner nor Toscanini were quite as strict in their control of tempo as some descriptions of them, and some of their own statements, would suggest.

Table 2. *Stravinsky, Petrushka*

Cue number (as in 1947 revision)	1911 score	1947 revision
beginning	♩ = 138	♩ = 138
after fig. 4	*poco a poco accel*	no marking
fig. 13 (and similar)	*stringendo* ♩. ♩ = 46 [i.e. ♩ = 161]	♪ = ♪
fig. 16 (and similar)	*come prima* ♩ = 138	no marking
fig. 60 (flute cadenza)	*ad lib* with pauses	values written out
fig. 81 onwards	*poco meno–pochiss.accel–a tempo–rall.*	*meno mosso*
fig. 98	♩ = 76	♩ = 76
fig. 100	♩ = 108 *furioso*	no marking
fig. 120	♩ = 144 *feroce stringendo*	♩ = 126
fig. 121	♩ = 112 *meno mosso pesante*	no marking
figs. 128–9	*stringendo–a tempo–stringendo*	no marking
fig. 153	♩ = 100 *agitato*	♩ = 100 *agitato ma tempo di rigore*
fig. 250	no marking	*tempo di rigore, non accelerando!*

In England, Henry Wood was noted for his straightforward attitude to tempo, though not always admired for it. A critic wrote of Wood's performance of Tchaikovsky's Symphony No. 5 in 1900,

Mr Wood and his orchestra were at their best in this Symphony, but why the conductor should completely ignore the composer's distinct direction, '*molto più tranquillo*' when attacking the yearning syncopated subject in the first *Allegro*, is a mystery. Those who heard Herr Nikisch's performance in the same hall some years ago will remember the great effect he produced with just this theme by taking it at a slower speed. Mr Wood scampers over it in feverish haste.[41]

As a number of examples given above have suggested, composers' scores are of only limited use as evidence for or against tempo changes. Mahler, Sibelius, and Elgar all seem to have had detailed tempo changes in mind, but did not indicate them in the published scores. Since flexibility of tempo was a general practice of the time, these composers presumably took it for granted that their scores would be treated in the usual way by their contemporaries, without the need for elaborate instructions. Similarly, early twentieth-century editions of earlier works provide only occasional evidence on the subject of tempo changes. Recommendations of tempo changes are to be found, for example, in a few of the many editions of Beethoven's Piano Sonatas. Bülow's detailed metronome markings were published in an edition by Lebert in 1902, together with a preface justifying the tempo changes but warning against 'the exaggerations

Table 3. *Beethoven, Piano Sonatas, tempo indications*

No. 21 in C major, Op. 53 ('Waldstein'), first movement

	Bar 1	Bar 35	Bar 43	Bar 50	Bar 54
Bülow (1902)	♩ = 168	152		160	168
Macpherson (1915)	♩ = 160–8	144–52		160	
Schnabel (1935)	♩ = etwa 176	160	152	160	168

No. 23 in F minor, Op. 57 ('Appassionata'), first movement

	Bar 1	Bar 24	Bar 34	Bar 35	Bar 47	Bar 51
Bülow (1902)	♩. = 126			112		126
Macpherson (1915)	♩. = 120			112		120
Schnabel (1935)	♩. = etwa 120	126	120	112	116	

so popular in modern playing'. Editions by Buonamici (1903) and Lamond (1923) reprint many of Bülow's indications, and editions by Macpherson (1909–23) and Schnabel (1935) give suggestions which, though not the same as Bülow's, often indicate a similar range of tempo (see table 3). Eric Blom (1938) takes a more cautious approach, and argues that slowing down is more acceptable than hurrying: 'Elasticity in the life of music, and an elastic will stretch, but cannot be pushed together. In other words, and words applied to Beethoven, the pace of any movement of his, slow or fast, can often be slightly spread out with advantage, whereas it can scarcely ever be tightened or hurried with anything but an untidy, scatter-brained effect.'[42] As the examples from records in the following section show, Blom's caution against hurrying is an indication of a changing fashion by the late 1930s.

In general, written sources suggest that the changing of tempo within movements was practised and accepted by the majority of performers and composers in the early twentieth century. Some writers urge caution, others do not. A number of musicians stand out against the general acceptance of tempo fluctuation, notably Weingartner, Toscanini and Stravinsky, and from the viewpoint of the late twentieth century we can see these as pioneers of a stricter attitude to tempo which was to influence a later generation of musicians. Once again, however, we are left feeling that the written sources provide as many questions as answers. What exactly do writers mean when they talk about fluctuations of tempo? Only occasionally do writers or editors go into detail, and provide metronome markings, and without them one cannot really know what degree of freedom is being recommended. As in other aspects of performance practice, it is only recordings which demonstrate what performers really did.

Recordings demonstrate that, in any movement containing contrasts of mood and tension, it was the general practice in the early twentieth century to underline the contrasts by changes of tempo. Lyrical and reflective passages would be played more slowly and energetic passages more quickly. This section illustrates this practice in a variety of works from the standard repertoire, ending with a number of examples in which twentieth-century works are performed by the composers themselves.

Beethoven, Violin Concerto, first movement

	bars 1–9	bars 28–41	bars 43–50
Kreisler, cond. L. Blech (rec. 1926)	♩ = 108	128	112
Szigeti, cond. Walter (rec. 1932)	96	132	112
Huberman, cond. Szell (rec. 1936)	108	120	116
Kreisler, cond. Barbirolli (rec. 1936)	108	120	116
Kulenkampff, cond. Schmidt-Isserstedt (rec. 1936)	108	120	116
Heifetz, cond. Toscanini (rec. 1940)	116	124	124
Menuhin, cond. Klemperer (rec. 1966)	104	108	104
I. Oistrakh, cond. D. Oistrakh (rec. c. 1971)	100	104	108
Szeryng, cond. Haitink (rec. 1973)	108	112	110
Grumiaux, cond. C. Davis (rec. 1974)	96	112	110
Zukerman, cond. Barenboim (rec. c. 1977)	104	112	112

No changes of tempo are indicated in the score during bars 1–50, but most of the recordings from 1926–40 have substantial changes of pace during the passage. Changes of tempo in the modern recordings are generally less noticeable.

Of the six old recordings, the one which comes nearest to a constant tempo through bars 1–50 is conducted by Toscanini, and this supports his reputation as a pioneer of firm control of tempo. The most striking feature of the other five old recordings is the considerable increase in tempo at bar 28. This increase is greatest in the two oldest recordings, conducted by Blech and Walter, and these two performances also have the greatest drop in tempo at bar 43. The five modern recordings have a slight increase in tempo at bar 28, and all but one have a barely perceptible relaxation of tempo at bar 43. Only in the performance conducted by Davis, however, does the increase in tempo at bar 28 approach the increases of the old recordings, and in all the modern recordings the maximum tempo at bars 28–41 is substantially slower than the maximum tempo of the old recordings. In none of the modern recordings is the drop of tempo at bar 43 as great as in the two oldest recordings.

This is typical of comparisons between pre-war and modern recordings. Performances of the orchestral, chamber and solo repertoire from the 1920s and (to a decreasing extent) 1930s very often show substantially greater fluctuations of tempo within movements than late twentieth-century recordings. The most striking differences are in the speeding up of energetic passages. As in Beethoven's Violin Concerto, the early recordings very often reach much faster maximum tempos than the modern recordings. The lyrical passages are not consistently slower than in modern performances, but the high speed of the vigorous passages creates greater contrast. Indeed, in the above examples, bars 43–50 are in most cases slower in the modern than in the old recordings. But the sense of relaxation into those bars is greater in the old recordings because of the faster tempo of the preceding passage. The G minor passage in the development section of this movement (bar 331ff.) makes a similar point. Modern performances, like those of the 1920s and 1930s, slow down substantially at these bars. The difference is in the tempos of the surrounding passages, which are vigorous in the old performances, and more restrained in the modern versions.

Rapid recovery to a fast tempo after slow passages is characteristic of the old recordings throughout this movement. These changes of tempo underline the contrast between the generally reflective nature of the solo sections and the more march-like character of the orchestral sections, so that a firm sense of forward motion is renewed whenever an orchestral tutti is reached. In modern performances the tempos of the orchestral sections are closer to the slower speeds of the solo passages, so that the contrasts in character between solo and tutti are less clearly defined than in the old recordings. It could be argued that the traditional drop in tempo at bar 331 formed a logical part of the tempo structure in the old recordings, but that in modern performances, which lack the counterbalancing fast tempos of the orchestral sections, this sudden relaxation of tempo stands out as an anachronism.

A number of other works contain passages which are still traditionally taken slowly. They include Dvořák's Symphony No. 9 ('From the New World'), where the second subject of the first movement (solo flute) is usually taken substantially slower than the basic tempo of the movement, and Brahms's Piano Concerto No. 2, the opening bars of which are often played at approximately half the eventual tempo of the movement. In both of these examples, tempos elsewhere in the movement used to be substantially faster in the 1920s and 1930s than in most modern performances, perhaps creating a more logical balance between fast and slow passages.

Traditional slow passages of this kind are the exception rather than the rule in modern performances. In most works, the range of tempo within movements is much narrower in modern performances than in those of the 1920s and 1930s. Beethoven's 'Kreutzer' Sonata provides a typical example.

Beethoven, Violin Sonata in A major, Op. 47 ('Kreutzer'), first movement

	bars 45–88	bar 91
Sammons/Murdoch (rec. 1927)	♩ = 160	112
Thibaud/Cortot (rec. 1929)	156	108
Huberman/Friedman (rec. c. 1930)	164	108
Kulenkampff/Kempff (rec. 1934)	152	108
Y. and H. Menuhin (rec. c. 1935)	132	104
Kreisler/Rupp (rec. 1936)	148	120
Szigeti/Bartók (rec. 1940)	160	108
Busch/Serkin (rec. 1941)	172	152
Szigeti/Arrau (rec. 1944)	160	114
Heifetz/Smith (rec. 1960)	160	128
Menuhin/Kempff (rec. 1970)	132	108
Perlman/Ashkenazy (rec. 1973)	148	120

The E major theme at bar 91 is marked *dolce*, but there is no specific indication of a change of tempo until the end of the theme, which is marked *adagio* at bar 115 with a pause at bar 116. 'Tempo I' resumes at bar 117.

The comparison between modern and old performances in this movement is not entirely consistent, but the general difference is clear: most of the old recordings make a much greater change of tempo into bar 91 than the modern recordings. Three of the old recordings make an unusually small change of tempo for their date. Kreisler and Rupp make exactly the same change of tempo as Perlman and Ashkenazy forty years later; Menuhin's tempos in 1935 are very similar to those in his 1970 recording; and Adolf Busch's change of tempo is unusually small even by modern standards. The other six recordings made between 1927 and 1944 all make a very great change of tempo into the E major theme, unlike the modern performances, which relax the tempo slightly but avoid making such an obvious change of pace. Once again, the wide range of tempo in the old recordings is created not by very slow tempos after the relaxation, but by very fast tempos before it. Heifetz, known for his fast tempos throughout his career, begins at ♩ = 160, an unusually fast starting tempo compared with most other modern performances. Of the old performances, however, more than half have starting tempos of ♩ = 160 or more, and only two (Kreisler and Menuhin) are substantially slower. Menuhin's starting tempo of ♩ = 132, which among modern performances is merely on the slow side, was in 1935 quite exceptionally slow.

Chopin, Piano Sonata No. 3 in B minor, first movement

	bar 1	bar 31	bar 41
Grainger (rec. 1925)	♩ = 108	124	72
Cortot (rec. 1933)	108	148	c. 84
Lipatti (rec. 1947)	120	128	80
Kempff (rec. c. 1959)	112	112	96
Rubinstein (rec. 1959/61)	104	120	84
Perahia (rec. c. 1974)	100	108	88
Barenboim (rec. c. 1975)	112	112	92
Ax (rec. c. 1975)	108	108	96

Chopin's Sonata in B minor provides a similar comparison between pre-war and modern practice. The first movement is marked *Allegro maestoso*, with no specific change of pace indicated in the entire movement. In the opening section of the movement, however, some players speed up at bar 31, and all pianists relax the pace into the second subject (marked *sostenuto*) at bar 41. The two earliest performances, by Grainger and Cortot, have the widest ranges of tempo. Of the two, Cortot has the greater increase of speed at bar 31, and Grainger has the greater decrease of speed at bar 41. None of the later recordings has as wide a tempo range. Rubinstein comes closest to it, with an increase at bar 31 as great as Grainger's, but with a much smaller change of speed at bar 41. All the other pianists are much more restrained in tempo at bar 31, and three of them make no increase at that point at all, although they are all flexible in detail. The drop of tempo at bar 41 is also much smaller in the modern versions than in the two earliest performances. The maximum tempo, at bar 31ff., is also faster in the early than in the modern performances, with only Rubinstein approaching the tempo of Grainger. Cortot, always a volatile pianist, has by far the fastest tempo at bar 31. Lipatti's 1947 performance also reaches a high tempo at bar 31, but his starting tempo is unusually fast so that the increase in tempo is only slight.

The scherzo of the same sonata also has no tempo change marked within the movement, but all pianists slow down for the trio at bar 61.

	bar 1	bar 61
Grainger	♩. = 120	60
Cortot	116	72
Lipatti	112	78
Kempff	92	76
Rubinstein	112	80
Perahia	96	80
Barenboim	116–20	64
Ax	116	84

The great change of tempo in the two earliest recordings is equalled only by Barenboim among the modern players. The starting tempos of the earliest two recordings are also as fast as in the fastest of the modern performances.

Great flexibility of tempo is found in pre-war recordings in a wide range of music. It is perhaps least surprising in Chopin and other late nineteenth-century music, because this is the period of music in which the greatest flexibility is allowed in modern performances – though, as the examples from Chopin's Sonata in B minor have indicated, modern flexibility tends to be less extreme, and less inclined to acceleration, than pre-war flexibility. The earlier examples from Beethoven's Violin Concerto and 'Kreutzer' Sonata have shown similar differences between old and modern practice. More surprisingly for modern listeners, Haydn and Mozart were in pre-war performances also treated with much greater volatility of tempo than is now considered appropriate.

Mozart, Symphony No. 40 in G minor, first movement

	bar 1	bar 28	bar 44
Berlin State Opera Orchestra, cond. Strauss (rec. c. 1926)	♩ = 112	116	100
Royal Opera House Orchestra, cond. Sargent (rec. c. 1928)	116	120	110
Berlin State Opera Orchestra, cond. Walter (rec. c. 1930)	90	108	92
London Philharmonic Orchestra, cond. Koussevitsky (rec. c. 1935)	92	120	108
London Philharmonic Orchestra, cond. Beecham (rec. 1937)	104	108	104
London Philharmonic Orchestra, cond. Kleiber (rec. c. 1950)	108	112	106
London Symphony Orchestra, cond. Krips (rec. c. 1953)	96	96	94
London Symphony Orchestra, cond. C. Davis (rec. 1961)	108	112	104
Columbia Symphony Orchestra, cond. Walter (rec. c. 1963)	96	100	84
English Chamber Orchestra, cond. Britten (rec. 1968)	108	108	98
Berlin Philharmonic Orchestra, cond. Karajan (rec. 1971)	104	104	104
Vienna Philharmonic Orchestra, cond. Böhm (rec. 1977)	88	92	92

Of the early recordings, Beecham's is the most straightforward performance, with only a very slight increase and decrease of tempo at bars 28 and 44. The other four pre-war recordings have a substantial relaxation of tempo into the second subject at bar 44, and those conducted by Walter and Koussevitsky also speed up considerably at the *forte* passage from bar 28. Koussevitsky's tempo is extremely volatile throughout the movement. His opening tempo ♩ = 92 is an average over the first sixteen bars. He takes the first three bars even more slowly, at about ♩ = 84, and he returns abruptly to this tempo at the repeat. Strauss and Sargent increase only slightly in tempo in bar 28, but their starting tempos are already the fastest of all the recordings, old or modern. Most of the modern recordings control the tempo more strictly, with little or no increase or decrease of tempo. Britten does relax more than most into bar 44, and Walter's modern performance has a substantial decrease of tempo at this point, which is exceptional among modern recordings. It is significant, however, that even Walter resists a noticeable acceleration at bar 28 in his modern recording, although in his pre-war performance he had increased the tempo substantially. Again this illustrates the point that in modern performance slowing down is more acceptable than speeding up, but in pre-war performance both were equally acceptable.

Similar tempo fluctuation in Mozart is found in many chamber and solo performances of the 1920s and 1930s.

Mozart, Piano Sonata in D, K.576, first movement

	bar 1	bar 16	bar 41
Kathleen Long (rec. c. 1929)	♩. = 88 (average)	100	76 (average)
Eileen Joyce (rec. c. 1941)	100	96	84

The performance by Kathleen Long is very characteristic of its period, with semiquaver passages almost invariably speeding up, and simpler, lyrical passages slowing down. Her tempo is flexible in detail, not just in the long term. The average tempo of the first few bars is ♩. = 88, but Long alternates between different tempos for each of the first four phrases: bars 1–2 are played at about ♩. = 100, bars 3–4 slow down to about ♩. = 84, and the same happens over bars 5–8. Similarly the second subject (bars 41ff) is played with alternating slower and faster phrases. Joyce's performance is much more straightforward. She begins at ♩. = 100, settling to ♩. = 96 by bar 16, and this remains the basic tempo to which she returns throughout the movement. The second subject at bar 41 is a little slower, but the change in tempo is much less abrupt than in Long's performance. Similar comparisons apply in the second movement of the sonata (Adagio), in which Long's tempo is very flexible, but Joyce's is carefully controlled.

The examples given so far in this chapter have included several pre-war performers who were, for their period, unusually strict in their control of tempo: Toscanini (Beethoven, Violin Concerto), Heifetz (Beethoven, Violin Concerto and 'Kreutzer' Sonata), Adolf Busch (Beethoven, 'Kreutzer' Sonata) and Beecham (Mozart, Symphony No. 40). Although Toscanini's reputation for tempo control is, in general, borne out by his recordings, his view of tempo was rather more complicated than his reputation for strictness might suggest. In some works, Toscanini's pre-war and post-war performances are very similar in tempo, for example Beethoven's Symphonies No. 4 (BBC Symphony Orchestra, rec. 1939 and NBC Symphony Orchestra, rec. 1951) and No. 6 (BBC Symphony Orchestra, rec. 1937 and NBC Symphony Orchestra, rec. 1952). But some recordings suggest that Toscanini in his late recordings became stricter in tempo in Classical works, in accordance with the general trend of the period, but at the same time became freer in tempo in Romantic works. In accordance with post-war taste, however, these fluctuations tended to favour relaxation of tempo rather than acceleration.

Mozart, Symphony No. 35 in D ('Haffner'), first movement

	bar 1	bar 19	bar 48
Philharmonic Symphony Orchestra of New York, cond. Toscanini (rec. 1929)	$\downarrow$ = 72	82	72
NBC Symphony Orchestra, cond. Toscanini (rec. 1946)	76	82	82

The earlier of these two recordings is much freer in tempo than the later one. The 1946 performance accelerates very slightly at the first continuous semiquaver passage (bar 19), but then remains constant in tempo. The 1929 performance begins more slowly, with additional rallentandos at bars 6–7 and 8–9. At the next tutti it soon reaches the fast tempo of the 1946 performance, but then relaxes in tempo at the next *piano* passage (bar 48). There are similar differences between the two performances in the slow movement.

Brahms, *Tragic Overture*

	bar 2	bar 106	bar 210
BBC Symphony Orchestra, cond. Toscanini (rec. 1937)	$\downarrow$ = 84	76	$\downarrow$ = 70
NBC Symphony Orchestra, cond. Toscanini (rec. 1953)	72	60	64

Tempos in the 1953 performance are generally slower and more flexible than in the 1937 performance. The later version slows down more into the second subject (bar 106), and the central section of the overture (bar 210, *molto più moderato*) is also much slower in the later than in the earlier performance.

Brahms, *Variations on a Theme by Haydn*, Variation 3

	bar 88	bar 108	bar 116 (as bar 88)
Philharmonic Symphony Orchestra of New York, cond. Toscanini (rec. 1936)	$\downarrow$ = 76	c. 70	76
NBC Symphony Orchestra, cond. Toscanini (rec. 1952)	76	c. 64	72

As in the *Tragic Overture*, tempos in several of the variations are slower and more flexible in the later than in the earlier recording. In variation 3, the opening tempo is identical in the two performances, but the second half of the variation (bar 108) opens with a very slight easing of tempo in the 1936 performance, and an expansive *meno mosso* in the 1952 performance, with a recovery of tempo at the recapitulation (bar 116). These fluctuations occur again at the repeat of the second half.

Weingartner's objection to 'tempo-rubato conductors' was quoted at the beginning of this chapter. Like Toscanini, Weingartner in recordings from the 1920s and 1930s often shows a narrower range of tempo within movements than most of his contemporaries. But he too was sometimes more flexible in tempo than his writings and reputation might suggest.

Beethoven, Symphony No. 3 ('Eroica'), second movement

	bar 1–	bar 69	bar 114
Vienna Philharmonic Orchestra, cond. Weingartner (rec. 1936)	♪ = 56	82	92–6

In the first movement of this symphony, Weingartner's tempo is slightly flexible, but hardly more so than in some modern performances. In the second movement, however, his changes of tempo go far beyond those heard in most pre-war and modern performances, in contradiction of Weingartner's own recommendations. In his book on Beethoven's symphonies (1897) he suggests a tempo of ♪ = 66–72, and specifically warns against hurrying at the *maggiore* (bar 69) or in the fugal section (bar 114).[43] Weingartner's range of tempo in his recording of this movement is ♪ = 56–96, with both the *maggiore* and the fugal section pushing forward noticeably.

Weingartner's other recordings, however, do often show an unusually strict control of tempo for their period. Brahms's Symphony No. 2 gives an opportunity for comparison between Weingartner, Beecham (another conductor with a firm control of tempo) and Max Fiedler (a conductor with a much more flexible attitude to tempo).

Brahms, Symphony No. 2, fourth movement

	bar 1	bar 23	bar 78	bar 98
Berlin Philharmonic Orchestra, cond. M. Fielder (rec. 1931)	♩ = 100	110	78	108
London Philharmonic Orchestra, cond. Beecham (rec. 1936)	104	108	96	104
London Philharmonic Orchestra, cond. Weingartner (rec. 1940)	108	118	100	116
Royal Philharmonic Orchestra, cond. Beecham (rec. 1956–9)	104	100	92	96
Vienna Philharmonic Orchestra, cond. Kertesz (rec. 1964)	104	110	94	100
Cleveland Orchestra, cond. Maazel (rec. 1976)	100	104	86	96

The performance conducted by Fiedler shows a degree of flexibility which is typical of the early twentieth century. Weingartner and Beecham are much more restrained in their tempo changes. Weingartner does increase tempo rather more than would be expected in modern performances at bars 23 and 98, but his relaxation at bar 78 is as subtle as in most modern recordings. Beecham's degree of flexibility hardly changed at all over twenty years, being typical of its period in 1956–9, but ahead of its time in 1936.

A number of pre-war musicians continued to make records through to the post-war period, and they provide an interesting light on the changing attitude to tempo fluctuation. Beecham and Heifetz, who were unusually restrained in their tempo fluctuations in the 1930s, changed very little in this respect in the post-war years. Toscanini, as we have seen, tended to become less flexible in Classical works and more flexible in Romantic works in his later recordings. Many musicians, however, changed their attitude to tempo fluctuation as the general fashion changed around them.

Brahms, Symphony No. 1, fourth movement

	bar 61	bar 94
Berlin State Opera Orchestra, cond. Klemperer (rec. 1928)	♩ = 116	140
Philharmonia Orchestra, cond. Klemperer (rec. 1958)	104	128
Philadelphia Orchestra, cond. Stokowski (rec. c. 1928)	132	148
London Symphony Orchestra, cond. Stokowski (rec. 1972)	124	132

These examples show the extent to which even musicians of the greatest individuality are influenced by the fashion of their time. Bar 94 is marked *animato*, and both Klemperer and Stokowski make a much greater increase of speed at this point in their 1928 recordings than in their modern performances. Klemperer, regarded as the great Classical conductor in the 1950s, was much more volatile in his tempos in the 1920s, and Stokowski, though still regarded by many as eccentric in the 1970s, was much more restrained in his tempo fluctuations than he had been in his pre-war performances.

Bruckner, Symphony No. 4, first movement

	bar 3	bar 67	bar 75	bar 141
Dresden State Opera Orchestra, cond. Böhm (rec. 1936)	♩ = 62	68	64	74
Vienna Philharmonic Orchestra, cond. Böhm (rec. 1972)	56	58–60	58	60

Not only is Böhm's 1936 performance of the movement generally faster than his 1972 performance, but he accelerates much more to the climaxes. The first recording has a tempo range of ♩ = 62–74 over the exposition, whereas the later recording has a much narrower range of ♩ = 56–60.

Mendelssohn, 'Hebrides' Overture

BBC Symphony Orchestra, cond. Boult   (rec. c. 1934)

bar 1	*bar 77*	*bar 96*	*bar 165*	*bar 180*	*bar 202*	*bar 226*
♩ = 108	128	120	140	116	96	148

BBC Symphony Orchestra, cond. Boult   (rec. c. 1960)

bar 1	*bar 77*	*bar 96*	*bar 165*	*bar 180*	*bar 202*	*bar 226*
♩ = 104	120	108	124	108	92	132

Boult's minimum tempos are similar in both recordings – at the beginning, and at the quiet passage for two clarinets at bar 202. But the loudest and most energetic passages are invariably much faster in the pre-war recording, particularly at the climaxes at bars 165 and 226.

Beethoven, Piano Concerto No. 4, first movement

	bar 74	*bar 82*	*bar 97*	*bar 105*	*bar 111*
Backhaus, London Symphony Orchestra, cond. Ronald (rec. c. 1930)	♩ = 116	96	116	88	116
Backhaus, Vienna Philharmonic Orchestra, cond. Schmidt-Isserstedt (rec. c. 1958)	112	100	104	92	104

Backhaus consistently uses a narrower range of tempo fluctuation in his c. 1958 performance than in his c. 1930 version, both in the first movement, shown here, and in the finale of the concerto. The greatest difference is in the maximum tempos, which are substantially faster in the earlier performance.

Chopin, Barcarolle, Op. 60

	bar 6	*bar 39*
Rubinstein (rec. 1928)	♩. = 60	c. 78
Rubinstein (rec. 1962)	56	c. 64

The earlier performance increases in tempo at bar 39 much more than the later version, as well as being much more volatile in detail in this section.

Chopin, Polonaise in A flat, Op. 53

	bar 17	*bar 85*
Rubinstein (rec. 1935)	♩ = 88	108
Rubinstein (rec. 1964)	♩ = c. 80	92

The tempos in the later performance are generally slower than in the earlier, and in the earlier performance the middle section has a greater increase in tempo.

As these examples show, most performers who lived through the period of change in attitude to tempo fluctuation reflected those changes in their own performances. If one compares pre-war and post-war recordings of the same work, the later performance usually shows a tighter control over tempo fluctuation than the earlier, and this generally applies whether the two recordings are by the same or different artists. In exceptional cases where the later recording is more flexible in tempo than the earlier, the flexibility almost invariably takes the form of slowing down for lyrical passages, rather than speeding up for energetic passages. Acceleration, which was part of the general interpretative practice in the 1930s and earlier, came to be thought of as uncontrolled in the post-war period, and the maximum tempos within movements tended to be slower than before the war.

The general practice of tempo fluctuation was part of the context within which early twentieth-century composers worked, and the examples which follow are chosen to show how composers, and performers approved by them, responded to that context.

Elgar stated that he wanted his works to be performed 'elastically and mystically' and not 'squarely and ... like a wooden box'.[44] He conducted recorded performances of almost all his major orchestral works, many of them twice, and so it is possible to establish just what degree of elasticity he had in mind. It soon becomes clear that Elgar's flexibility of tempo went far beyond the indications given in his scores.

Elgar, Symphony No. 1, fourth movement, allegro

	start	fig. 118	fig. 120	fig. 130	fig. 134
Markings in score	$\d = 84$	none	none	none	none
London Symphony Orchestra, cond. Elgar (rec. 1930)	76	108	100	80	96
Philharmonia, cond. Barbirolli (rec. 1963)	64	76	84	76	80
London Philharmonic Orchestra, cond. Boult (rec. 1967)	72	80	88	80	84
London Philharmonic Orchestra, cond. Solti (rec. c. 1972)	80	96	100	76	108
London Philharmonic Orchestra, cond. Barenboim (rec. c. 1974)	80	88	88	68	88

Elgar's own recording of the symphony, the only one made before the war, is here compared with four modern recordings. After the slow introduction, the allegro of the fourth movement is marked ♩ = 84 with no other change of tempo indicated until the final climax of the movement (*Grandioso, poco Largamente* at fig. 146). Elgar's own performance begins slightly below his metronome marking, at ♩ = 76, rising to ♩ = 108 at fig. 118. For the *cantabile* melody at fig. 130 he drops to ♩ = 80, recovering to ♩ = 96 at fig. 134. There are similar fluctuations throughout the movement, none of which are indicated in the score. The four modern performances do not take the movement at a constant speed, but the changes of tempo are almost invariably less extreme. In particular, although modern conductors slow down for quiet and lyrical passages they are generally much more reluctant than Elgar to speed up at moments of increasing tension. Solti studied Elgar's performance before making his own recording, but even he is sometimes less volatile in his tempo fluctuations than Elgar. His first acceleration reaches only ♩ = 100 (at fig. 120), compared with Elgar's ♩ = 108 at fig. 118. Solti does, however, reach ♩ = 108 at fig. 134, a higher tempo than Elgar at this point.

Boult, Barbirolli, and Barenboim all have a much smaller range of tempo than Elgar, with much slower maximum speeds. Compared with Elgar's tempo range of ♩ = 76–108, Boult has ♩ = 72–88, Barbirolli ♩ = 64–84, and Barenboim ♩ = 80–88 over the first acceleration with a drop to ♩ = 68 at fig. 130. The first movement of the symphony provides similar comparisons, with Elgar reaching faster maximum speeds than modern conductors (with the exception of Solti).

Despite Elgar's claim that 'I've done all I can to help players' with detailed markings,[45] it is clear that in this most fundamental aspect of interpretation, tempo fluctuation, he left a great deal unstated in his scores. To make matters more confusing, some of his detailed tempo instructions are flatly contradicted by his own performances. In the score of his second symphony, there is a point at the first climax of the first movement (fig. 7) where Elgar writes, after an acceleration, *Tempo primo (subitamente)*. Elgar ignores this instruction in both of his two recordings of the symphony (1924 and 1927), whereas modern recordings (with the exception of Solti's) observe it. In 1902 Elgar wrote to Richard Strauss, who was to conduct 'Cockaigne' in Berlin, 'There are several omissions in the score of "Cockaigne" regarding indications of Tempi: . . . General time (Hauptzeitmass) ♩ = 112 the first *two* bars a little broader (etwas breiter) with humorous distinction ♩ = 104 and at ② p. 7 the same two bars also somewhat broader . . . '[46] Elgar's three recorded performances of 'Cockaigne' (1917, 1926 and 1933) only partly obey these instructions. They all play the opening bars slightly more slowly than the eventual tempo, but the tempo range is not ♩ = 104–112 as suggested in the letter, but ♩ = 108 rising to ♩ = 120 by bar 5, and, in the 1926 version, accelerating to about ♩ = 132 before fig. 3, a much faster maximum tempo than in the letter. The last part of Elgar's instruction, that the opening bars of the theme should be broadened again at fig. 2, is completely ignored in all three recordings, indicating either that his letter did not describe what he did in practice, or that he had changed his mind between 1902 and 1917.

Even where Elgar's changes of mind about tempo are clearly stated, his last thoughts on paper do not necessarily reveal his actual practice. Sketches for the 'Enigma' Variations contain several metronome markings which differ from the published figures.[47] In the sketch of 'Nimrod', an original pencil marking of ♩ = 66 is dimly visible. This was then rubbed out and replaced by ♩ = 72, but for the published score Elgar reverted to ♩ = 66. Four years later, in 1903, he wrote to Nimrod himself (A. J. Jaeger of Novello), 'I always take Nimrod slower than M. M. in score. [Frederic] Cowen says it shd. be altered, what do you think?'[48] Jaeger agreed, and the marking in the score was changed to ♩ = 52. However, in Elgar's 1926 recording, he begins at ♩ = 40, rising to ♩ = 48 after fig. 34 and accelerating to about ♩ = 56 before the climax. This demonstrates that, even when Elgar had thought long and hard about his tempo markings, he did not indicate the full extent of his own habitual tempo fluctuations. The practice of varying the tempo at changes of tension was so fundamental a part of performance practice in the early years of the century that either Elgar was not fully aware of it, or he took it for granted as obvious to anyone who might conduct his scores.

Rachmaninoff, Piano Concerto No. 2 in C minor

Rachmaninoff, Philadelphia Orchestra, cond. Stokowski   (rec. 1929)

first movement	*mm in score*	*recording*
fig. 1	moderato ♩ = 66	♩ = 82
9th bar of fig. 4	none	♩ = c. 80 (flexible)
fig. 6	none	♩ = c. 72
17th bar of fig. 6	poco più mosso ♩ = 72	♩ = 104
9th bar of fig. 7	moto precedente ♩ = 72	♩ = 90
fig. 8	più vivo ♩ = 76	♩ = 108
17th bar of fig. 8	più vivo ♩ = 80	♩ = 108
17th bar of fig. 9	allegro ♩ = 96	♩ = 112
9th bar of fig. 10	maestoso (alla marcia)	♩ = 90
fig. 11	meno mosso ♩ = 76	♩ = c. 76
fig. 13	moderato ♩ = 69	♩ = 69
fig. 16	meno mosso ♩ = 63	♩ = 72

third movement	mm in score	recording
start	allegro scherzando ♩ = 116	♩ = 126–130
		♩ = 138 by fig. 30
24th bar of fig. 30	moderato ♩ = 72	♩ = 72
fig. 32	meno mosso ♩ = 48	♩ = 38
13th bar of fig. 32	moto primo ♩ = 116	♩ = 124
fig. 33	più mosso ♩ = 120	♩ = c. 130
9th bar of fig. 33	presto ♩ = 126	♩ = c. 158
7th bar of fig. 36	più vivo ♩ = 132	♩ = c. 160
23rd bar of fig. 36	moderato ♩ = 72	♩ = 64
31st bar of fig. 37	meno mosso ♩ = 48	♩ = 42
fig. 38	moto primo ♩ = 116	♩ = 140
fig. 39	agitato ♩ = 76	♩ = 96
33rd bar of fig. 39	presto ♩ = 132	♩ = c. 156
38th bar of fig. 39	maestoso ♩ = 60	♩ = 80
62nd bar of fig. 39	più vivo ♩ = 80	♩ = c. 104
66th bar of fig. 39	risoluto ♩ = 100	♩ = c. 116

Like Elgar, Rachmaninoff recorded many of his major works, and he too shows greater flexibility of tempo than his scores suggest. Where metronome markings are given, as in the second piano concerto, the performance often reaches faster maximum tempos than those indicated in the score. The first movement of the concerto is played faster than the printed indications almost throughout. Only at figs. 11 and 13 is the tempo as slow as the marking on the score. The difference between performance and score is most striking at the 17th bar of fig. 6 and at fig. 8, where the performed tempo is 50 per cent faster than that indicated in the score. In the third movement, the maximum tempos of the performance are again much higher than those in the score, but the minimum tempos (at fig. 32 and at the 31st bar of fig. 37) are substantially slower than in the score. The overall range of tempo has therefore been increased in performance, though, as in most of Rachmaninoff's recordings, it is the vigour and directness of the fast passages which most determine the character of the performance as a whole.

Richard Strauss's attitude to tempo fluctuation has already been suggested by his remark in 1887 that Mahler was 'one of the few modern conductors to understand "modifications of tempo"'.[49] Leo Wurmser's memories of Strauss's conducting later in life are more contradictory, with reports of unmarked tempo changes in his own and other composers' works, but also of Strauss's objections to a conductor's freedom of tempo in *Arabella*.[50]

Strauss's many recordings of his own and other composers' orchestral music reveal considerable flexibility of tempo.

Beethoven, Symphony No. 5, first movement

Berlin State Opera Orchestra, cond. Strauss   (rec. 1928)
Berlin Philharmonic Orchestra, cond. Nikisch   (rec. 1913)

	Strauss	Nikisch
bar 6	$\lrcorner = 92{-}104$	84
bar 44	108	92
bar 63	84	80
bar 109	108	92
bar 221	92	76
bar 484	80	80

Strauss's flexibility in Mozart's Symphony No. 40 has already been illustrated. His recording of Beethoven's Fifth Symphony is a much more extreme example. Comparison with Nikisch's 1913 recording (admittedly an early acoustic recording) shows Strauss using a much greater range of tempo than Nikisch, although Nikisch had a reputation for flexibility. The figures given above show the broad range of Strauss's tempos, but they do not show his dramatic use of acceleration. After each of the pauses at bars 5 and 24, Strauss begins slowly, $\lrcorner = 92$, and accelerates through the continuous quaver passages to $\lrcorner = 104$. After a steady tempo of $\lrcorner = 108$, the second subject (bar 63) is played with a sudden drop in tempo to $\lrcorner = 84$. The tempo ebbs and flows throughout the movement, and at the end, the quiet bars after the pause (bar 484) are played slowly $\lrcorner = 80$, but the final fortissimo is suddenly much faster. This performance is one of the most vivid examples of the pre-war use of tempo fluctuation to emphasise changes of mood and tension.

R. Strauss, *Don Juan*

Berlin State Opera Orchestra, cond. Strauss   (rec. 1929)
Dresden State Opera Orchestra, cond. Böhm   (rec. 1938)

	principal markings	*Strauss*	*Böhm*
bar 9	$\lrcorner = 84$	$\lrcorner = 84$, soon 92	$\lrcorner = 104$
19th bar of D	tranquillo	$\lrcorner = 64{-}8$	$\lrcorner = 68$
3 before H	a tempo $\lrcorner = 84$	$\lrcorner = 92$	$\lrcorner = 96$
4th bar of L	a tempo ma tranquillo $\lrcorner = 76$	$\lrcorner = 60$	$\lrcorner = 60$
19th bar of N	a tempo $\lrcorner = 84$	$\lrcorner = 84$	$\lrcorner = 92$
9th bar of P	a tempo giocoso $\lrcorner = 92$	$\lrcorner = 92$	$\lrcorner = 108$

The tempo range of Strauss's recording is greater than that of his metronome markings in the score (a few transitional markings have been omitted). The range of the principal markings from the opening to the horn theme (19th bar of N) is only $\lrcorner = 84{-}76$ in the score (apart from the *tranquillo* after letter D which has no metronome marking), but Strauss's performance has a range of

♩ = 92–60. The *a tempo* at the 19th bar of N is performed at the speed marked in the score, ♩ = 84, but since Strauss's predominant tempo in the first section of the work was ♩ = 92, his tempo here is slower than a literal *a tempo*. Although Strauss's tempo is more flexible than the metronome markings in the score, it is not exceptionally volatile by pre-war standards. Böhm (1938) has an even greater tempo range of ♩ = 104–60 over the same passage.

Holst, *The Planets*, 'Mars'

	start	fig. 6	fig. 8
London Symphony Orchestra, cond. Holst (rec. 1926)	♩ = 184	c. 168	176
BBC Symphony Orchestra, cond. Boult (rec. 1945)	♩ = 156	128	152

In Holst's letter to Boult after the first performance of *The Planets* in 1918 (p. 11), he asks for more 'row' and 'sense of climax' in 'Mars', and suggests that he should 'perhaps hurry certain bits?' Boult's 1945 recording was made many years after the first performance, and does not necessarily show how he took it in 1918, but the comparison between the two recordings is interesting. Holst is no more flexible in tempo than Boult, he does not 'hurry certain bits', but his tempos are very fast, substantially faster than Boult's and other more modern performances. When Holst's recording was reissued in 1972, Imogen Holst wrote that 'the work sounds just as it did when Holst used to conduct it before a Queen's Hall audience half a century ago. Rhythm, to Holst, was the most important thing in life, and in the recording he never for one moment allows the rhythm to sag, with the result that *Mars* sounds even more relentless than usual.'[51]

Stravinsky, *Petrushka*

[Straram Orchestra] cond. Stravinsky (rec. 1928)
London Symphony Orchestra, cond. Coates (rec. 1927–8)
Danish Radio Orchestra, cond. Malko (extracts, rec. 1933)
Philadelphia Orchestra, cond. Stokowski (rec. 1937)
Columbia Symphony Orchestra, cond. Stravinsky (rec. 1960)

Stravinsky's attack on 'interpreters' of his music has already been quoted, and as we have seen, revisions of some of his scores, particularly *Petrushka*, show attempts to prevent tempo fluctuations. Compared with composers writing in more conventionally late-Romantic styles – Elgar, Richard Strauss, Rachmaninoff – Stravinsky provides fewer obvious opportunities for tempo fluctuation; much of his music is written in distinctly contrasted sections, rather than developing gradually through tension and relaxation in the nineteenth-century manner. Stravinsky's own performances of the late 1920s and early

1930s are fairly clear-cut in their tempos, but they contain occasional slight tempo fluctuations which he did not allow in his post-war performances. Some other conductors of Stravinsky in the late 1920s and 1930s are much freer in tempo, in a manner which Stravinsky guarded against in his revised scores of the 1940s.

At a number of points in *Petrushka*, Stravinsky in his 1928 recording already performs the work as he was to revise it in 1947, rather than according to the 1911 original (cue numbers are as in the 1947 revision). At fig. 102–3 the original edition has a change of tempo from *Adagietto* ♪ = 54 *dolente*, accelerating to *Andantino* [♪] = 84 at fig. 103.[52] Stravinsky in 1928 plays the whole passage at ♪ = 76, approximately as in his revised 1947 score (*Andantino* ♪ = 80 from fig. 102).

There are a few slight accelerations and decelerations in Stravinsky's 1928 performance which are avoided in the 1960 recording. The very opening begins in 1928 at ♩ = 136 (very close to the metronome mark ♩ = 138), but settles by fig. 7 to ♩ = 128. The 1960 performance stays firmly at ♩ = 136. The 'Dance of the Coachmen' (fig. 213) begins in the 1928 version at ♩ = 96 (with poor co-ordination), settling to ♩ = 112 by fig. 230. The 1960 performance has a much slighter acceleration, from ♩ = 104 to ♩ = 112. In both editions of the score the marking is ♩ = 112 straight away at fig. 213.

To a modern listener, these accelerations and decelerations in the 1928 recording sound like moments of poor control or indecisiveness, though there is no evidence that they struck Stravinsky like that at the time. In 1936 he described this and his other recordings of the late 1920s as 'documents which can serve as a guide to all executants of my music', particularly as regards 'the pace of the movements and their relationship to each other'.[53]

Stravinsky's adjustments of tempo are, however, very slight compared with some of the much greater fluctuations in other pre-war recordings of *Petrushka*. Coates accelerates very markedly in the final bars of the 'Russian Dance' (fig. 90), from ♩ = 112 to c. ♩ = 144. At the 'Dance of the Coachmen' (fig. 213) Coates accelerates more than Stravinsky in 1928, from a starting tempo of ♩ = 88 to ♩ = 108 by fig. 228. At the marked *agitato* at fig. 234, Coates accelerates to a very rapid ♩ = 144 by fig. 237, compared with Stravinsky's ♩ = 132 (the tempo which he specifies in the 1947 revision at this point).

Stokowski also inserts a number of tempo changes which would certainly have displeased Stravinsky. At fig. 127, he anticipates the tempo change indicated at fig. 130, suddenly increasing to ♪ = 140. Long before the indicated *agitato* marking at fig. 234, Stokowski is already accelerating from fig. 199, through fig. 230, and he also accelerates to the climax at fig. 250, where, in the 1947 revision, Stravinsky was to write *Tempo di rigore, non accelerando!* Malko, in a recording of extracts from *Petrushka*, has a sudden increase from ♩ = 112 to ♩ = 144 at fig. 228, where no change is marked, and he accelerates even faster than Stokowski to the climax at fig. 250.

These recordings of *Petrushka* give a revealing picture of Stravinsky's practice in the 1920s and its relationship with the general habits of the time. Stravinsky was less strictly controlled in tempo in 1928 than in 1960. This corresponds with the general change in fashion between these two dates, and also ties in with the differences between the 1911 and 1947 editions of *Petrushka*. However, other pre-war recordings show that Stravinsky even in 1928 was much less free in his tempos than some other conductors of his work. Stravinsky's recordings from the late 1920s may have a certain lack of control compared with his post-war recordings, but we can see that in comparison with other pre-war conductors, he was ahead of his time in the strictness of his tempos.

Sibelius, Symphony No. 5, first movement

London Symphony Orchestra, cond. Kajanus (rec. 1932)

markings in score	Sibelius's mm.	Kajanus
Tempo molto moderato (start)	♩. = 66	♩. = 63 up to ♩. = 68 after D
Largamente (p. 25)	♩. = 63	♩. = 56
Allegro moderato (ma poco a poco stretto) (p. 30)	♩. = 80	♩. = 86
D (p. 39)	♩. = 96	♩. = 92 up to ♩. = 96 at F
K (vivace molto) (p. 49)	♩. = 104	♩. = 104
M (p. 52)	♩. = 112	♩. = 112
N (p. 54)	♩. = 126	♩. = 110
Presto (p. 60)	♩. = 138	♩. = 120
Più presto (p. 64)	none	♩. = c. 138 (from S)

This recording conducted by Kajanus and the following example conducted by Koussevitsky provide interesting comparisons with Sibelius's own tempo suggestions, which were discussed earlier in this chapter (pp. 10–11). Kajanus collaborated closely with Sibelius from the turn of the century until his death in 1933, and the majority of his tempos in this movement, and the gradual transitions between them, are close to Sibelius's indications, which were published during World War II. The only major difference between Kajanus's and Sibelius's tempos is towards the end of the movement. The increase in tempo between letter M and the *Presto* on p. 60 is much slighter in Kajanus's performance than in Sibelius's suggestion (though Kajanus does make a brief further accelerando over the last few bars from letter S). Kajanus's tempo at the

Presto is quite fast by modern standards, and this underlines the point made earlier, that Sibelius's suggested maximum tempos are very fast indeed.

Sibelius, Symphony No. 7

BBC Symphony Orchestra, cond. Koussevitsky (rec. 1933)

markings in score	Sibelius's mm.	Koussevitsky
Adagio (start)	♩ = 76	♩ = 52–56
letter B	none	♩ = 70
letter D	gradual accel. to	♩ = 86
Un pochett. meno adagio (p. 12)	♩ = 76	c. ♩ = 60
Poco affrett. (p. 13)	♩ = 84	♩ = 100 accel.
bar before G	none	meno
letter I	none	♩ = 90
6/4 (p. 20)	♩. = 104 gradual accel. to	subito ♩. = 80
Vivacissimo (p. 23)	♩. = 152	subito ♩. = 144
Adagio (p. 30)	♩ = 56	♩ = 56
Poco a poco meno lento al (p. 35)		brief accel.
letter N	none	♩ = 90
Allegro molto moderato (p. 40)	♩. = 76	♩. = 76
Allegro moderato (p. 42)	♩. = 84	♩. = 84
Poco a poco meno moderato (p. 43)		a tempo
Vivace (p. 59)	♩. = 126	♩. = 132
Presto (p. 64)	♩. = 160	♩. = 152
Adagio (p. 68)	♩ = 56	♩ = 52

Unlike Kajanus, who collaborated with Sibelius for many years, Koussevitsky only began to take an interest in Sibelius a few years before he made this recording. His very fast maximum tempos are typical of the period, but Sibelius's own indications are sometimes even faster (*vivacissimo* on page 23, and *presto* on p. 64). At the *poco affrett.* on p. 13 Koussevitsky's tempo is substantially faster than Sibelius's suggestion, and he then accelerates until a sudden hold in tempo one bar before fig. G. This is one of a number of instances which make it clear that Koussevitsky was unaware of, or chose to ignore, some of Sibelius's intentions (Sibelius's metronome markings were not published until several years after Koussevitsky made this recording). At the *vivacissimo* on p. 23, Koussevitsky suddenly increases the tempo, whereas Sibelius indicates a gradual accelerando over the preceding three pages. Koussevitsky also ignores a number of markings in the published score. The score has *poco a poco meno moderato* on p. 43, but Koussevitsky keeps to the same basic tempo (with occasional surges) through to a sudden increase in speed at the *vivace* on p. 59. At the change of time signature to 6/4 on p. 20, Sibelius suggests an increase in tempo, but Koussevitsky suddenly slows down. This is despite a marking in the score five bars before, *poco a poco affrettando il tempo al*, which Sibelius's later instructions clarify as an acceleration right through to the *vivacissimo* on p. 23. These and other 'liberties' which Koussevitsky takes with the score might have been expected to displease Sibelius. But Sibelius (unlike Stravinsky) seems to have had a liberal attitude to conductors' interpretations, and declared himself 'completely captivated' by Koussevitsky's recording of the seventh symphony.[54]

A number of points emerge from the recorded examples given in this chapter. The most obvious is that a greater range of tempo within movements was generally used in the 1920s and 1930s than in modern performances. But the trend over the last 60 years has not been simply a narrowing of the accepted tempo range. In pre-war performances, slowing down at points of low tension and speeding up at points of high tension were both used frequently, and with equal emphasis. Modern performers still sometimes slow down at lyrical passages, particularly in works of the Romantic period, but accelerations at energetic passages are generally very restrained. The degree of acceleration heard in many pre-war recordings would be considered uncontrolled in modern performance. One of the results of this modern caution is that the maximum tempos within movements are usually slower in post-war than in pre-war performances, so that the average tempo of a movement has generally dropped. And what is true within movements is true also of complete multi-movement works. In pre-war performances, fast movements were often very fast, so that the contrast between fast and slow movements was very great. In modern performance, fast movements are usually more moderate in pace, so that the difference between fast and slow movements is less clearly defined. This is particularly noticeable in works with lyrical fast movements, such as Brahms's Symphony No. 2. A sceptic might argue that tempos on 78 r.p.m. records cannot be taken to represent those used in concert performance, because of the need to fit the music on to the sides. This was sometimes an important factor in the days of acoustic recordings, before 1925, when records were no substitute for concert performance, and when it was common practice both to speed up tempos and to cut the music to fit the sides. But from 1925 onwards, with the advent of electrical recording, and as the maximum length of a side increased, gramophone records were treated more and more seriously by performers, and so the practice of speeding up the music became much less common. Records of the late 1920s still have to be treated with some caution when the music is a tight fit on the record. There are a number of examples of works recorded in the late 1920s, then re-recorded in the 1930s by the same performers, when the maximum length of a side had increased from four to four and a half minutes. In some of these cases, the tempo in the later recording is substantially slower than in the earlier version, and there is therefore some reason to suspect that the earlier performance was speeded up for the record.

Such examples, however, do not undermine the overwhelming evidence for the general use of very fast maximum tempos in pre-war performances. There are countless examples of very fast performances from the 1920s and 1930s on records which have plenty of room left at the end of the side, and in such cases there is no reason to doubt that the performers were close to their normal tempos. Recordings containing very fast tempos were praised by composers, performers and critics. Stravinsky specifically approved his recordings of *Petrushka*, *The Firebird* and *The Rite of Spring* made in the late 1920s, which contain examples of very fast tempos compared with his post-war recordings.[55] Rachmaninoff's approval of his recordings included particular praise for his records of Schumann's *Carnaval*, some of which is played at great speed. Elgar approved of both his 1926 and his 1933 versions of 'Cockaigne', although the 1926 version accelerates to a faster tempo than either his metronome marking or his 1933 performance. Pencilled comments by Elgar relating (almost certainly) to his 1926 recording of the 'Enigma' Variations are to be found in his copy of the published piano arrangement of the variations.[56] He seems to have had reservations about his tempo for one of the slower variations, variation 8, because he writes at the head of it, 'Agree with Dr. R. a leetle slower' – probably a reference to Hans Richter who conducted the première of the variations, and who presumably used to take this variation more slowly than Elgar did. However, Elgar praises two of the variations in which his tempo is substantially quicker than the metronome mark in the score. Variation 2, which Elgar takes at $\downarrow$ = 80 compared with the score's $\downarrow$ = 72, has 'delightful' at the fifth bar of fig. 6, and 'lovely' over the ending. Variation 7 ('Troyte') has 'fine' over the opening bars, and Elgar takes it at $\circ$= 84 compared with the printed $\circ$= 76.

Despite suspicions about particular recordings, therefore, very fast maximum tempos were a genuine part of the flexible musical style of the early twentieth century. Over the succeeding decades there has been a gradual change in attitude to tempo, and to flexibility of tempo, and this has been part of a more general change in the rhetoric of musical rhythm. Toscanini's principle that one should perform what is in the composer's score and nothing more has been very influential on later generations. As far as tempo is concerned, Toscanini did not quite practise what he preached, as we have seen, and few musicians even in the late twentieth century are absolutely inflexible in tempo. Nevertheless, modern taste insists on careful control, particularly of acceleration. This goes with a requirement that every detail should be considered and clearly placed. By comparison, early twentieth-century performance was more volatile. Rhetorical flexibility was applied not just to overall tempo, but also to the shaping of phrases and the relationship between individual notes. This detailed flexibility is the subject of the next chapter.

2

Tempo rubato

INTRODUCTION

In the early part of the twentieth century, there was general agreement about the need for flexibility in performance, not only in overall tempo, but also in more detailed phrasing. The pianist Josef Lhevinne was expressing a widespread view when he wrote, 'Rhythm should not be thought of as something dead. It is live, vital, elastic.'[1] The violinist Achille Rivarde similarly wrote,

Rhythm is elasticity of movement. In physical life when the arteries harden and lose their suppleness, old age sets in and the decrease of vitality begins, and in music the analogy holds good. When the natural rhythmic ebb and flow, the elastic give-and-take of movement is resisted, the performance is characterised by a certain lifelessness and affects the listener as being spiritless. This elasticity of movement, this rhythm should be felt in every bar.[2]

This view was supported by both performers and composers. Elgar's demand for elasticity has already been quoted, and his own flexibility in rhythmic detail was commented on by contemporary reviewers: 'Credit is due to the orchestra for its response to Sir Edward's uneasy, wilful beat';[3] 'the orchestra ... were responsive to Sir Edward's very personal *rubato*'.[4] H. C. Colles writes of Elgar that 'Such things as the pauses and accents, directions for *rubato* ... acquire their authoritative interpretation only from him. He knows where to throw the emphasis in each phrase, so as to give it eloquence.'[5] Mahler, as well as requiring frequent changes of tempo, was rhythmically very flexible in his conducting. Admirers praised him for his 'freedom of rhythm',[6] detractors criticised his 'arbitrary nuances' and his 'seeking after effects'.[7] Natalie Bauer-Lechner writes, 'Conducting, according to Mahler, should be a continual elimination of the bar (des Taktes), so that it retreats behind the melodic and rhythmic content, like the fabric of a Gobelin under the pattern of the embroidery.'[8] Mahler's piano accompaniments to his lieder were, according to Robert Heger, even freer than his conducting.[9] Reger is similarly reported to have accompanied freely not only his own lieder but also the works of other composers.[10] Marguerite Long remembers Fauré's call for 'suppleness in the fluctuation of the phrasing' in the performance of his piano music,[11] and

about Debussy's piano-playing she writes, 'How could one forget his suppleness, the caress of his touch?'[12] Recalling Ravel's instructions in the Menuet
of the Sonatine, Vlado Perlemuter writes, 'Above all he asked me to play it
flexibly.'[13] Otto Klemperer remembers the 'great freedom' of Bartók's piano
playing,[14] and Bartók himself praises the conductor Václav Tálich for his
'wonderful plasticity' in Czech music.[15] These last two remarks have already
been quoted in the discussion of flexibility of tempo, but general comments of
this kind seem also to imply more detailed rhythmic flexibility.

Similar quotations, praising or calling for rhythmic freedom, are very
common in writings of the early twentieth century. But although they convey
strong negative feelings against rigidly metronomic performance, words such
as 'elasticity', 'freedom' and 'suppleness' give no positive information about
what actually happens to the rhythm during a rubato passage. The problem, as
so often in the documents of earlier periods, is that the writers assume in the
reader a knowledge of the general performance practice of the time.

In the case of tempo rubato, the picture is further complicated, because,
although most writers in the early twentieth century were broadly in favour of
rhythmic flexibility, there was considerable controversy and confusion about
what kind of flexibility was appropriate, and even about the meaning of the
term *tempo rubato*. The writings and recordings of the period shows that three
kinds of rhythmical freedom were involved: the use of accelerando and
rallentando, the use of the tenuto or agogic accent, and the rhythmical
independence of a melody from its accompaniment ('melodic' rubato). In
practical performance these three aspects of tempo rubato rarely occur in
isolation from each other, but they provide a convenient way of separating the
different elements of the subject. After sections on each of these three topics,
they are brought together again in a discussion of recordings.

ACCELERANDO AND RALLENTANDO

Stainer and Barrett's Dictionary of Musical Terms (1898 ed.) defines tempo rubato
as 'robbed or stolen time. Time occasionally slackened or hastened for the
purposes of expression', and this is the sense in which many writers understood
the term.[16] Hugo Riemann's *Dictionary of Music* (1897 English ed.) has 'free
treatment of passages of marked expression and passion, which forcibly brings
out the *stringendo-calando* in the shading of phrases, a feature which, as a rule,
remains unnoticed'.[17] Paderewski writes that tempo rubato consists 'of a more
or less important slackening or quickening of the time or rate of movement'.[18]
Other keyboard players to recommend this kind of rubato include Landowska
and Gieseking, though both make it clear that they are talking about a very
subtle effect.[19]

Several writers caution against excess, and some of them suggest that this
kind of rubato is to be used principally in modern music ('modern' at this

period meaning music from about the 1820s onwards). Franklin Taylor writes, 'All such variations in tempo as have been described above are in their proper place in modern music, from Weber onwards, and should be employed very sparingly, if at all, in the works of earlier composers, the measured and strict character of whose music demands a like strictness of time.'[20] The violinist Hans Wessely remembers that the Chaconne by Bach, as played by Joachim, 'received in all phrases the most wonderful elasticity of time', though he warns that 'The moment that the shape of a phrase cannot be felt, the execution of it must be styled an indifferent one.' By contrast, 'more recent (French) compositions demand greater freedom of phrasing and time changes'.[21]

Writers on singing, like instrumentalists, often recommend a rubato consisting of accelerando and rallentando. In the *Voice-Training Primer* (1893) by Mrs Emil Behnke and Charles W. Pearce, this kind of rubato is to be used routinely: 'Ascending phrases, as a rule, should be sung *crescendo*, and with a slight quickening of speed (*tempo rubato*) ... Descending phrases should, on the other hand, be sung *diminuendo*, and with a slight slackening of speed (*tempo rubato*).'[22] David Ffrangcon-Davis (1906), in a book prefaced by Elgar, stresses the importance of elastic tempo, but warns that 'rejection of inelastic *tempi* must not run riot and develop into universal *tempo rubato*'.[23] Here we are back to the problem of definitions: where does 'elasticity' end and 'universal *tempo rubato*' begin? Charles Lunn (1904) is similarly unspecific: 'Lawlessness is one thing, liberty quite another. Liberty is a reward given by Nature for past and present obedience to Law.'[24] Giovanni Clerici (1906) is more specific, introducing the notion of balance, when talking about variations in pulse: 'These variations will consist of slight and almost unnoticeable accelerations, followed by retards (which just balance each other, the hurrying being in approaching a climax, and the retard to allow time to cool down afterwards) ...'[25]

The idea of balance was at the root of a controversy about tempo rubato in the early twentieth century. Prominent among writers on the subject was the piano teacher Tobias Matthay, who identifies two principal forms of rubato:

The most usual is that in which we emphasise a note (or a number of notes) by giving *more* than the expected Time-value, and then subsequently make-up the time thus lost by accelerating the *remaining* notes of that phrase or idea so as to enable us accurately to return to the pulse ... In the opposite form of Rubato ... we begin with a pushing-on or hurrying the time. This we must necessarily follow up by retarding the subsequent notes of the phrase.[26]

Matthay was one of a number of theoreticians who insisted that the time 'borrowed' must be 'payed back', to maintain what he called the 'Tempo outline'.[27] The controversy about this theory is clearly represented in the first three editions of *Grove's Dictionary*. In *Grove I* (1879–89) J. A. Fuller Maitland writes about rubato, 'This consists of a slight *ad libitum* slackening or quickening of the time in any passage, in accordance with the unchangeable rule that in all such passages any bar in which the licence is taken must be of exactly the same length as the other bars in the movement ...'[28] This entry is reprinted in *Grove II* (1904–10), but in *Grove III* (1927–8) A. H. Fox Strangways bluntly dismisses the theory as a misconception:

The rule has been given and repeated indiscriminately that the 'robbed' time must be 'paid back' within the bar. That is absurd, because the bar line is a notational, not a musical, matter. But there is no necessity to pay back even within the phrase: it is the metaphor that is wrong. *Rubato* is the free element in time, and the more it recognizes the norm the freer it is. The law which it has to recognize is the course of the music as a whole; not a bar but a page, not a page but a movement. If it does not do this it becomes spasmodic and unmeaning, like correspondence which is too much underlined.[29]

General notions of balance in rubato are quite common in writings of the period, but strict acceptance of the rule of compensation is rare in writings by the most prominent performers. Among pianists, Josef Hofmann (1909) comes unusually close to the ideas of Matthay and Fuller Maitland: 'What you shorten of time in one phrase or part of a phrase you must add at the first opportunity to another in order that the time "stolen" (rubato) in one place may be restituted in another.'[30]

Such ideas of balance and compensation are firmly rejected by Paderewski (1909):

Some people, evidently led by laudible principles of equity, while insisting upon the fact of stolen time, pretend that what is stolen ought to be restored. We duly acknowledge the high moral motives of this theory, but we humbly confess that our ethics do not reach to such a high level ... the value of notes diminished in one period through an *accelerando*, cannot always be restored in another through a *ritardando*. What is lost is lost.[31]

Similarly, Landowska writes, 'Rubati must not be symmetrical. A rubato occurring in the course of a progression, for instance, should never be repeated. Otherwise it ceases to be "stolen time". Can one steal systematically?'[32]

A number of writers from the early twentieth century reject not just the theory of compensation, but the whole idea that rubato should consist of accelerando and rallentando. Frederick Niecks (1913) writes against this kind of rubato, stating that 'The continuous use of time-modifications is as ridiculous as the continuous use of vibrato ...'[33] J. Alfred Johnstone (1914) deplores 'the modern tempo rubato of the ultra-romantic school, which plays havoc with both form and time'. He describes this modern rubato in the following way: 'This curious artificial device may be described thus: the first few notes of the passage selected for the operation are taken slowly, and then during the remainder of the passage, the pace is gradually increased until the regulation speed is attained.'[34] According to George Woodhouse, Leschetizky did not teach this modern kind of rubato, 'which tends inevitably to reduce expression to whimsical play upon tempo'.[35] These writers were not, however, advocating strictly metronomic performance. They, and many other writers from the early years of the century, thought of rubato in terms of detailed rhythmical adjustment, by a combination of tenuto and shortened notes.

TENUTO AND AGOGIC ACCENTS

Dictionary entries often define rubato in terms of rhythmic adjustment rather than accelerando and rallentando: 'Taking a portion of the time from one note of a melody and giving it to another, for the sake of expression';[36] 'Indicates that the music is not to be performed in strict time, certain notes being given more, others less, than their absolute value.'[37] Hugo Riemann, in *Musikalische Dynamik und Agogic* (1884) was the first writer to develop a theory of 'agogics', by which he meant the use of small modifications of rhythm and tempo (as opposed to dynamics) for expressive performance. He uses the now familiar term 'agogic accent' to describe the lengthening of a note for purposes of accentuation. Notes to be lengthened include particularly 'notes which form centres of gravity' within a phrase, and 'more especially, in suspensions, whereby the harmonic value is rendered clearer'.[38] Riemann published editions of standard keyboard works in which agogic accents were marked with the sign ∧. His instruction book for pianists, which illustrates the use of agogic accents, reached an eighth edition in 1922.[39]

The use of agogic accents (though not usually called that) was widely recommended by writers in the early years of the century. J. Alfred Johnstone, whose attack on 'modern' tempo rubato was quoted above, refers to the use of agogic accents as 'quasi tempo rubato', and notes with pleasure that 'modern editors are coming to recognize it as one of the important principles of expressive interpretation'. He recommends Riemann's editions, and gives his own illustration of agogic accents in the opening bars of Mendelssohn's *Andante and Rondo Capriccioso* op. 14. Although the rhythm is notated as equal quavers, they are not (according to Johnstone) to be played all the same length. The quavers on each crotchet beat are to be lengthened, with the highest quaver of each phrase longest of all. Unlengthened quavers are to be shortened in proportion as the others are lengthened.

When the chords are struck, as they so often are, in exactly even time, and with exactly even accentuation, the effect produced is as unlike the real music intended as the monotonous outflow of a pianola or a barrel-organ is unlike the playing of an artist. The very life of this passage consists in a delicate give-and-take in the proportionate lengths of the notes; a variety of touch; and a constant rise and fall of tone.

Elsewhere Johnstone remarks of this 'quasi tempo rubato' that 'Joachim produces wonderful effects by its use.'[40] Fuller Maitland (1905), whose statement of the theory of compensation in rubato was quoted above, also praises Joachim for his agogic accents:

The kind of accent that consists, not of an actual stress or intensification of tone on the note, but of a slight lengthening out of its time value, at the beginning of the bar, and at points where a secondary accent may be required. All the greatest interpreters of the best music have been accustomed to lay this kind of accent on the first note of the bar, or of a phrase, as taste may suggest, but none have ever carried out the principle so far or with such fine results as Joachim has done.[41]

Leschetitzky, according to George Woodhouse, emphasised, rather than 'whimsical play upon tempo', the importance of 'rhythm and nuance – those revealing accents, hoverings, the hundred and one subtleties of phrasing which give life and soul to musical form'.[42]

Several writers liken this rubato by agogic accents to declamation in speech. Henry T. Finck (1909) writes that Paderewski's playing differs from that of other pianists 'particularly in this greater number of *rhetorical pauses* ... The pause is either a momentary cessation of sound or a prolongation of a note or chord.'[43] Finck also quotes Busoni's advice: 'The bar-line is only for the eye. In playing, as in reading a poem, the scanning must be subordinate to the declamation; you must *speak the piano*.'[44]

This declamatory aspect of rubato is emphasised by several writers on singing. M. Sterling Mackinlay (1910) describes tempo rubato in terms of rhythmical adjustment, 'the lengthening of certain syllables being equalised by the shortening of others. It is a style of singing principally useful for the interpretation of strong feelings, being governed by the accent which is given in ordinary speech.'[45] Gordon Heller (1917) advises the singing student that 'He must look upon each phrase as a sort of music sentence', and he gives specific advice about the placings of agogic accents:

If groups of notes happen to occur, which have to be sung to one word, the student must be careful to make the first note very slightly longer – though only very slightly – than the rest of the group. Should a triplet be written by the composer, care must be taken here to make the first note of the three a trifle longer than the rest, and thus give a musicianly rendering of it. To hurry the time in such a place would spoil the rhythm . . .[46]

W. H. Breare (1904) gives more general advice to singers which implies the need for agogic accents: 'there is nothing more unattractive than the slavish observation of strict time. To execute any passage with grace, it becomes necessary to make a distinction between accented and unaccented notes.'[47]

MELODIC RUBATO

Where tempo rubato frees a melody from strict note values, either by agogic accents or by accelerando and rallentando, the question arises whether the accompaniment should follow the melody or retain strict time, so that the melody is momentarily out of step with the accompaniment. Josef Hofmann (1909) poses the problem in the form of an answer to a question from a student:

I find an explanation of *tempo rubato* which says that the hand which plays the melody may move with all possible freedom, while the accompanying hand must keep strict time. How can this be done?

The explanation you found, while not absolutely wrong, is very misleading, for it can find application only in a very few isolated cases ... I assume that you are able to play each hand alone with perfect freedom, and I doubt not that you can, with some practice, retain this freedom of each hand when you unite them, but I can see only very few cases to which you could apply such skill, and still less do I see the advantage thereof.[48]

Max Pauer (1913) describes his astonishment when he first heard a recording of his own piano playing: 'Was I, after years of public playing, actually making mistakes that I would be the first to condemn in any one of my own pupils? I could hardly believe my ears, and yet the unrelenting machine showed that in some places I had failed to play both hands exactly together...'[49]

Despite these comments, there is a great deal of evidence for a well-established tradition in which the accompaniment does not follow the rubato of the melody. Franklin Taylor (1897) writes, 'It should be observed that any independent accompaniment to a rubato phrase must always keep strict time, and it is, therefore, quite possible that no note of a rubato melody will fall exactly with its corresponding note in the accompaniment, except, perhaps, the first note in the bar.'[50] Frederick Niecks (1913) similarly advises, 'Where there is an accompaniment rhythmically distinct from the melody, the former should be in strict time, whilst the melody, within certain limits, may proceed on her course with the greatest freedom.'[51]

It was not only pianists who practised this independence of melody and accompaniment. The link between this style of piano-playing and singing was clearly stated in the 1880s, by Adolph Christiani, when advising pianists to keep strict time in the left hand during rubato passages: 'Now it may be said that this is impossible. But such is, by no means, the case. Listen, in Italian opera, to a first-class singer, and notice how steadily the orchestral accompaniment proceeds, while the soloist retards and accelerates, at almost every moment.'[52]

Among violinists at the turn of the century, Ysaÿe was particularly admired for his rubato. According to Carl Flesch, 'He was master of the imaginative rubato',[53] and Henry Wood remembers his 'marvellous singing quality and perfect rubato ... if he borrowed he faithfully paid back within four bars'.[54] This might seem like Matthay's theory of compensation in action, with the orchestra and soloist accelerating and slowing down together. But Emile Jacques-Dalcroze, Ysaÿe's accompanist, makes it clear that his rubato proceeded independently of the accompaniment (not a procedure recommended by Matthay). He describes a rehearsal with Ysaÿe of Beethoven's 'Kreutzer' Sonata:

In *rubato* melodic passages, he instructed me not to follow him meticulously in the accelerandos and ritenutos, if my part consisted of no more than a simple

accompaniment. 'It is I alone', he would say, 'who can let myself follow the emotion
suggested by the melody; you accompany me in strict time, because an accompaniment should always be in time. You represent order and your duty is to
counter-balance my fantasy. Do not worry, we shall always find each other, because
when I accelerate for a few notes, I afterwards re-establish the equilibrium by slowing
down the following notes, or by pausing for a moment on one of them' . . . In the train
he would try to make up violin passages based on the dynamic accents and cadences of
the wheels, and to execute 'rubato' passages, returning to the first beat each time we
passed in front of a telegraph pole.[55]

Discussion of the origins of this independent rubato belongs to a later
chapter, but it is worth mentioning here that some early twentieth-century
musicians and writers were aware that this style of rubato had a long tradition,
and in particular was associated with Chopin's playing. Marguerite Long's
description of the 'suppleness' of Debussy's playing has already been quoted,
and she writes that Debussy was 'fully preoccupied with Chopin's method,
particularly Chopin's phrasing . . .' Later she elaborates:

In his music this all adds up to a series of nuances that are not to be defined unless they
are felt, and which are represented by *rubato* that is as much part of the interpretation of
Debussy as of Chopin . . . This delicate *rubato* is difficult to obtain in both Chopin and
Debussy. It is confined by a rigorous precision, in almost the same way as a stream is
the captive of its banks. *Rubato* does not mean alteration of time or measure, but of
nuance or *élan*.[56]

This description is not without ambiguities – a 'nuance' can be dynamic,
agogic or tonal – but it does seem as if Long is describing a style of rubato in
which freedom in a melody does not affect the pace of the accompaniment.
Similarly, Long writes about the rubato recommended by Fauré, '*Rubato* in
Fauré is close to Chopin, and derives from freedom in the rounding of the
phrases and respect for the underlying pace.'[57] Whether 'respect for the
underlying pace' really means that Fauré disliked the accelerando–rallentando
style of rubato is open to debate. Certainly Fauré considered Cortot superior to
Long in musicianship, and as an example later in this chapter will show,
Cortot's rubato involved a very volatile approach to tempo which might be
thought to contradict Long's claim.

RECORDINGS

As we have seen in this chapter, different writers recommended or rejected
three different aspects of tempo rubato: the use of accelerando and rallentando
(either strictly 'paid back' or not), the use of tenutos or agogic accents, and a
style of rubato in which the melody was free while the accompaniment
maintained strict tempo. The kinds of rubato used in practice on recordings of
the early twentieth century show a strong relationship to these three descrip-

tions. Rubato of any kind is found at its most extreme, and most frequently, in recordings of pianists (not surprisingly, since solo pianists are free of the constraints of ensemble playing), but also in recordings of other instrumentalists and singers. However, recordings reveal that, whatever some writers might have liked, practising musicians did not adhere strictly to one or other theory of rubato. John McEwen (Principal of the Royal Academy of Music, 1924–36) published in the 1920s an interesting study of rubato among pianists, using Duo-Art piano rolls of Busoni, Pachmann, Carreño and others as evidence.[58] By a visual analysis of the rolls, measuring the lengths of the notes represented by the perforations, he examined the two 'laws' of rubato most frequently put forward by theorists, which he stated in the form of two questions:

1 Have the artists who recorded these rolls, when 'playing an independent accompaniment to a rubato melody or phrase', kept strict time in the accompaniment?

2 Have these artists, when employing time variations (rubato), so balanced these variations that the 'duration of the whole phrase remains the same as it would have been, if played in strict time throughout'?[59]

McEwen finds that the answer to the first question 'is obviously and clearly in the negative'. The illustrations which he gives to prove this are taken from rolls of Pachmann playing Chopin's Nocturne in F sharp, Op. 15 No. 2, and Carreño playing Beethoven's 'Moonlight' Sonata. He demonstrates that the length of the notes in the accompaniments – regular quavers in the Chopin, regular triplet quavers in the Beethoven – vary considerably, and are by no means in strict time. The following is his analysis of Pachmann's recording of the accompaniment in the first four bars of the Chopin Nocturne, notated as equal quavers.

The lengths of these quavers, measured from perforation to perforation on the music-roll, are (in millimetres) as follows:

	♩	♩	♩	♩
1st bar	32.5	34	31.5	25
2nd bar	33	39	30	39.5
3rd bar	33	32	25	23
4th bar	41.5	42	44	53

The reader will see that so far from these quavers being equal in length, as they would be in strict time, there is variation extending from 23mm to 53mm.[60]

McEwen finds similar variations in Carreño's roll of Beethoven's 'Moonlight' Sonata. Here, the first twelve triplet quavers vary in length from 12mm to 19mm, and the crotchet beat varies in length over the first three bars from 32mm to 55mm.

As to the second 'rule', that rubato should be balanced 'so that the duration of the whole phrase remains the same as it would have been, if played in strict time throughout', McEwen points to an absurdity in this theory: 'It is obvious that under this law a performer can bring any vagary or irregularity of time whatsoever, and justify it as "Tempo Rubato", provided he waits till the end of the phrase before defining the value of the average pulse according to which his strict time progresses.'[61] In other words, the theoretical 'strict pulse' can be defined as the average pulse of whatever has been played, which allows total freedom. The same principle can be applied to the average pulse of an entire movement. If what the theoreticians mean is that the average pulse should remain the same over the entire piece, because rubato is 'balanced' within each phrase, then the piano rolls again show that the rule falls down in practice. McEwen uses the same recording by Pachmann to demonstrate this, measuring the lengths of phrases in milimetres. There is no evidence in this performance for an underlying regular pulse continuing through Pachmann's rubato. The opening phrase (to the third quaver of bar 2), ought, according to the rule of compensation or balance, to be the same overall length as its repetitions (from the fourth quaver of bar 2 to the third quaver of bar 4, and from the fourth quaver of bar 8 to the third quaver of bar 10). However, the length of this phrase on the roll is 293.5mm the first time, 252mm the second time, and 287mm the third time.

McEwen gives only a small number of examples to support his case, but if, as he claims, he found similar evidence in a large number of Duo-Art rolls, this would strongly suggest that the two rules of rubato – strict time in the accompaniment, and balance or compensation – were inventions of theoreticians, rather than reflections of actual practice. They are not quite so easily dismissed, however. The chief proponents of the theories were distinguished musicians – Franklin Taylor was a well-known pianist and a pupil of Clara Schumann, Tobias Matthay was a successful teacher whose pupils included Myra Hess, Irene Scharrer, and McEwen himself.

Listening to early twentieth-century recordings with late twentieth-century ears, it is possible to discern at least some relationship between practice and theory, and to understand how these rules may have come to be developed. The theory of compensating rubato, as put forward by Taylor, Matthay, and others, is based on the notion that any accelerando should be balanced by a rallentando or tenuto, and vice versa. This is certainly not a style of rubato familiar in the late twentieth century. In the chapter on flexibility of tempo, it was observed that modern performers were much more reluctant to speed up than to slow down, and the same applies to rubato. Many modern examples of rubato, particularly of pianists, correspond with that 'curious artifical device' to which J. Alfred Johnstone objected in 1914: 'the first few notes of the passage selected for the operation are taken slowly, and then during the remainder of the passage, the pace is gradually increased until the regulation speed is attained'.[62] The most common use of rubato among late twentieth-century pianists is to linger at points of particular emphasis, any acceleration usually being no more a gradual return to tempo after such lingerings. In modern performances, therefore, the pulse is almost invariably held back by rubato. In early twentieth-century rubato, by contrast, pianists were equally likely to accelerate *to* a point of emphasis; and, as in broader tempo changes, so in detailed rubato pianists not only slowed down to underline particular turns of phrase, but also speeded up to emphasise the character of more energetic passages. This does create the impression of 'ebb and flow' and 'give and take' recommended in writings of the period, and even if the strict rule of compensating rubato is nothing more than a theory, it can at least be seen as an attempt to rationalise this genuine practice of a rubato which is flexible either side of the basic pulse.

Similarly, the rule that an accompaniment continues in strict time during a rubato passage is, if taken literally, quite divorced from the practice of the early twentieth century. But, as we shall see in chapter 8, it has too long and respectable a history to be dismissed out of hand, and as with the theory of compensation, recordings show that it is at least loosely based on aspects of real practice.

The rhythmic dislocation of melody from accompaniment is one of the most obvious features of much early twentieth-century piano playing. Like the early twentieth-century tendency to accelerate, this practice has been firmly discouraged in the late twentieth century, and failure to play the left and right hands together is now generally regarded as carelessness. But until the 1920s, many pianists, particularly those of the older generation (Paderewski, Pachmann, Rosenthal *et al.*), made a habit of this non-synchronisation. Most often this took the form of delaying a note of a melody in order to create an accent, or sometimes to draw attention to an inner part. The separation of melodic note and accompaniment was sometimes undisguised, at other times the separation was softened by spreading a chord. McEwen, in his book on tempo rubato, while examining the rule that the accompaniment should keep strict time, makes no mention of this widespread practice. However, one of his examples, which he uses for another purpose, contains clear illustrations of it. It is a photographic reproduction of two bars (bars 50–2) of the Duo-Art piano roll of Chopin's Nocturne in F sharp recorded by Pachmann, showing the perforations of the roll aligned with the musical notation of the passage, so that the distances between the notes show the precise rhythm played by the pianist (see example 2.1). Of the three points in this passage at which a note in the melody theoretically coincides with a note in the bass, only one is played even approximately synchronously. This is the low C sharp in the melody against F sharp in the bass (first beat of the last bar of the passage). Even here the bass note is slightly later that the melody note. The first full bar of the passage begins with B natural in the melody played much later than the F sharp in the bass. The last quaver of the bass part is played after the melody note (C sharp), and the three notes of the chord are clearly separated with an arpeggio.

Ex.2.1   Chopin, Nocturne in F sharp, Op. 15 No. 2, bars 50–2, showing the perforations on
Duo-Art piano-roll performed by Pachmann. From McEwen, *Tempo Rubato or Time-Variation in
Musical Performance*.

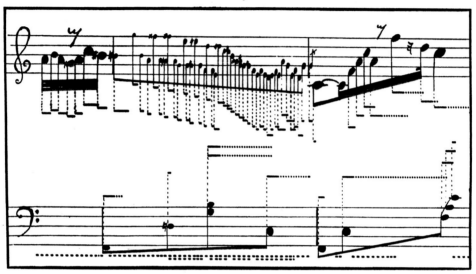

This example illustrates in graphic form a very widespread practice among
pianists of the early twentieth century, and it is this practice which must be at
the root of the rule insisting on strict time in an accompaniment. In passages
where melody and bass are dislocated, the apparent position of the beat is often
defined by the bass, whether it is in strict tempo or not. In such cases the
melody, if played rubato, appears free in relation to a pulse defined by the bass.
It is only a short step from this observable phenomenon to a theory that the
accompaniment proceeds in strict time. Again, like the theory of compensation
in rubato, this rule can be seen as an attempt to rationalise actual practice. The
practice itself is, however, more complex than it might appear, as examples will
show.

The third aspect of tempo rubato already discussed in this chapter, though
not mentioned by McEwen, is the use of tenutos or agogic accents, as distinct
from accelerando and rallentando. Here, too, modern practice has moved a
long way from the early twentieth century. Agogic accents are still used by
modern pianists (and other instrumentalists and singers), but the general
practice is that, as in Johnstone's 'curious artificial device', after the lengthened
note (or notes) 'the pace is gradually increased until the regulation speed is
attained'. What distinguishes much early twentieth-century use of the tenuto
from this modern practice is that the lengthened note is immediately followed
by a shortened note rather than by a gradual return to tempo. The effect is to
emphasise a note without drawing out the phrase as a whole. It leads, as several
writers quoted above suggest, to a style of rubato much closer to declamatory
speech rhythm than the smoother, less volatile rubato of late twentieth-century

playing. At its most extreme, this rhythmical adjustment goes so far as to create dotted or triplet rhythms from even note-values, a common feature of Paderewski's playing, although he makes no mention of it in his article on tempo rubato quoted above. More subtle versions of this rhythmic adjustment, which often amount to momentary *notes inégales*, are found in the playing of many instrumentalists during the period.

As was mentioned at the beginning of this chapter, these three kinds of rubato – detailed tempo fluctuation, agogic accents, and separation of melody and accompaniment – have been separated in discussion for convenience, but in practice each one rarely occurs singly in recordings of the early twentieth century. They are therefore discussed together in the examples which follow.

Schubert, Impromptu in B flat, D. 935 No. 3, theme and variation 3

Paderewski   (rec. 1924)
Edwin Fischer   (rec. 1938)
Schnabel   (rec. 1950).

To a late twentieth-century listener, the most striking feature of Paderewski's performance of the theme of this Impromptu is the frequent rhythmic separation of the melody and the accompaniment, a habit which is not mentioned in Paderewski's own remarks on tempo rubato or in the description of his playing by Finck. There are sixteen main beats in the first eight bars of the theme, and on seven of them the bass anticipates the melody note. Between the main beats, the melody and accompaniment are also separated in the first half of bar 5 and in both halves of bar 7, where the exceptional amount of dislocation has the effect of emphasising the arrival at the climax of the melody. At the end of bar 4, the sudden appearance of the two inner parts, moving in thirds, is picked out by playing the lower part slightly ahead of the upper. Similarly in bar 8 Paderewski emphasises the appearance of the inner part by playing its first note (B flat) much earlier than the outer parts. The end of the phrase is then finished off with a slow arpeggio in the right hand. The most noticeable other instance of rhythmic flexibility is a slight acceleration and tenuto in the first half of bar 3. Paderewski plays the first time and the repeat in almost exactly the same way, except at bar 4 where he slows down the second time but not the first.

By comparison with Paderewski, both Fischer and Schnabel play the theme in a much more straightforward manner, and neither of them uses noticeable dislocation of bass and melody. Fischer eases slightly into the second beat of bar 2, making room for Schubert's appoggiatura, but otherwise plays straight through the eight bars. Schnabel's most noticeable flexibility is at bars 4 and 8. In both instances he slightly lengthens the first quaver of the bar and then plays the following semiquavers slightly fast. This is very characteristic of this pianist, and also ties in with the general tendency in the early decades of the century to hurry the short notes (a habit discussed in the next chapter).

Rubato and the treatment of long and short notes are inextricable from each other in Paderewski's performance of Variation 3 of the Impromptu. His treatment of the dotted rhythms is not just a matter of over- or under-dotting, but is related to his use of tenutos, the emphasising of beats, and the relationship between melody and bass. The rhythm ♫ in the melody is played as ♩．♪ throughout, with the semiquaver therefore coinciding with the third quaver of the triplet group in the bass. This has the effect of bringing together melody and bass notes which would be separated if played strictly according to the notation. In many cases, the triplet which follows this dotted rhythm is played with a lengthened second quaver and a shortened third quaver, so that the third quaver is played after the bass. This shortened quaver is therefore played shorter than the semiquaver of the dotted rhythm. The rhythm ♪♪ is played in three different ways, creating a variety of relationships between melody and accompaniment. Where the quaver is an upbeat to a phrase, as at the end of the second, fourth, and sixth bar of the variation, it is played short, falling after the last triplet quaver in the bass. In the first half of the first bar, however, the quaver is played more or less as a duplet quaver, falling before the third quaver of the triplet group in the bass, and the last quaver of this bar is in a similar relationship to the bass. Where this phrase is repeated, at the fifth bar, the equivalent two quavers are played as triplet quavers, coinciding with the bass. Treatment of dotted rhythms is discussed in the next chapter, but the point here is that Paderewski's flexible interpretation of these rhythms creates a constantly changing relationship with the bass, and subtly varies the impetus towards the next beat. This is further complicated by the separation of melody and bass, which, in the first half of the variation, occurs on seven out of the sixteen main beats. The second bar is particularly complex. In the right hand, the semiquaver is lengthened to coincide with the triplet quaver in the bass, the following triplet begins with an accelerando, and is distorted by a lengthened second quaver and shortened third quaver, and then the bass slightly anticipates the next beat. The effect, as so often in Paderewski's playing, is a volatile exploration of the rhythmic progression of the melody, with a flexible relationship between the melody and the bass. In the eighth bar, bass and melody are separated not only on the final beat, but also on the preceding two quavers, giving weight to the end of the rallentando.

As in the theme, Fischer and Schnabel both give a more straightforward performance of Variation 3, with none of Paderewski's tenutos during triplet groups, no separation of bass and melody on main beats, and no significant variations in tempo. However, their treatment of dotted rhythms still retains some early twentieth-century characteristics. The rhythm ♫ is played ♬♩. by Schnabel, and even more overdotted by Fischer, both consistently throughout the variation. Schnabel gives quaver upbeats in the second, fourth, and sixth bars their full duplet value, but shortens the final quavers of the first and fifth bars to triplet quavers coinciding with the bass. He maintains this pattern throughout the variation. Fischer reverses this pattern, though a little less consistently. In the second and fourth bars he shortens the quaver upbeats to triplet quavers, but in the sixth bar he makes the upbeat quaver even shorter. The quavers of the first and fifth bars, which Schnabel shortens, Fischer plays full length.

Chopin, Mazurka in C sharp minor, Op. 63 No. 3 (examples 2.2a and 2.2b)

Paderewski   (rec. 1930)
Pachmann   (rec. c. 1928)
Rachmaninoff   (rec. 1923)

This example shows Paderewski using many tenutos and other rhythmic distortions in the performance of Chopin, for which he was particularly celebrated. The basic rhythm of the Mazurka is played with tenutos which vary subtly throughout the piece. At the beginning he establishes a rhythm with a long first beat and a short second beat (descriptions of Chopin's own perform-ance of a mazurka rhythm specify a lengthened first beat). This is varied at points of particular emphasis. For example, the approach to the highest point of the melody at bars 4–5 is emphasised by shifting the tenuto to the second beat. At bar 4 the phrase is rounded off by a slight lengthening of the second beat, then a shortened third beat gives an impetus into the climactic phrase. At bar 5 the lengthening of the second beat underlines the start of the phrase, and further emphasis is given by arpeggiating the accompaniment and delaying the melody note. The passing of the melodic climax is signalled by a sudden return in bar 6 to the original rhythmic pattern with a shortened second beat. This pattern then continues for the next few bars, until, from bar 16, the predominance of quavers in the melody tends to even out the three beats of the bar. At bar 19 the dotted rhythm and twist of harmony are emphasised by tenutos on the first two beats of the bar, with a shortened third beat, as well as by a rallentando (at bar 27, which is identical, all three beats are lengthened). At bar 24, the brief appearance of a countermelody in the bass is picked out not only by a tenuto on the second beat, but also by playing the bass note early. In the middle section of the mazurka, from bar 33, the predominant pattern of tenutos changes. Where tenutos occur, they are on the second beat of the bar, not the first. At the recapitulation of the first section, from bar 49, distortions of the beat are generally less marked than at the beginning of the Mazurka, but where they occur they tend to shorten the second beat or lengthen the third, as before. Dislocation of melody and bass, however, is much more frequent than in the opening section. In the coda of the Mazurka, from bar 65 (example 2.2b),

Ex.2.2   Chopin, Mazurka in C sharp minor, Op. 63 No. 3, Paderewski. ⌐ unequal
quavers (dotted ryhthm, except where marked 'less'); ‒ lengthened note;
ᴗ shortened note. (a) bars 1–26; (b) bars 65–9.

Paderewski points the canonic countermelody by a subtle combination of tenuto and rhythmic dislocation. The first note of the countermelody, at bar 66, is picked out by being played early and held long. At bar 69 two more notes of the countermelody are played early. Together with general flexibility of tempo over this passage, this gives an extraordinary impression of rhythmic independence to the countermelody.

As well as lengthening and shortening beats, Paderewski adopts a flexible (by modern standards, cavalier) approach to rhythms within the beat. Many pairs of quavers are played with unequal lengths, often to the extent of a dotted rhythm, sometimes to a lesser extent. (Pairs of quavers marked with a square bracket are played as dotted rhythms; those marked 'less' are played with subtler inequality.) At first, it seems as if Paderewski is simply taking the dotted rhythm from the recapitulation (bars 50 and 52) and playing the opening of the Mazurka in the same manner. However, it soon becomes clear that his use of unequal quavers is both more extensive and more flexible than that. The subtlest examples of unequal quavers occur at climactic moments: at the highest points of the phrase, at bars 6 and 14, and at the climax before the coda, at bars 62–4. At bars 50 and 58, the upbeat pairs of quavers are played late and fast, after the bass (these quavers do not occur in the first section of the Mazurka). In the middle section, Paderewski modifies some of the dotted rhythms, playing equal quavers at bars 40 and 44, and underdotting the rhythm at bar 36. Such modifications of even and dotted rhythms are frequently encountered in Paderewski's recordings, though rarely in such concentration as in this Mazurka.

Perhaps surprisingly, Pachmann, who had a certain reputation for eccentricity, interprets the rhythm of this piece much more literally than Paderewski. He plays the pair of quavers in bar 2 slightly fast, but there are no noticeable examples of unequal quavers. It is in the relationship between melody and bass that Pachmann shows the most flexibility. As in Paderewski's performance, the separation of melody and bass is sometimes used to underline important moments in the structure of the music, though at other times it seems haphazard. At bar 6, Pachmann marks the descent from the highest point of the melody by playing the first and second beats slightly later than the bass. At bar 17 the move to a new phrase with a new rhythm is signalled by a delayed melody note (the same phrase is played in the same way at bars 21 and 29). At bars 47–8 the modulations back to the original key of C sharp minor are emphasised by increasing rhythmic dislocation. At bar 47 the E flat in the melody is played slightly after the bass, at bar 48 the E natural in the melody is played still later than the bass, and at bar 49 the return to the home key is underlined by arpeggiating the chord on the second beat. Pachmann's treatment of the canon at bars 65–71 is less striking, and less subtle, than Paderewski's. He does not separate melody and countermelody to a noticeable extent, but he emphasises the beginning of the passage in a more general way by playing the right hand after the left on the second beat of bar 65 and the second beat of bar 67. In slower music, the separation of melody and bass is a continual feature of Pachmann's playing, as a later example will show.

Rachmaninoff's performance gives a generally more modern impression than Paderewski's and Pachmann's. He is much less volatile in tempo than Paderewski and he does not dislocate the melody and bass. He does, however, modify pairs of quavers and make use of occasional tenutos, though not as frequently as Paderewski. He plays a dotted rhythm instead of equal quavers at the upbeat into bar 1. At bar 25, he bends the group of three quavers, lengthening the first and second quavers and shortening the third, an example of short-term give and take which is highly characteristic of Rachmaninoff (see the following example). He plays the beginning of the recapitulation with many more examples of modified quavers than the opening. Between bars 50 and 59 he turns six pairs of equal quavers into dotted rhythms. Then, somewhat like Paderewski, he plays more subtly unequal quavers towards the climax, turning them into something more like a triplet rhythm at bars 60 and 61, but then reverting to dotted rhythms at the last beat of bar 63 and bar 64. At bars 66–7 he again uses subtle tenuto to bring the inner countermelody into relief. In bar 66, the first note of the inner part is slightly lengthened and the second note shortened (approximately in triplet rhythm), and in bar 67 the second phrase of the inner part is again emphasised by a tenuto on the F sharp. There are further examples of pairs of quavers turned into a triplet rhythm at bars 72 and 73. Rachmaninoff's performance, therefore, though it gives a general impression of being straightforward in an almost modern way, contains elements of rhythmic adjustment which are characteristic of early twentieth-century piano-playing.

Rachmaninoff, Rhapsody on a Theme of Paganini, Variation 18

Rachmaninoff, Philadelphia Orchestra, cond. Stokowski   (rec. 1934)

This passage (the famous 'big tune' of the Variations) illustrates a characteristic way in which Rachmaninoff often subtly adjusts rhythmic values in his own music. Several times during the variation he adjusts the recurring upbeat group of four semiquavers, slightly lengthening the first three and shortening the fourth. Sometimes he also adjusts the triplet groups in a similar way. There are many examples of this sort of rhythmic adjustment in Rachmaninoff's performances of his own works (another striking example is to be found in the second subject of the first movement of his Piano Concerto No. 2). It illustrates how Rachmaninoff, unlike many modern performers of his music, often achieves subtle rhythmic emphasis and expression without drawing out the phrase as a whole.

Chopin, Nocturne in E flat, Op. 9 No. 2

Paderewski   (rec. 1930)

Chopin, Nocturne in D flat, Op. 27 No. 2

Pachmann   (rec. c. 1925)

These two examples provide particularly clear illustration of the use of the rhythmic separation of melody and bass. Paderewski's performance of the Nocturne in E flat is flexible in a number of ways. The triplet groups in the accompaniment often have a lengthened first quaver and shortened second and third quavers, particularly when the melody is at its simplest (throughout bar 3, for example). This effect of 'leaning' on the main beats is rather similar to the predominant rhythm in Paderewski's performance of the Mazurka in C sharp minor. The most striking feature of the performance, however, is the dislocation of melody and bass. Of the 32 dotted-crotchet beats in the first eight bars, 27 are played with the bass note in advance of the melody note. There are also fourteen examples of melody notes between the main beats being played after the chord in the accompaniment. Pachmann's performance of the Nocturne in D flat is, as in the earlier comparison between these two pianists, more straightforward in general flexibility, but it too has many instances of dislocation of melody and accompaniment. Admittedly, fewer of the main beats are treated in this way than in the Paderewski example – only eight of the first 24 beats of the Nocturne. But there are striking examples of dislocation between the main beats, particularly at bars 6 and 8, where semiquavers become increasingly late towards the end of the bar. Slow-moving and rhythmically fairly simple examples like these force one to consider just what is involved in such dislocation. The descriptions of 'melodic rubato' quoted earlier in this chapter suggest that, where a note of the melody is played either before or after the accompaniment, the beat is conveyed by the accompaniment, and the freedom occurs in the melody. But is this how one actually perceives the relationship between melody and bass? The answer, as these two examples demonstrate, is that it depends on the circumstances. In Pachmann's performance, the continuous semiquavers of the accompaniment do give the impression that they carry the main responsibility for conveying the beat. Melody notes which occur after the bass note are, on the whole, heard as being late. On main accents, as at the first beats of bars 4 and 5, this has the effect of a deliberate accentuation by delay. Where a succession of melody notes becomes dislocated from the bass, as in bars 6 and 8, there is a sense of the melody drifting out of phase with the accompaniment and then returning, as in Ysaÿe's rubato (see example 2.6). Again, the accompaniment is perceived as maintaining the pulse. The Paderewski example is rather different. Where dislocation occurs *between* the main beats, then the melody notes seem to be delayed, as in the Pachmann example. This happens, for example, at the beginning of bar 4. The leap upwards in the melody is accentuated by delaying the second quaver of the bar, then the third quaver is also delayed, but shortened, so that on the following main beat the melody and bass are again (roughly) synchronised. The same pattern occurs at the beginning of bar 8, and several other subsidiary quavers during the passage also give a definite impression of delayed melody notes. By contrast, the principal beats, most of which are dislocated, sound as if the bass anticipates the beat, rather than the melody being late. In other words, the beat seems to be carried principally by the melody rather than by the bass. This is the reverse of the way melodic rubato is usually described by writers. Certainly, in music where the bass maintains a rhythmic pattern at a fast enough pace for the exact position of the beat to be unambiguous, as in the Nocturne in D flat, the tendency is for any dislocation to sound like a delay in the melody. But where the bass is slow-moving and the rhythmic impulse of the melody strongly defined, as in the Nocturne in E flat, then a dislocated beat can often sound like an anticipation in the bass rather than a delay in the melody. Of course, there is room for ambiguity, and in many instances different listeners might disagree as to whether the bass leads or the melody follows. What is certain is that the situation is a great deal more complex than most writers of the early twentieth century would have us believe.

Chopin, Nocturne in F sharp, Op. 15 No. 2 (example 2.3)

d'Albert   (rec. 1916)

D'Albert, a pupil of Liszt, shows in this example less of a tendency than Pachmann and Paderewski to dislocate melody and bass. Dislocation does occur on the first beats of bars 3 and 6, and in bar 6 the chords in the left hand on the second and fourth quavers are arpeggiated. But the most notable rhythmic feature of this performance is the adjustment of note-lengths in the melody. This takes the form of shortening the last semiquaver of the beat, in bars 1, 5, 6, and 9. In bar 1, there is a compensatory lengthening of the first semiquaver of the group, but in the other examples there is no compensation for the shortening of the final semiquaver, so that the effect is of an unexpected, or at least unprepared, lurch into the next beat. The final quaver of bar 3 is shortened in a similar way. In the sense that these shortened notes are all 'upbeats' into the next beat, this ties in with the general tendency in the early years of the century to shorten upbeats, but the lack of compensatory lengthening of the preceding notes is striking. McEwen's analysis of Pachmann's piano-roll of these bars, which was quoted earlier, clearly shows the shortening of the last quaver of bars 1 and 3, and in bar 1 the last quaver is much shorter than any of the other three quavers of the bar. This probably gives a similar

Ex.2.3 Chopin, Nocturne in F sharp, Op. 15 No. 2, bars 1–10, d'Albert.

effect to d'Albert's shortened final quaver in bar 3, but McEwen gives no information about Pachmann's treatment of semiquavers.

Chopin, Sonata in B minor, Op. 58, first movement, bars 41–56

Grainger   (rec. 1925)
Cortot   (rec. 1933)
Rosenthal   (rec. 1939)

Rosenthal, like d'Albert a pupil of Liszt, was in his late seventies when he made this recording, and demonstrates an earlier style of playing than Cortot and Grainger. Much of the performance suffers from obvious clumsiness because of old age, but this passage, the second subject of the first movement, shows the characteristic rhythmic nuances of his generation which have already been illustrated in the examples of Paderewski, Pachmann, and d'Albert. There are several instances of dislocation of melody and accompaniment which, because of the continuous flow of quavers in the bass, are generally heard as delayed melody notes rather than anticipated bass notes. These become most frequent and most marked where the playing is quietest and most intimate, at bars

49–50. Rosenthal's frequent adjustment of the length of quavers is also characteristic of his generation. In the accompaniment the triplet quavers are sometimes irregular, most noticeably in the first two bars of the passage. This irregularity consists of shortening the third quaver of a triplet group, on the first and third beats of bar 41, and on the third beat of bar 42. This has the effect of a push into the next beat, similar to the effect noticed in d'Albert's playing of the Nocturne in F sharp. In the melody, Rosenthal on four occasions adjusts a pair or group of quavers so as to shorten the last quaver, creating shortened 'upbeats'. On the last beats of bars 41 and 45, this has the effect of turning equal quavers into a dotted rhythm. Other instances of irregular quavers occur on the second beat of bar 50, and in the quintuplet group in bar 51, which is reshaped into a fast triplet followed by a tenuto and a short final quaver. On three occasions quavers are adjusted to fit the triplets of the accompaniment – on the second beat of bar 49, the first beat of bar 50, and the second beat of bar 51. All these rhythmic adjustments are in addition to fluctuations in tempo.

In one important respect Cortot's performance is less old-fashioned than Rosenthal's: he uses dislocation of melody and bass only occasionally, and it always occurs on the first beat of the bar, except in bar 41 where it highlights the first note of the melody. However, Cortot makes much use of tenutos and tempo fluctuations, accelerating and slowing down many times during this theme. Changes of pace are sometimes quite abrupt. For example, over the first four bars of the passage there are three sudden changes to a faster pace, each preceded by a brief point of repose. During the rest of the passage few notes pass without an accelerando, rallentando, or tenuto. This produces an impression which is characteristic of this pianist – an extremely volatile exploration of the detailed shape of the music. There are also several examples of detailed rhythmic adjustment of the length of quavers. At the end of bar 41, Cortot plays the pair of quavers unequally. In the second half of bar 45, the lengthened first three quavers are followed by a shortened final quaver. There are other examples of unequal quavers in bars 50–1. In some instances these unequal quavers are not as unequal as in Rosenthal's performance (at bars 41 and 45), but at the beginning of bar 50 Cortot adjusts the pair of equal quavers to a dotted rhythm, whereas Rosenthal plays a triplet rhythm. By contrast, Cortot underdots the dotted rhythm at bars 47 and 49, lengthening the final semiquaver to make a triplet rhythm. In description these rhythmic adjustments might seem as obvious as Rosenthal's, but to the modern ear they sound less crude, and so much a part of Cortot's generally volatile approach that they do not stand out as much as in Rosenthal's performance.

By comparison with Rosenthal and Cortot, Grainger plays the passage in a very straightforward manner – unusually so for the 1920s. The high points of phrases at bars 43–4 and 47–8 are marked by a slight suggestion of dislocation of melody and bass, but in general there is even less dislocation than in Cortot's performance, and much less than in Rosenthal's. The only marked example of rubato in Grainger's performance is at bar 51, where the quintuplet group is played late.

J. S. Bach, Italian Concerto, second movement (example 2.4)

Gordon-Woodhouse   (rec. c. 1927)
Landowska   (rec. 1935–6)

Gordon-Woodhouse, the first harpsichordist to make records, was trained as a pianist (under Beringer), and her playing carries over the traditional character-istics of early twentieth-century piano rubato on to the harpsichord without any noticeable dilution. It is particularly striking to a modern listener to hear Bach played on the harpsichord much as Paderewski, Pachmann, or Rosenthal play Chopin on the piano. Her use of tempo fluctuations, like Cortot's, is extremely volatile. Several times, for example at bars 7, 10, and 11, an accelerando begins or ends with a definite tenuto, which has the effect of providing a firm anchor-point to which the acceleration is tied. In bars 10 and 11 the tenuto occurs at the end of the accelerando, not on a quaver beat, nor even on a semiquaver sub-beat, but simply on the last demisemiquaver of the run, producing a sudden halt quite unlike anything in later twentieth-century rubato. She makes extensive use not just of arpeggiated chords, a device used by modern harpsichordists as a historical eighteenth-century habit, but also of the dislocation of melody and accompaniment common in piano playing in the early twentieth century. Melody notes are most delayed in order to accentuate leaps, at the end of bar 13 and the beginning of bar 20. At bar 13 the approach to the leap is also prepared by more subtle dislocation on the two preceding quavers. Dislocation in the first two bars of the melody, bars 4–5, immediately establishes a sense of freedom in the relationship between melody and accom-paniment, which is maintained by occasional dislocation throughout the passage, in conjunction with the general rhythmic freedom created by the continual fluctuations in pace.

Landowska, in an essay quoted earlier in this chapter, writes of 'the thousand and one minute particles of stolen time, of inserted breathings, of phrases brought into relief . . . that I obtain through retards or deliberate infinitessimal rushings!'[63] What emerges most strikingly from the comparison between these two recordings is how much more closely that quotation describes Gordon-Woodhouse's playing than Landowska's. Landowska does not play this passage in strict time, but she is much closer to it than Gordon-Woodhouse. Gordon-Woodhouse's accelerations are often quite sudden and short-lived; most of Landowska's accelerations are subtle and long-term. Her most marked acceler-ation is at bars 19–20, resulting in a sustained increase in tempo through to the rallentando in the second half of bar 22. Landowska uses dislocation of melody and accompaniment much less frequently than Gordon-Woodhouse, on the

Ex.2.4   J. S. Bach, Italian Concerto, second movement, bars 1–14, Gordon-Woodhouse.

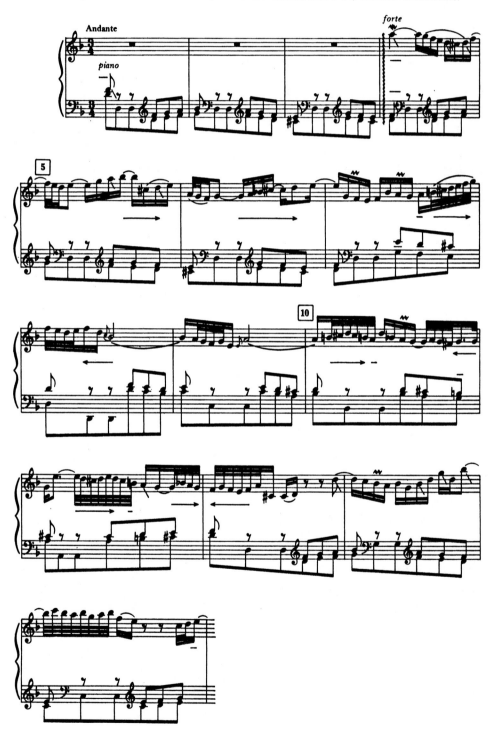

first note of the melody, and twice in bar 7 to accentuate trills. There are only occasional suggestions of rhythmic alteration, most noticeably at the end of bar 24, where a rallentando culminates in a tenuto on the penultimate note of the bar, so that the final pair of demisemiquavers is played as a dotted rhythm. Landowska's performance conveys much more impression of rhythmic regularity than Gordon-Woodhouse's, in the long term and the short term, and seems less 'pianistic' in early twentieth-century terms. This is despite the fact that Landowska's harpsichord is made much more piano-like than Gordon-Woodhouse's by the use of crescendos and diminuendos. In general, Landowska's playing is rhythmically at its most characteristic in fast movements, and although it has rhythmic flexibility, and moments of rhythmic eccentricity, it obtains its sense of rhythmic vigour more by articulation, and particularly by the use of staccato, than by rubato.

Beethoven, Piano Sonata in C minor, Op. 13 ('Pathétique'), first and second movements

Lamond (rec. 1926)

Lamond's playing of Beethoven shows many of the usual rhythmic characteristics of the early twentieth century – sudden changes of pace, tenutos and unequal notes, and dislocation of melody and accompaniment. In the first movement, at bars 56, 64, 68, and 72, Lamond distinguishes the ongoing melody in the treble from the brief 'aside' in the bass by playing the phrase in the bass suddenly faster than the melody either side of it. Slurred pairs of crotchets with a trill on the first of the pair, which first appear at bars 58–9, are in many cases played unequally. This happens three times in a row at bars 58–9, 66–7, and 74–5, and four times in a row at bars 86–7, creating an effect of habitual *notes inégales*. At bar 76, and again at bar 80, the sudden movement of the left hand after the constantly repeated A flat of the preceding bars is brought out not only by accentuation but also by playing the descending minims ahead of the beat. This passage is played with very similar rhythmic adjustments where it recurs at the recapitulation.

Lamond's performance of the second movement is notable for the varied use of rhythmic dislocation. The first statement of the theme (bars 1–8) has no noticeable dislocation. In the second statement (bars 9–16), three important notes of the melody are separated from the accompaniment by being played late (the first beat of bar 12, and both beats of bar 13), and the statement is also made more emphatic by the use of several tenutos at the beginning of beats. The episode which follows at bar 17 is played in quite a different manner. The separation of the melody from its accompaniment is emphasised in Lamond's performance by frequent rhythmic dislocation, with notes of the melody being played late not only at the principal beats but also at several of the intervening semiquavers. This has the effect of underlining the contrast in texture between the opening theme, with its closely juxtaposed melody and accompaniment, and the episode, in which the melody is isolated from the accompaniment.

Beethoven, Violin Sonata in G, Op. 96, first movement, bars 1–59

Fachiri, Tovey   (rec. c. 1928)

This example of a Beethoven violin sonata is rhythmically as flexible as the previous example of a solo piano sonata. Tovey's piano-playing in particular shows many examples of changing pace and rhythmic adjustment in this passage. From bar 11 the change to a continuous pattern of quavers is underlined by an acceleration to a substantially faster pace. This pace is interrupted at the highest point of the passage at bar 17 by a tenuto, followed by a gradual return to tempo. Tenutos on the first beats of bars 20 and 21 are followed by a sudden ritenuto into the abrupt *piano* at bar 22. Over bars 23–4 there is another slight accelerando, with the sudden ritenuto repeated into the *piano* at bar 25. Later on in the passage, the most marked accelerandos and rallentandos occur over bars 44–59. Here Beethoven twice specifies *ritard* followed by *a tempo*, but Fachiri and Tovey go far beyond any implications of these markings. They begin to slow down two bars earlier than the marked *ritard*, at the end of bar 46, then the *a tempo* at bar 49 is followed by an acceleration at bar 51. Another brief hold-up at bar 54, emphasising the arrival at the sforzando chord, is followed by a further acceleration over bar 55 before arriving at the marked *ritard* at bar 57. Tovey makes much use of tenutos. Several times single tenutos are used to emphasise a strong beat (as at the first beats of bars 20 and 21), to create a slight separation from the following phrase (the first notes of bars 33, 35, and 37), or to mark the climax of a phrase (the highest notes of bars 17, 38, and 40). Elsewhere they stress the first of a pair of quavers, or of a triplet, creating unequal quavers. In bar 9 both pairs of quavers are unequal, and in bars 47–8 Tovey lengthens the first of each triplet to a gradually increasing extent as he slows down, so that by the second beat of bar 48 the triplet quavers have almost become a quaver followed by two semiquavers. It is noticeable that Fachiri's playing is rhythmically much more straightforward than Tovey's. The general flexibility of tempo applies as much to Fachiri as to Tovey, of course, but detailed rhythmic adjustment is largely absent from Fachiri's playing. The pairs of quavers in the opening theme, which Tovey plays unequally at bar 9, are played equally by Fachiri (though she plays a portamento between them at bars 3 and 8, which creates a different kind of rhythmic emphasis). It is particularly striking that the triplet rhythm of bars 47–8, which Tovey plays with increasing inequality, is played without noticeable inequality by Fachiri at bars 55–6. This greater degree of freedom by the pianist than by the violinist helps to give an impression of a performance whose character is dominated by the pianist.

J. S. Bach, Sonata in G minor for Unaccompanied Violin, Adagio
(example 2.5)

Joachim   (rec. 1903)
Kreisler   (rec. 1926)
Arnold Rosé   (rec. c. 1931)

Fachiri, the violinist in the previous example, was a pupil of Joachim, and Tovey was also associated with Joachim in his early years. Joachim's own rhythmic style, on the evidence of his few recordings, is nearer to Tovey's than Fachiri's. This recording of the Adagio in G minor was made when his playing had already declined through old age, and there are clear signs of clumsiness in rhythm, for instance a tendency to snatch anxiously at some of the chords. Nevertheless the performance does also provide clear evidence of the frequent use of very marked tenutos and unequal rhythms. This accords with the descriptions of Joachim's agogic accents quoted earlier in this chapter. *Notes inégales* occur more frequently in this example than in any of the performances discussed so far. Four consecutive pairs of semiquavers are treated in this way at bars 5–6, and again at bar 11, and there are other examples in bars 3, 12, 16 (where the inequality creates a dotted rhythm), 17, 18, and 19. Other aspects of Joachim's rhythmic style are more difficult to judge. The performance is extremely volatile in tempo, and some of the hurrying sounds like the result of insecurity – for example at bar 15, where Joachim plays the last two quavers of the bar at almost double speed. But the general tendency to play groups of the shortest note values fast seems like a genuine stylistic feature. The most exaggerated examples are the rising scales on the third beat of bars 2 and 15, but there are less extreme examples throughout the movement.

By contrast with Joachim, Kreisler's performance is the most modern in rhythmic style of the three, with Rosé intermediate between Joachim and Kreisler. This is not to say that Kreisler is inflexible. His performance contains a number of tenutos, accelerandos, and rallentandos, but they are used in a gradual and subtle way, avoiding Joachim's abrupt changes of pace and rhythmic adjustments. In the very first bar, the two runs of demisemiquavers each begin slowly and accelerate slightly, and there are slight pauses on the chords before and between the runs. The rising scale on the third beat of bar 2 is played with a tenuto on the first note (G), with the following notes slightly fast. The same applies at the equivalent passage at bar 15. Joachim also plays these rising scales fast, but whereas Joachim, here and elsewhere, rushes ahead in a manner which seems uncontrolled (by modern standards), Kreisler keeps the pace much more firmly in check, and the performance as a whole is much less volatile than Joachim's. Kreisler's tenutos are generally of the modern type –

Ex.2.5 J. S. Bach, Unaccompanied Violin Sonata in G minor, first movement, bars 1–13, Rosé, Kreisler, and Joachim.

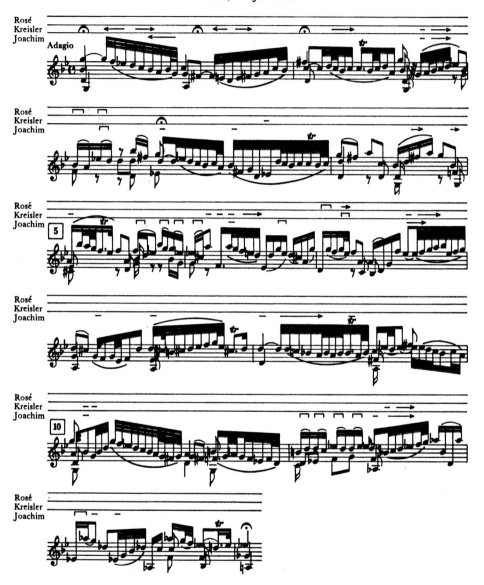

points of emphasis which are followed not by a compensating adjustment of the next note-value, but by a more gradual return to tempo. Kreisler interprets rhythmic detail much more literally than Joachim. There is only one noticeable example of *notes inégales*: in bar 7, on the pair of demisemiquavers at the end of the first beat.

Rosé's performance is the most constant in tempo of the three, but his interpretation of rhythms is less modern (in the sense of less literal) than Kreisler's. In particular, he uses the device of *notes inégales* almost as frequently as Joachim. At the beginning of bar 3 the two pairs of slurred semiquavers are played slightly unequally, and at the end of bar 18 the two pairs of semiquavers are played very unequally. There are other examples of individual pairs of unequal semiquavers at the beginning of bar 7, the beginning of bar 16, and on the third beat of bar 19. On the other hand, the four pairs of slurred semiquavers in bar 11, all of which are played unequally by Joachim, are played with equal note-values by Rosé.

J. S. Bach, Partita in E for Unaccompanied Violin, Gavotte

Willy Burmester   (rec. 1909)

J. S. Bach, Partita in B minor for Unaccompanied Violin, Sarabande

Huberman   (rec. 1936)

J. S. Bach, Suite in D for Unaccompanied Cello, Sarabande and Gavotte I

Casals   (rec. 1936–7)

These brief examples provide further illustration of *notes inégales* in both fast and slow movements from Bach's works for unaccompanied strings. Burmester's performance of the Gavotte from the Partita in E is fast and rhythmically pointed throughout (he plays it in an arrangement with piano accompaniment). Unequal quavers occur from time to time during the movement, but they reach a climax at bars 34–5, creating an almost jazz-like swinging of the rhythm. In the Gavotte from the Cello Suite in D, Casals similarly swings the rhythm with unequal pairs of quavers as he approaches the final statement of the gavotte theme (bar 19). The remaining two examples, by Casals and Huberman, are both from sarabandes, and in each case *notes inégales* are used to give a sighing emphasis to the phrasing of a sequence of descending pairs of notes, at bar 15 of the Sarabande in B minor, and at bars 17–20 of the Sarabande in D.

Ex.2.6   Vieuxtemps, Rondino, Op. 32 No. 2, Ysaÿe. (a) bars 14–20; (b) bars 38–41.

Vieuxtemps, Rondino Op. 32 No. 2 (examples 2.6a and 2.6b)

Ysaÿe, Decreus   (rec. 1912)

This recording is of particular interest for two reasons. The first is that Ysaÿe studied with Vieuxtemps. This not only lends significance to Ysaÿe's performance of this piece, but also provides a link with one of the great violin schools of the nineteenth century. The other reason is that Ysaÿe's rubato was particularly praised, and writers, including Ysaÿe himself, insisted that his rubato was achieved without disrupting the beat in the accompaniment (see pp. 43–4). This is the classic claim for melodic rubato in pianists, which, as we have seen, is not borne out by recordings, even though melody and accompaniment often part company. In the case of Ysaÿe the evidence given by writers is very specific, so it is interesting to examine the rubato in this recording. In both of the extracts given here Ysaÿe does play with considerable freedom while the accompanist continues with a constant beat. At bar 16 the upward arpeggio is played fast and thrown off with panache, and then Ysaÿe inserts a comma after the arpeggio so as to return to the beat. The continuous semiquavers in bars 18–19 are played with subtle freedom. In the second half of bar 18 the B sharp is played early so as to make room for the first three semiquavers to spread out; the last two semiquavers are played fast, and the beat is rejoined at the beginning of bar 19. All but the last two notes of bar 19 are played fast; the two halves of the bar are separated by a slight comma, and the A sharp which begins the second half is slightly ahead of the beat. The hurrying of most of this bar is compensated for by a tenuto on the E natural, then the last note of the bar is played short, creating a dotted rhythm. In the second extract Ysaÿe twice falls behind the beat and then catches up. At bar 38 the first three semiquavers are lengthened, and are then compensated for by accelerating over the descending scale in the second half of the bar. Similarly at the beginning of bar 40 Ysaÿe lingers on the F double-sharp and G sharp, then accelerates over the descending scale, and slows down at the last two notes of the bar to join the beat at the beginning of bar 41. Through all of this the pianist maintains an accompaniment of equal quavers. An analysis of Ysaÿe's rubato on paper looks complicated and contrived. But the effect when heard is simple and elegant, underlining the rhythmic shape of the melody, and swaying either side of the beat in a manner which is elastic but highly disciplined. How much if any of this style derives from Ysaÿe's association with Vieuxtemps is impossible to know, but it is not difficult to understand why Ysaÿe's rubato was so much admired in the early years of the century.

Mozart, String Quartet in D minor, K. 421, first movement (examples 2.7a and 2.7b)

Lener Quartet   (rec. c. 1927)
Flonzaley Quartet   (rec. c. 1928)

The previous examples in this chapter have been of soloists and of single instruments with piano. The constraints of ensemble-playing become greater in a string quartet, and the opportunities for rhythmic freedom are more restricted. Nevertheless, both of these performances show the use of different kinds of rubato and rhythmic adjustment. In this movement, the Lener Quartet plays at a more constant tempo than the Flonzaley, but with more examples of detailed rhythmic adjustment. Lener (the leader) plays unequal semiquavers at bars 8, 25, and 26. At bar 8 three pairs of semiquavers are played as *notes inégales*.

Ex.2.7   Mozart, String Quartet in D minor, K. 421, first movement, violin ɪ, Lener and Flonzaley
Quartets. (a) bars 7–8; (b) bars 25–6.

Bars 25–6 are more complicated. Here too, Lener plays pairs of semiquavers
unequally, but the rhythm is also affected in each bar by a portamento over the
rising fourth. In bar 25 the portamento makes the beginning of the B flat less
defined than it would be without a portamento, and so Lener establishes the note
clearly by lengthening it, and then compensates by shortening the following A.
The same happens in bar 26, though here the portamento is also preceded by an
unequal pair of semiquavers. This passage is an illustration of the rhythmic effect
of portamento. In fairly fast-moving music a portamento often makes the start of
a note, and therefore its relationship to the beat, rhythmically vague. The effect is
somewhat akin to the dislocation of melody and bass by pianists.

There are fewer examples of unequal note-values in the Flonzaley Quartet's
performance of the first movement. The only example of real *notes inégales*
occurs during the recapitulation, at bar 87, where the climax of the phrase is
emphasised by unequal semiquavers. A tendency to shorten upbeats is shown in
bars 1–2. Not only is the last quaver of bar 1 shortened as a result of
overdotting, but the third quaver of bar 2 is also shortened, as an 'upbeat' to the
second half of the bar. Unlike Lener, the leader of the Flonzaley Quartet plays
the semiquavers in bar 8 fairly evenly. But where this phrase recurs at the
recapitulation (bar 77) he plays the fourth semiquaver of each beat short, again
like a shortened upbeat on a small scale. Elsewhere the Flonzaley hurry groups
of notes. At bar 9 the trill and the two notes after it are played fast. At bar 18 the
first beat is lengthened and the semiquavers on the second beat are played
slightly fast. At bar 26 there is another example of hurrying which, like the
Lener's performance of this bar, is complicated by a portamento. The first three
semiquavers of the bar are played fast, then there is a portamento up from G to
B flat. The portamento is slow enough to delay the B flat, but the fast
semiquavers before it enable the B flat to arrive on the beat. This gives the
impression that the violinist has made room for the portamento by the fast
semiquavers before it. The reverse happens at bar 4. Here a portamento from

F to B flat lengthens the first beat, and the two quavers of the second beat are hurried in compensation. Finally, at bar 20 the cellist draws attention to his entry by starting early and then holding the rhythm slightly, rather as a pianist might emphasise an inner part by playing the first note early.

CONCLUSION

Early twentieth-century rubato is extremely varied. As these examples have shown, the three main elements – accelerando–rallentando, melodic rubato, and tenuto – are all used together, and each performer has a characteristic way of using them. They add up to a rhythmic style which is flexible in quite a different way from late twentieth-century rubato. A number of writers quoted at the beginning of this chapter talk about rubato in terms of rhetoric, and the volatility and detailed emphasis of the style does suggest analogies with the stresses of speech. For Leschetizky, rubato gives 'life and soul to musical form', and Lhevinne and Rivarde refer to the natural elasticity of life as the source of rubato. Early twentieth-century rubato is certainly extremely eventful; it is rarely dull. But from the perspective of the late twentieth century some kinds of rubato are more convincing than others. Two players who still sound particularly eloquent are Ysaÿe, with his swaying either side of the beat, and Rachmaninoff, with his subtle use of tenuto. Cortot's very detailed tempo variations sometimes seem highly expressive, but at other times seem over-done. Tovey's rubato gives, appropriately, an almost analytical impression, as if he is explaining each turn of phrase. With the oldest generation of players on record, one sometimes gets a hint of a lost language which is no longer quite understood, as with d'Albert's unprepared lurches on to the beat. Similarly, the rubato of Paderewski and Pachmann now sounds rather clumsy and disorderly, because it relies so much on dislocation of melody and accompaniment. Admittedly, Pachmann was in his late seventies when he recorded Chopin's Nocturne in D flat, so he had probably lost some of the subtlety of his earlier years. But he must surely have used a great deal of dislocation even in his prime, when he was considered one of the greatest of all Chopin players.

The differences between early twentieth-century and modern rubato are very striking, and it is tempting to speculate what a musician from the early years of the century would make of the modern style. Old-fashioned playing uses rubato to create a sort of relief, in which significant details are made to stand out. By comparison, a modern performance is much smoother and more regular. Any points of emphasis are carefully incorporated into the whole, nothing is allowed to sound out of place; the relief has been, so to speak, flattened out. If we now find some old-fashioned rubato clumsy and eccentric, perhaps a musician from the early twentieth century would find modern playing lacking that life and rhetorical eloquence which rubato was supposed to create.

3

Long and short notes

As the previous chapter has shown, early twentieth-century performers made extensive use of tenutos or agogic accents followed by shortened notes. There was also a very general tendency, in patterns of long and short notes, to lengthen the long notes and hurry and lighten the short notes. To a late twentieth-century listener, the effect is a rather casual, 'throwaway' style of rhythm, because short notes, whether single or in groups, tend to receive less emphasis and clarity of definition than we expect in modern performances, and because the practice of shortening short notes often leads to acceleration. It also produces a tendency to overdot dotted rhythms.

References to this treatment of short notes are very sparse in the writings of the early twentieth century. Writers who argue about tempo rubato and the use of agogic accents rarely make any mention of it. If we take 'accented notes' to include long notes in passages of long and short notes, then the advice by W. H. Breare (already quoted) might imply the shortening of short notes: 'there is nothing more unattractive than the slavish observation of strict time. To execute any passage with grace, it becomes necessary to make a distinction between accented and unaccented notes.'[1] August Wilhelmj and James Brown (1898–1908) give advice to violinists about accentuation which implies the lightening (if not necessarily shortening) of short notes: 'It should be remembered that accent is the result of *difference* in force, and that it is secured by weakening the weak notes, as well as by strengthening the strong ones.'[2]

Rowsby Woof (1920) warns the violin student against any tendency to shorten the long notes in dotted rhythms: 'The only way of curing this evil practice is to insist on a disproportionate lengthening of the dotted notes, and a consequent exaggerated shortening of the short notes.[3] Woof, however, seems to suggest this is a temporary measure to correct a fault, without implying that the rhythm should eventually be played in this way. Arnold Dolmetsch (1916) does give a specific example of overdotting in the early twentieth century, but states that it is exceptional: 'In instruction books, be they old or new, we learn that "a dot after a note makes it half as long again." In spite of the intended modern precision, there are still exceptions to that rule. In military marches, for example, figures like ♩. ♪ and ♩♩ are played ♩.𝄾♪ and ♩𝄾♩ but such instances are rare.'[4]

The interpretation of dotted rhythms is occasionally mentioned in editions, and in other discussions of specific works. For example, Frederick Corder's edition of Beethoven's piano sonatas (1924) has this to say about the opening bars of the 'Pathétique' Sonata: 'The short notes in the opening phrase are *quite* short; those in the first half of bar 5 not quite so abrupt.' This suggestion that the note values of a dotted rhythm should vary depending on the character of the music, is borne out by many recordings of the period, as this chapter will show. About the first movement of the 'Moonlight' Sonata, Corder writes that the rhythm ♫ should be played ♪♪♪. Tovey and Craxton's edition (1931) writes about the same movement, 'You need not worry about the exact length of the semiquaver so long as it does not become a triplet quaver. Half a triplet quaver [as in Corder's edition] will do quite well; far better than a meticulous click that attains the accurate value of ♪ ♪ at the cost of natural accent and tone.'

Two pianists who studied with Ravel, Marguerite Long, and Vlado Perlemuter write that Ravel insisted on a light siciliano rhythm in the Forlane from *Le Tombeau de Couperin*. Long writes, 'It is not often enough recognized that the *Forlane* is a lively, gay dance ... with a too slow tempo and the semiquavers not short enough, it becomes sad, and with all the repeats monotonous.'[5] Perlemuter confirms this: 'Ravel asked me not to make the dotted quaver heavy ... There is only a little difference between that and playing it [the semi-quaver] like a grace note.'[6] In 'Les Oiseaux Tristes' from *Miroirs* Perlemuter also gives an example of a group of short notes which Ravel wanted played more quickly than written: 'it is the arabesque of the sorrowful bird which must not be played strictly in time, but more quickly ... Ravel himself wrote that on my music. If one plays strictly what is written it becomes characterless' (example 3.1).[7]

There are no doubt many more such references scattered through the editions and commentaries of the period, but they are certainly scattered very thinly; and though they indicate a flexible attitude to note values in certain circumstances, they hardly add up to a general policy on the treatment of long and short notes.

Writers of the early twentieth century occasionally object to the inexact treatment of dotted rhythms. Weingartner (1905) insists, in the rhythm from Beethoven's 'Egmont' Overture shown in example 3.2, on 'preventing the last quaver of the first bar from being turned, as so often happens, into a semi-quaver ...'[8] Alberto Bachmann (1925) gives similar advice to violinists in examples from Mendelssohn and Saint-Saëns. About the second movement of Saint-Saëns's Violin Concerto No. 3 in B minor, Op. 61, he writes, 'As regards the beginning there exists a controversy among violinists which deserves to be explained: the second note of measure 1 is often played as though it were a thirty-second note, as follows' (example 3.3a), 'instead of being played in this

Ex.3.1   Ravel, *Miroirs*, 'Lex Oiseaux Tristes', motif quoted by Perlemuter.

Ex.3.2   Beethoven, 'Egmont' Overture, bars 82–3, as quoted by Weingartner.

Ex.3.3   Saint-Saëns, Violin Concerto No. 3 in B minor, second movement, bar 5. (a) 'wrong'
version, according to Bachmann; (b) the same, as printed.

wise' (example 3.3b).[9] Adrian Boult was present in 1923 at rehearsals of the
Casals Orchestra in Barcelona, and reports that Casals was both flexible and
precise in his approach to rhythm:

The same rhythmic figure occuring in a work by Schubert and in a work by Tchaikovsky
would be handled in a totally different manner. Modern works were given a certain
freedom, but a mathematical exactness of rhythm would put glowing life into the
classics. It was a thrilling experience to hear how a simple figure like the first subject of
the Schubert C major Symphony, or the minim-followed-by-crochet so often found in
classical scherzos, played in *absolutely* strict time, gained in character and point.[10]

Charles Reid recalls Barbirolli's insistence, even in the 1920s, on full-length
dotted notes, with 'every demisemiquaver like the crack of a whip!', a description which certainly suggests clarity, but not necessarily strict note values.[11]
    Landowska, discussing double-dotting in eighteenth-century music, writes:

nineteenth-century romanticism went so far as to reject completely this manner of
shortening the note after the dot. Busoni said in his edition of *The Well-Tempered
Clavier* [1894], apropos of the D major Fugue from Book I: 'Take care not to play the
dotted note too long or the sixteenth-note too short – mistakes to which teachers' ears
have long since grown accustomed; not this way [example 3.4a] but so' [example 3.4b].
    It is thus that my revered master Michalowski taught it to me. According to him,
the prolongation of the dot brought vulgarity to the phrase. Oh, the puerility of
aesthetics! That which from Lully to Bach was proud, chivalrous, and magnificent
became vulgar in the nineteenth century!'[12]

It is instructive to imagine how we would interpret these remarks about long
and short notes if we did not have recordings of the period to guide us.

Ex.3.4 Motif from J. S. Bach, 48 Preludes and Fugues, I No. 5 in D as quoted by Landowska.
(a) 'incorrectly' double-dotted, according to Michalowski; (b) the same, 'correctly' played.

(a)   (b)

Comments of any kind about this subject are not only rare, but also confusing
and contradictory. Busoni, Weingartner, and Bachmann argue strongly in
favour of strict interpretation of dotted rhythms, but all of them state that overdotting is common practice. Casals is reported to have required strict rhythmic
interpretation in classical works. Ravel, Tovey, and Corder recommend overdotting in particular circumstances, Dolmetsch observes that double-dotting is
only rarely encountered, Woof recommends overdotting as a corrective to
underdotting, and this is also a possible implication of Barbirolli's insistence on
full-length dotted notes. Breare and Wilhelmj write more generally about the
need to lighten unaccented notes, which presumably include short notes in
patterns of long and short notes.

If any sort of coherent picture emerges from these comments, it is that the
overdotting, and perhaps lightening, of dotted rhythms was to some extent
practised in the early twentieth century, but that some musicians argued for it,
others strongly against it. It is impossible to deduce from such sources how
widespread the practice really was, and the one characteristic which all these
quotations have in common – their rarity – suggests that it was not a subject of
general concern or controversy.

Before we turn to recordings, however, there is one other source which
sheds some light on the possible treatment of dotted rhythms, and that is the
notation of the period. A number of writers in recent years have discussed
interpretation of dotted rhythms when they occur against triplets, not only in
eighteenth-century music, in which such problems have long been familiar to
scholars and performers, but also in nineteenth-century music. The question is
whether the dotted rhythm in such cases is intended to be interpreted literally,
or adjusted to fit the triplets.

Schubert provides many instances in which a dotted rhythm is written, but
performance as a triplet rhythm may be, and in some cases certainly is,
intended. Writers have pointed to similar ambiguities in Beethoven, Schumann, and Chopin, and Gwilym Beechey (1972) extended the argument as far
as Brahms, Liszt, Wolf, and even Debussy and Rachmaninoff.[13] Nineteenth-
century examples of this and other ambiguities will be discussed briefly in
chapter 8. One of the early twentieth-century examples mentioned in passing
by Beechey is Rachmaninoff's Prelude in B flat Op. 23 No. 2 (published 1904),
the theme of which, he writes, 'may admit of more than one possible
interpretation'.[14] Admittedly, this edition is full of notational inconsistencies,

but the differences in rhythmic notation between bars 3–4 and bars 11–12 are particularly striking. At bar 3, the short notes of the dotted rhythm in the right hand are notated as semiquavers, against running sextuplet semiquavers in the accompaniment. At bar 11, the theme is repeated, but here the dotted rhythm is adjusted to fit the sextuplet accompaniment. Did Rachmaninoff really expect the rhythm of bar 3 to be interpreted literally, or is it to be fitted with the accompaniment, as at bar 11? Exactly the same inconsistency occurs again at the recapitulation of this theme (bars 38 and 46). In other works, Rachmaninoff's notation does provide clearer evidence of a flexible attitude to dotted rhythms. In the opening bars of the Moment Musical, Op. 16 No. 4 (published 1896) the question is again whether the upbeat semiquavers in the right hand are intended to be shortened to fit with the accompanying sextuplets. The notation of bar 48, where they are placed amid continuous sextuplets, strongly suggests that they are. It might be argued that in this work, which is marked *Presto* ♩ = 104, the difference between a literal and a sextuplet semiquaver would hardly be noticed, but the notational ambiguity remains. Other works by Rachmaninoff provide less ambiguous examples, for example the Prelude in F minor Op. 32 No. 6 (published 1922), bars 49 and 51, where the same note doubles as the last of a group of sextuplets and the semiquaver of a dotted rhythm. Very similar examples can be found in the Prelude in D flat, Op. 32 No. 13, the first movement of the Sonata, Op. 36, and in the first movement of the Piano Concerto No. 3 (at figure 20).

It is not unusual in works from the early part of the century to find dotted rhythms which, for similar reasons, cannot be interpreted literally. An example is Fauré's Nocturne No. 6 (published 1894; example 3.5). About this passage Marguerite Long writes, 'The theme will be shown to advantage by playing with great evenness of touch, without becoming confused by the balanced but immutable rhythm of the quaver triplets which accompany it.'[15] This advice may or may not be derived from Fauré himself, but if the triplets are played with 'immutable rhythm' the dotted rhythms of the theme will clearly be underdotted. Long does not mention this point, nor does she discuss how to play the dotted rhythms at bar 11, where the dotted rhythm and the triplets are in separate hands. Should the dotted rhythm still be underdotted to fit the accompanying triplets, or should it now revert to its 'correct' values? Granados supplies several problematic examples. *Escenas Romanticas* (published 1923; example 3.6) has a clear instance of notated overdotting at the end of bar 11, where the semiquaver of the melody coincides with the accompanying sextuplet semiquavers. This calls into question the interpretation of the dotted rhythm at bar 9, which could be interpreted literally or overdotted. And is the final quaver of bar 10 to be played as notated, or should it be played as a triplet quaver to follow the triplets in the left hand? Examples of this kind raise questions about dotted rhythms wherever they occur together with triplets. In the first of Granados's *Goyescas*, 'Los Requiebros' (published 1930), the dotted

Ex.3.5   Fauré, Nocturne in D flat, Op. 63 No. 6, bars 1–2.

Ex.3.6   Granados, *Escenas Romanticas*, No. 3, bars 9–12.

rhythms could be played as notated throughout, or it could be argued that the dotted quaver should vary in length, depending on whether there are duplets or triplets in the accompaniment.

Problems of overdotting also occur occasionally in the notation of Debussy and Ravel. Ravel's *Miroirs* No. 1, 'Noctuelles' (published 1906) has an example of a notationally 'incorrect' dotted rhythm at bar 18. But in practice it is rhythmically unambiguous: the dotted rhythm has to be overdotted. In Debussy's *Danse Profane* (published 1904), 3 bars before fig. 5, the harp part is also unambiguously overdotted. The second violin part, however, is notated in simple dotted rhythm. If, as might seem likely, the violins are intended to match their rhythm to that of the harp, how are they to know that they too must overdot the rhythm?

Finally, Berg's piano arrangement of the 'Song of the Wood Dove' from Schoenberg's *Gurrelieder* (published 1912) provides another example of notated overdotting in conjunction with sextuplets (example 3.7). As in some earlier examples, the overdotting at the second beat of the second bar (right hand) seems unambiguous. But is the dotted rhythm in the left hand to be matched to it, and if so, are all the dotted rhythms in this passage to be overdotted?

Ex.3.7 Schoenberg, *Gurrelieder*, 'Song of the Wood Dove', piano arrangement by Berg, 4 bars before fig. 108.

If a pianist were to interpret the rhythm in this way, how would this compare with the probable rhythmic interpretation of the full score at this point? In orchestral performance, the same problem does not arise, because the sextuplets and dotted rhythm are in separate parts. Does this mean that we can imagine an orchestral performance with literal interpretation of dotted rhythms, but a piano performance with overdotting, or would the orchestra be expected to overdot simply because of the prevalence of sextuplets?

The deeper one delves into this problem the more obvious it becomes that, without recordings, the subject is a bottomless pit filled with unanswerable questions. The notated overdotting in the above examples could be an indication of a generally flexible attitude to the length of dotted notes, or it could be argued that it is simply a notational convenience. After all, why should a composer take the trouble to write [♩] or [♩] when it is perfectly clear what is meant by [♩] even if it is theoretically incorrect?

The suggestion that such notated overdotting might indicate a general tendency to overdot would be no more than a theory, if we did not have recordings. In fact, they demonstrate that the reason why most writers did not comment on the interpretation of dotted rhythms is that the practice of overdotting was universal in the early twentieth century.

RECORDINGS

Of the writers quoted at the beginning of this chapter, a few seem to be arguing in different ways against a casual or careless attitude to dotted rhythms. Rowsby Woof writes of the 'evil practice' of underdotting dotted rhythms, Weingartner argues against letting a rhythm become overdotted 'as so often happens', and Barbirolli and Casals are described as trying to overcome rhythmic carelessness by rehearsal. A casual attitude to dotted rhythms, and to other patterns of long and short notes, is certainly the impression given to a late twentieth-century listener by many early twentieth-century recordings, both in the interpretation of note values, and in the clarity and definition of the rhythm. In many recordings up to the 1930s, dotted rhythms are overdotted, and short notes are light, often resulting in a general lack of clarity and control. However, we have to be very careful how we judge this impression. The modern listener expects clarity and control in modern performances, and the lack of it in early recordings sounds at first like simple incompetence. One of the most important tasks, therefore, is to try to distinguish the element of incompetence from points of genuine style. This is nowhere more difficult than in orchestral performance.

If one takes any of the standard orchestral works, and examines recordings from the 1920s to the 1940s, a clear trend in the treatment of long and short notes is revealed, from uncontrolled, imprecise, and often unclear rhythms in the early recordings, to generally controlled, precise, and clear rhythms in the later recordings. The simplest explanation for what one hears on the earlier recordings is the lack of rehearsal, and there can be little doubt that the degree of clarity and control achieved by an orchestra is to some extent governed by the amount of rehearsal time available, and the regularity of the orchestra's membership. However, as the earlier part of this chapter has already suggested, the problem is rather more complicated than that. Even the most unrehearsed orchestra of the 1990s could never play with the style of dotted rhythms and other long–short patterns shown by the orchestras of the 1920s. Lack of rehearsal, then as now, can be expected to lead to a generally imprecise performance, and most of the orchestras of the 1920s certainly rehearsed less than those of the 1990s. But lack of rehearsal time cannot, by itself, account for the most striking rhythmic practice of the 1920s and (to a diminishing extent) 1930s – the almost universal habit of overdotting and of lightening short notes.

Schubert, Symphony No. 9 in C major, second movement, bars 1–43

London Symphony Orchestra, cond. L. Blech   (rec. c. 1928)
Hallé Orchestra, cond. Harty   (rec. c. 1928)
BBC Symphony Orchestra, cond. Boult   (rec. c. 1935)
London Symphony Orchestra, cond. Walter   (rec. c. 1938)
Philadelphia Orchestra, cond. Toscanini   (rec. 1941)
Vienna Philharmonic Orchestra, cond. Karajan   (rec. c. 1949)

These performances demonstrate very clearly the changing treatment of long and short notes. The two earliest performances are the least literal of the six in their playing of dotted rhythms, and the least controlled. At the beginning of the second movement (bars 1–7) both overdot the dotted rhythms, but the Hallé Orchestra defines the short notes more clearly than the London Symphony Orchestra. Where the dotted rhythms become louder (bars 38–43), the short notes become weaker in both performances, and the London Symphony Orchestra tends to play them early so that the passage accelerates. The two performances from the 1930s have more literal dotted rhythms, and are more controlled, though in both the rhythm weakens and accelerates a little at bars 38–43, more noticeably in the BBC Symphony Orchestra than in the London Symphony Orchestra. Both of the performances from the 1940s have stronger and clearer short notes and are more controlled in tempo, although Toscanini's tempo is unusually fast. Similar comparisons can be found in the other movements of the symphony, notably in bars 78–130 of the first movement.

Beethoven, Symphony No. 3 ('Eroica'), first movement, bars 45–71

Symphony Orchestra, cond. Coates   (rec. 1926)
Vienna Philharmonic Orchestra, cond. Weingartner   (rec. 1936)
NBC Symphony Orchestra, cond. Toscanini   (rec. 1939)
Boston Symphony Orchestra, cond. Koussevitsky   (rec. 1945)

These recordings show variable overdotting and the general shortening of upbeat quavers, even when they are not part of a dotted rhythm. In Coates's performance the wind instruments play the dotted rhythms quite literally, but the violins overdot throughout the passage. At bar 66, and other bars with similar rhythm, the final upbeat quaver of each bar is shortened, as it might be if it were preceded by a dotted crotchet.

In the light of Weingartner's attack on overdotting, quoted at the beginning of this chapter, it comes as a surprise to find very noticeable overdotting in his recording (though admittedly not double-dotting, to which he specifically objected). The rhythm from bar 45 is played with full-length quavers at first, but the last two dotted rhythms in the woodwind (bars 53–4) are slightly overdotted, and the fortissimo dotted rhythm at bar 55 is substantially overdotted. As in Coates's recording bar 66 is played with a short final quaver, and so is bar 68. However, the effect is less exaggerated, and the quaver is more clearly defined, than in Coates's recording.

Even Toscanini's orchestra, noted for its strict discipline, sometimes overdots dotted rhythms, and the final quaver of bar 66 is short (though not as short as in Coates's recording). Even when overdotted, however, the rhythms are always very clear. Of these four performances, the Koussevitsky is the most literal in its rhythmic interpretation, though even here there are occasional instances of slight overdotting. Neither of the two American performances gives any suggestion of a casual approach to rhythm. The impression is rather that the hurrying of short notes is caused by the intensity and drive of the performances, and in both performances the overdotting is much more incisive, and much more subtle, than in Coates's version.

Beethoven, Symphony No. 8, first movement, bars 70–92

Vienna Philharmonic Orchestra, cond. Schalk   (rec. c. 1928)
Vienna Philharmonic Orchestra, cond. Weingartner   (rec. 1936)

This comparison shows that Weingartner's recordings with the Vienna Philharmonic Orchestra in the 1930s, though they sometimes contain overdotting as in the 'Eroica' Symphony, were more literal in their rhythmic interpretation than the Vienna Philharmonic's recordings from the late 1920s. The orchestra plays the dotted rhythm at bars 70–2 a little more clearly under Weingartner than under Schalk. More strikingly, at bars 90–2 the final quaver of each bar is very short under Schalk, so that the first beat of the next bar arrives early. Under Weingartner the rhythm is much more controlled, though the quavers are still slightly short.

Beethoven, Symphony No. 4, first movement, bars 158–85; second movement, bars 1–10

Casals Orchestra of Barcelona, cond. Casals   (rec. 1932)

In an article quoted earlier in this chapter, Boult reported in 1923 that Casals insisted, in his extensive rehearsals with his orchestra, on strict rhythms in classical works. He cited the opening theme of Schubert's 'Great' C major Symphony as an example, and since the principal rhythmic feature of that theme is its dotted rhythms, the clear implication is that Casals did not allow overdotting in classical works. As with Weingartner, therefore, it comes as a surprise to find very noticeable overdotting in this recording by Casals. At bars 161 and 165 of the first movement the rhythm is considerably 'overdotted' and hurried. Similarly at bars 180 and 184 the crotchet upbeat is short and weak. At the beginning of the second movement, the dotted rhythms are not always clearly audible. But where they are, they are very overdotted. Indeed Casals's orchestra, far from being strict in its dotted rhythms, shows a more noticeable tendency to overdot than most other orchestras of the period.

Ex.3.8   Mozart, Serenade in G, K. 525 ('Eine kleine Nachtmusik'), first movement, bars 22–4.

Mozart, Serenade in G, K.525 ('Eine kleine Nachtmusik'), first movement, bars 22–4 (example 3.8)

Barbirolli's Chamber Orchestra, cond. Barbirolli   (rec. c. 1929)

The general standard of rhythmic clarity in Barbirolli's Chamber Orchestra is high by the standards of British orchestras in the 1920s, but the description, quoted earlier, of Barbirolli's demisemiquavers being 'like the crack of a whip', and the implication that he insisted on the clarity of all short notes, are not borne out by this example. Here the quaver and two semiquavers are not clearly differentiated in length, because the quaver is short and weak.

Elgar, Overture, 'Cockaigne', bars 1–26

Royal Albert Hall Orchestra, cond. Elgar   (rec. 1926)
BBC Symphony Orchestra, cond. Elgar   (rec.1933)

These two performances, both conducted by the composer, show considerable differences in the style of their short notes. In the earlier recording the rhythms ♫♪,♫♫♪ and ♪♫♩ are played with fast, light semiquavers, and in the rhythm ♫♫♫,♫♪♩ the semiquavers tend to be hurried. In the later version, semiquavers are generally less hurried and, in patterns of repeated notes, more clearly separated from each other.

The examples given so far are typical of performances of the period, and it is worth pausing at this stage to consider some of the implications. Those from the 1920s are strikingly different in their rhythmic style from later twentieth-century performances, because of a general tendency to overdot dotted rhythms, and to lighten and shorten (or hurry) short notes, which often leads to acceleration. To the modern listener this style of rhythm sounds rather casual because of a general lack of clarity and control. But it is important to realise that this is a late twentieth-century view which cannot have been widely shared by musicians of the early twentieth century. As we have seen, comment of any kind on the treatment of long and short notes is sparse, and there is no evidence, despite Weingartner and others, of a general dissatisfaction with this aspect of rhythmic practice. This point is underlined by a comment relating to the last pair of recordings, written by Elgar in a letter to the Gramophone Company. When the Company first proposed, in March 1933, that Elgar should re-record 'Cockaigne' Overture now that it could be fitted on to three sides, instead of the four sides of his 1926 recording, he replied, 'By all means do "Cockaigne" again: is there anything wrong with the old four side records?'[16] The BBC Symphony Orchestra was more thoroughly rehearsed than the Royal Albert Hall Orchestra, and Elgar, after recording 'Cockaigne' with them, is reported to have said 'that he had greatly enjoyed conducting them, and what a fine orchestra they had become under Adrian Boult'.[17] But the difference in rhythmic practice between the two recordings is one of style, not just competence. The Royal Albert Hall Orchestra played in the style of its day, and this was the style to which Elgar and his contemporaries were accustomed. The point is further reinforced by recordings of Elgar's 'Enigma' Variations.

Ex.3.9 Elgar, Variations on an Original Theme ('Enigma'), Variation 3, bars 2–3. (a) as printed; (b) the same, as played by RAH Orchestra, Elgar.

Elgar, Variations on an Original Theme ('Enigma'), Variation 3 and Variation 7 (examples 3.9a and 3.9b)

Royal Albert Hall Orchestra, cond. Elgar   (rec. 1926)
Hallé Orchestra, cond. Harty   (rec. 1932)
BBC Symphony Orchestra, cond. Boult   (rec. 1936)
Hallé Orchestra, cond. Barbirolli   (rec. 1947)

In the earliest two recordings it is again difficult to separate rhythmic style from matters of competence. In both performances, Variation 7 is played very fast (faster than Elgar's metronome marking) and with less control of the rhythm than would be expected in a late twentieth-century performance. In patterns of minims and crotchets, which occur throughout this variation, the crotchets are often hurried and weak under Elgar, and only a little clearer and more controlled under Harty.

In Variation 3, both performances show a rhythmic adjustment which is similar to overdotting. In the recurring motif shown in example 3.9a, The Hallé and Royal Albert Hall Orchestras play the triplet rhythm as if it were written as shown in example 3.9b.

We know that Elgar was satisfied with his recorded performance of the Variations because the pencilled comments on this recording in his copy of the piano score, some of which were quoted earlier (see p. 36), include several expressions of enthusiasm.[18] Over the beginning of Variation 7 he writes 'fine', and his only comments on Variation 3 are 'delightful' (over bar 8) and 'perfect!' (four bars from the end). Again, we have to remind ourselves that this style of performance, which to modern ears sounds somewhat slapdash, was the accepted style of the day. By comparison the later versions conducted by Boult and Barbirolli are much more controlled in their rhythms, and both play the triplet rhythms of Variation 3 as they are written, without 'overdotting'.

Elgar, Overture, 'In the South'

London Symphony Orchestra, cond. Elgar   (rec. 1930)

This recording demonstrates that the rhythmic style of Elgar's performances includes not only the lightening and shortening of short notes, but also the variable overdotting of dotted rhythms. In the opening theme the dotted crotchet is always overdotted and the quaver is very short. The other recurring dotted rhythm ♩.♪♩ is usually overdotted in lively passages (for example at figure 2), but it is played more literally in quiet and sustained passages (as at figures 10–13).

Holst, *The Planets*, 'Mars' (example 3.10)

London Symphony Orchestra, cond. Holst   (rec. 1926)

By comparison with most late twentieth-century performances of 'Mars', this performance conveys an exceptional nervous energy, largely because of the impression that the orchestra only just manages to fit in the rhythmic details at the very fast tempo (an impression which is very often conveyed by recordings of the 1920s). In particular, the short notes of the dotted rhythms are not always as firmly placed as they would be in a modern performance. This is most noticeable at bars 54ff and at bar 80. This performance also demonstrates a flexible attitude to dotted rhythms in Holst's notation. The trumpet-call at bar 70 (and elsewhere) is notated as in example 3.10. The trumpets in Holst's recording play the dotted rhythm as a triplet (indeed, it would be very difficult to play a literal dotted rhythm at Holst's tempo).

Ex.3.10   Holst, *The Planets*, 'Mars', bar 70, trumpets

Stravinsky, *Firebird*, 'Danse infernale'

[Straram Orchestra] cond. Stravinsky   (rec. 1928)

The rhythm in this performance, conducted by the composer, sounds very unstable, principally because the quavers in the syncopated rhythm of the opening bars are hurried. In Stravinsky's later recordings from the 1950s and 1960s, the quaver is placed more emphatically, and without hurrying. Similar comparisons can be made between Stravinsky's different recordings of *Petrushka* (for example, the treatment of the rhythm at figure 73 in the 1947 edition).

Richard Strauss, *Don Juan*

Orchestra of the Berlin State Opera, cond. Strauss   (rec. 1929)

Beethoven, Symphony No. 5, second movement, bars 1–10

Orchestra of the Berlin State Opera, cond. Strauss   (rec. 1928)

These two recordings show contrasting treatment of dotted rhythms, although they are both played by the same orchestra under Richard Strauss. The opening of *Don Juan* is played with impressive clarity of rhythm compared with many recordings of the 1920s. The dotted rhythms are generally quite clear and incisive, although the tempo is brisk. Strauss's concern for the clarity of the rhythm is shown by his careful notation, in which accents are placed over some of the semiquavers of dotted rhythms (as at bar 9). By contrast, the example from Beethoven shows overdotting and, by modern standards, lack of clarity. The different rhythms of bars 4 and 5 are played in almost the same way, because the dotted quaver in bar 5 is virtually double-dotted. At bar 8, the final demisemiquaver is very short and weak.

Although the changing rhythmic practice of orchestras between the 1920s and the 1940s must have been affected by improving orchestral discipline, the preceding examples show that there was also a clear stylistic change over the period, with performances from the earlier years often showing overdotting and the lightening of short notes. The remaining orchestral examples in this chapter are taken from recordings from the 1920s and 1930s in which this stylistic, or interpretative, aspect of overdotting is unmistakable. They are chosen to emphasise how widespread this practice was, the examples being taken from French, German, Dutch, and American recordings.

Debussy, *Nocturnes*, 'Fêtes', figures 10–12

Berlin State Orchestra, cond. Klemperer   (rec. 1926)
Philadelphia Orchestra, cond. Stokowski   (rec. c. 1928)
Colonne Orchestra, cond. Pierné   (rec. c. 1928)
Paris Conservatoire Orchestra, cond. Gaubert   (rec. c. 1929)
Paris Conservatoire Orchestra, cond. Coppola   (rec. c. 1939)

Pierné's recording is of particular interest, because Debussy admired his performances of the *Nocturnes*.[19] None of these five performances plays the rhythm of the middle section of 'Fêtes' as written. Of the five, only Gaubert's version makes a clear distinction between the lengths of semiquavers after dotted quavers (in the first and fifth bars of the theme) and demisemiquavers after dotted semiquavers (in the sixth bar). The versions conducted by Pierné, Coppola, Klemperer, and Stokowski play all the short notes of the dotted rhythms virtually the same, as demisemiquavers, so that the first and fifth bars of the theme are double-dotted. Gaubert's performance is not so consistent in its overdotting. The trumpets play the dotted rhythms fairly literally (13th–14th bars of fig. 10), but the woodwind slightly overdot the dotted quavers (5th–6th bars of fig. 11). Both trumpets and woodwind shorten the initial semiquaver of the theme.

Brahms, Symphony No. 4, first movement, bars 53–64

Berlin Philharmonic Orchestra, cond. De Sabata   (rec. 1939)

Throughout this passage the dotted crotchets are approximately double-dotted, but the resulting rhythm is played very clearly. Modern performances sometimes slightly overdot this passage, but rarely to the extent of double-dotting.

Brahms, Academic Festival Overture, bars 45–53

Concertgebouw Orchestra of Amsterdam, cond. Mengelberg   (rec. 1930)

At bars 45–9 the rhythm is markedly overdotted, but at bars 49–52 the brass plays the dotted rhythm much more literally. Like Elgar's recording of 'In the South', this illustrates a tendency to overdot more in loud passages than in quiet ones.

Donizetti, *Don Pasquale*, Overture

Orchestra of La Scala, Milan, cond. Toscanini   (rec. 1921)

Toscanini's recording of the Overture to *Don Pasquale* is rhythmically one of the most remarkable performances of the pre-electric period. The reduced size of the orchestra and the cramped conditions of the acoustic recording studio created great problems of ensemble. It is therefore not surprising that many orchestral recordings of the early twenties are, at best, rhythmically dull, and at worst, somewhat chaotic. This performance, however, demonstrates the highest standard of precision, and the utmost clarity and incisiveness in its dotted rhythms.

Brahms, Variations on a Theme by Haydn, Theme and Variation 7

Philharmonic Symphony Orchestra of New York, cond. Toscanani   (rec. 1936)

Brahms's Variations demonstrate that Toscanini had a flexible attitude to the length of dotted notes even though the clarity is again consistent. In the dotted rhythm of the theme the semiquaver is clearly emphasised, but the rhythm is considerably overdotted at each appearance. In Variation 7, the siciliano rhythm is overdotted to a varying extent throughout the variation. Modern performances sometimes overdot these passages a little, but rarely as noticeably as in this recording.

J. S. Bach, Suite No. 2, Polonaise

Chicago Symphony Orchestra, cond. Stock   (rec. c. 1929)
Busch Chamber Players   (rec. 1936)

This final pair of orchestral examples once again illustrates the difficulty of deciding where genuinely stylistic overdotting ends and casual inattention to detail begins. The Busch Chamber Players overdot the rhythm, playing a short but crisply defined semiquaver (except in the first bar, which is not quite unanimous). The Chicago Symphony Orchestra also plays a very overdotted rhythm, but the semiquaver is weak and the result is, to modern ears, ill-defined, and much more old-fashioned in style than the Busch performance.

The orchestral examples in this chapter have demonstrated that the shortening and lightening of short notes was a widespread stylistic feature of the performances of the 1920s. Any lingering doubts about the genuinely stylistic character of this practice are removed by examining chamber and solo recordings of the period. Here too we find that the practice of lightening and shortening the short notes was prevalent among the most admired soloists and chamber ensembles of the day.

Ex.3.11   Mozart, String Quartet in D minor, K. 421, first movement, bars 1–2, violin I.

Mozart, String Quartet in D minor, K.421 (example 3.11)

Lener Quartet   (rec. c. 1927)
Flonzaley Quartet   (rec. c. 1928)

Both quartets show a lightness in the placing of rhythmic details which sounds casual to the modern listener. In the first movement, the Flonzaley Quartet hurries details more noticeably than the Lener. In the opening phrase (example 3.11) the Flonzaley Quartet shortens the two marked quavers. At bar 9 the dotted rhythm is overdotted and hurried, and at bars 59–69 the repeated phrase of triplets is played as a casual aside, without the clear accentuation and separation of repeated notes which would be expected in a modern perform-ance. In the first movement it is the Flonzaley Quartet which seems the more casual of the two quarters. In the third movement (minuet), however, it is the Lener Quartet which seems the more casual, by playing the upbeat dotted rhythm with hardly any separation of the semiquaver. Here the Flonzaley distinguishes the rhythm more clearly. In the trio the Flonzaley plays with subtle accelerandos and ritardandos which have obviously been carefully rehearsed (for example at bar 48). But the semiquavers are placed less clearly than by the Lener, so that they sound like grace notes before the beat, rather than semiquavers on the beat. By contrast, at the opening of the fourth movement, the Lener plays the siciliano rhythm with a short and insignificant semiquaver, whereas the Flonzaley makes the rhythm sharper, with a more audible semiquaver. There can be no question of casual rhythmic detail of this kind being the result simply of inadequate rehearsal.[20] Similar placing of short notes can be found in the other well-known string quartets recording in the 1920s, such as the Catterall, London, International, Budapest (led by Hauser), Capet, and Bohemian Quartets.

The leaders of the Busch and Pro Arte Quartets were almost exact con-temporaries of Jenö Lener, leader of the Lener Quartet. But the Busch and Pro Arte Quartets played in a style which was generally more emphatic in rhyth-mic definition than that of the Lener and Flonzaley Quartets, though it still incorporated some overdotting and lightening of rhythms.

Ex.3.12   Beethoven, String Quartet in F minor, Op. 95, third movement, bars 5–8.

Beethoven, String Quartet in F minor, Op. 95 (example 3.12)

Busch Quartet   (rec. 1932)

The Busch Quartet is similarly much more emphatic in rhythmic style than most quartets of the 1920s. They play the first movement of Beethoven's F minor quartet in a much more forceful style than the Lener Quartet (rec. c. 1927). The triplet rhythm at bar 24, however, sounds casual, because of the lightness of the quavers, and the dotted rhythms at bars 66–9, though clearly placed, are allowed to accelerate. Similarly, the third movement has a general impression of great nervous energy, and the dotted rhythms often accelerate. In the rhythm of bars 5–6, which recurs throughout the movement, the semiquaver is not always clearly defined, and the quaver at the end of the bar is played as a semiquaver (example 3.12). Modern performances do not always play the quaver quite according to its strict length, but they usually differentiate between semiquaver and quaver.

Mozart, String Quartet in E flat, K428

Pro Arte Quartet   (rec. c. 1937)

The Pro Arte Quartet plays in a rhythmic style which is generally precise and firmly defined. Occasional details, however, are reminiscent of the style of the 1920s. In the first movement at bar 5 the first violin tends to hurry the semiquavers a little. In the third movement (minuet), bars 12ff, the demisemiquavers are not always clearly defined.

By the 1930s, some quartets, notably the Kolisch Quartet and the Budapest Quartet (now led by Roisman), were playing in a rhythmic style which had largely lost the lightness of short notes characteristic of the 1920s. The changes in rhythm style heard in recordings of string quartets are encountered to the same extent in recordings of other chamber works. Comparisons between earlier and later performances almost invariably show a more literal and emphatic treatment of patterns of long and short notes in the later examples.

Brahms, Hungarian Dance no. 1 in G minor

Joachim   (rec. 1903)
Leopold Auer   (rec. 1920)

Joachim was seventy-two when he recorded this Hungarian Dance, and it contains many instances of rhythmic awkwardness which are presumably the result of physical difficulties.[21] It is nevertheless possible to hear a rhythmic style in which short notes are often hurried and lightened. In the first theme Joachim gives the rhythm a characteristic swing, by lingering on the dotted crotchets and shortening the quavers. Auer overdots the first phrase of the theme much as Joachim does. But in the second phrase (bars 7–12) he emphasises the changing direction of the melody by lengthening the quavers. Joachim's recording of the Adagio from Bach's Unaccompanied Sonata in G minor (rec. 1903) also contains instances of shortened and hurried short notes which are discussed in the chapter on tempo rubato.

Beethoven, Violin Sonata in G, Op. 96, first movement

Fachiri and Tovey   (rec. c. 1928)

The rhythmic flexibility of this performance is illustrated in chapter 2. Both players overdot all dotted rhythms, for example at bars 27ff, and the second theme at bars 41ff is double-dotted.

Mozart, Violin Sonata in A, K526

Catterall and Harty   (rec. c. 1924)
Y. and H. Menuhin   (rec. 1933)

As well as showing flexible tempo, rubato and non-synchronisation of the pianist's hands, Catterall and Harty also tend to hurry short notes and overdot. By contrast, the Menuhins are rhythmically much more straightforward. In the first movement at bars 28–30, Harty places a tenuto on the first note of each phrase and accelerates the triplet group. At bars 75–89 Harty and Catterall hurry each of the runs, and often place a tenuto on the first quaver of the bar. At bars 52–3 of the second movement Harty overdots the dotted rhythms. The Menuhins show an occasional tendency in the outer movements to rush (the tempos are already substantially faster than those of Harty and Catterall), but they invariably play rhythmic detail in a more literal manner.

Brahms, Violin Sonata in A, Op. 100, second movement

Busch and Serkin   (rec. 1932)

Adolf Busch's solo recordings show the extent to which the rhythmic style of the Busch Chamber Players and the Busch String Quartet was determined by the style of their leader. The second movement of the sonata contains a particularly delightful instance of rhythmic lightening by overdotting. Busch overdots the rhythm consistently at bars 56–59, and at bars 63–4 (and again at bars 67–9) he 'overdots' the rhythm across the bar line by shortening the quaver. Because the piano accompaniment contains triplet quavers throughout these bars, the effect of Busch's overdotting is to turn the passage into 9/8 rhythm.

Ex.3.13   Schubert, Impromptu in B flat, D. 935 No. 3, Variation 1, bar 1, as played by Paderewski.

As with the various kinds of rubato, it is solo pianists who show the greatest freedom in the treatment of dotted rhythms and other combinations of long and short notes. As in orchestral and chamber music, the earlier recordings show the greatest freedom, though some overdotting and lightening of short notes continued to be heard throughout the 1930s.

Schubert, Impromptus in A flat, D935 No. 2, and in B flat, D935 No. 3

No. 3 in B flat, Paderewski   (rec. 1924) (example 3.13)
No. 2 in A flat, Paderewski   (rec. 1926)
No. 2 in A flat, Pouishnoff   (rec. c. 1928)
both Impromptus, Fischer   (rec. 1938)
both Impromptus, Schnabel   (rec. 1950)

In Paderewski's performance of the Impromptu in B flat, the treatment of dotted rhythms is very variable, in a way which would be unthinkable in a modern performance. At bar 14 of the theme the dotted rhythm is, for once, very much underdotted, with the demisemiquavers played more or less as semiquavers. By contrast the first variation is slightly overdotted. Paderewski plays the rhythmic pattern as two overlapping sets of dotted rhythms, one within the beat, the other across the beat, as in example 3.13. He overdots *both* sets of dotted rhythms to a varying extent, creating irregularity throughout the variation. Fischer does not overdot the rhythm of this variation. Schnabel clarifies the distinction between the dotted rhythm of the melodic line and the semiquavers of the accompaniment by a tendency to play the second semiquaver of each group fractionally late and fast. But this irregularity is very slight, and is much more subtle than Paderewski's rhythmic adjustment.

In the Impromptu in A flat Paderewski plays the first sixteen bars with a variety of dotting. The rhythm ♩ ♩.♪ is sometimes played quite literally, sometimes slightly overdotted. However, the most exaggerated overdotting occurs at the forte passage from bar 16, which is almost double-dotted. This is another example of a dotted rhythm becoming more overdotted in loud passages.

Pouishnoff slightly shortens the quavers throughout the Impromptu in A flat, but does not vary their length as Paderewski does. Fischer slightly varies the length of the quavers, but makes no distinction between the loud and soft passages. The quaver in bar 1 is full-length, but the quaver in bar 2 is shortened. The same distinction is made between bars 9 and 10, and in both instances the effect is to lend impetus to the following phrase.

Schnabel plays the quavers their notated length during quiet passages (bars 1–16 and bars 31–46), but slightly shortens them during loud passages (bars 17–24). In both Impromptus Fischer and Schnabel are much more subtle in their overdotting than Paderewski.

The variety of overdotting heard in Paderewski's recordings of these Impromptus is typical of his rhythmic style. As with his rubato his freedom of rhythmic interpretation was more extreme than that of most of his contemporaries. Other pianists of his generation, however, also interpreted dotted and similar rhythms liberally.

Rachmaninoff, Prelude in G minor, Op. 23 No. 5

Rachmaninoff   (rec. 1920)
Lhevinne   (rec. 1921)

In both performances the rhythm of the principal theme of this prelude is much lighter than in late twentieth-century performances, because the semiquavers are fast and late.

Mozart, Rondo in A minor, K511

Schnabel   (rec. 1946)

Although Schnabel and Fischer survived into the 1950s, their rhythmic styles were largely derived from the early twentieth century. They have already been compared with Paderewski and found to be more straightforward in their rhythmic interpretation. But their recordings show that the hurrying of short notes and overdotting and lightening of dotted rhythms were prominent features of their playing. Here, Schnabel overdots the siciliano rhythm of the principal theme. Throughout the rondo, groups of demisemiquavers are often played late and fast, for example at bars 142 and 144.

Beethoven, Piano Sonata in B flat, Op. 106 ('Hammerklavier')

Schnabel   (rec. 1935)

The hurrying of groups of short notes is characteristic of all Schnabel's recordings. Where it seems under control, as in the preceding recording of Mozart, it has the effect of bringing the rhythm of phrases into sharp relief – a characteristic for which Schnabel is still admired. Some of Schnabel's performances, however, seem to modern listeners rather slapdash and out of control, and this is usually because hurrying of short notes results in lack of rhythmic definition. This is true of his famous recording of Beethoven's 'Hammerklavier' Sonata. The breathless impression given by the first movement results not just from the attempt to play the movement nearly at Beethoven's very fast metronome marking, but also from his treatment of short notes. In the opening theme the quavers are all fast and light, and therefore, to modern ears, ill-defined.

Mozart, Piano Concerto in G, K453, first movement

Fischer and his Chamber Orchestra   (rec. 1937)

Like Schnabel, Fischer seems rhythmically hasty because of the lightness and speed of the semiquavers, for example in the dotted rhythms of the opening theme, where the semiquavers are short and unemphatic.

Chopin, Etude in C minor, Op. 10 No. 12 ('Revolutionary')

Cortot   (rec. 1933)

Cortot's rhythmic style is characterised by both haste and flexibility in the playing of short notes. Often his treatment of dotted rhythms is inextricably tied up with his exceptionally free use of tenuto and rubato. In the 'Revolutionary' Etude the recurring rhythmic motif ♫♩. ♪|♩ is played with a variety of tenutos and note-lengths. For example, at the beginning of the theme (bars 10–14), Cortot plays this rhythm in two different ways. At bars 10 and 12 he lingers on the dotted quaver and plays the semiquaver short, and at bars 11 and 13 he lengthens the semiquaver.

These examples have shown that the practice of lightening and shortening short notes was very widespread among pianists in the 1920s and 1930s, as it was in orchestral and chamber performances. Some evidence that composers of the period accepted this style as the norm has already been provided by orchestral performances conducted by Elgar, Holst, Stravinsky, and Strauss. This point is underlined by the remaining examples in this chapter, which are taken from performances by three composer-pianists, Rachmaninoff, Poulenc, and Bartók.

Chopin, Waltz in A flat, Op. 42

Rachmaninoff   (rec. 1919)

Rachmaninoff's recording of his Prelude in G minor has already illustrated his fast and light short notes. This waltz contains instances in which Rachmaninoff plays quavers and semiquavers both as semiquavers. At bars 229ff the rhythm ♫ ♩. ♪ is played ♫ ♩. ♪, and the rhythm is adjusted in this way throughout bars 229–61.

Rachmaninoff, Rhapsody on a Theme of Paganini, Variation 20

Rachmaninoff, Philadelphia Orchestra, cond. Stokowski (rec. 1934)

Rachmaninoff's performance of his Rhapsody is characterised throughout by light and vigorous rhythms. Specifically, he overdots the rhythm of Variation 20, and plays the semiquavers much less emphatically than modern pianists.

Poulenc, Caprice in C ('d'après le Final du Bal Masqué')

Poulenc (rec. c. 1932)

Poulenc plays short notes very hastily and lightly, for example in the opening bars where the upbeat groups of semiquavers are played as fast grace notes.

Bartók, Suite, Op. 14, first movement

Bartók (rec. 1929)

Like Poulenc, Bartók tends to play groups of short notes fast and lightly, with emphatic accents on the main beats. There are instances of this throughout this recording, for example in the pattern of quavers and semiquavers which first occurs at bars 5–6. At bars 55–67 Bartók plays the slurred semiquavers as fast swirls, in a manner which, in a modern pianist, would be thought unclear and casual.

CONCLUSION

Flexibility of tempo, different kinds of rubato, and the variable treatment of long and short notes add up to a rhythmic style which is very different from that of the late twentieth century. The problem of accepting some of these old-fashioned habits as stylistic has already been mentioned. Lightened short notes now sound unclear, accelerated loud passages seem uncontrolled, dislocated rubato sounds poorly co-ordinated. To put it at its most negative, early twentieth-century rhythm sounds somewhat chaotic. But the range of examples in this section, from under-rehearsed orchestras to the most famous soloists and string quartets of the period, shows that we have to accept the chaos as part of the style of the time.

There are more positive ways of looking at the disorderliness of early twentieth-century rhythm. There is an informality, an improvisational quality about it. The rhythmical repertoire of the early twentieth-century musician seems designed to explore different possibilities as one plays a piece of music. There is an impression that it could all be different at the next performance. A certain amount of disorderliness is necessary to make this possible. In a concerto, a soloist could alter the rubato from one performance to another, because some freedom was allowed either side of the beat. Only the broad changes of tempo needed to be rehearsed and predictable. In modern performance, in which perfect co-ordination is expected, this would be impossible. There is much less give and take between soloist and accompaniment than there used to be, and a soloist cannot indulge in sudden whims of unrehearsed rubato without the danger of losing the conductor. This applies not just to concertos, but to any music involving more than one performer, instrumental or vocal, and almost any recording from the 1920s or earlier illustrates the point.

So modern rhythm has not just become more orderly. It has lost much of the informality and rhetorical unpredictability of early twentieth-century playing. The relationships between notes are closer to a literal interpretation, and there is less emphasising of contrasts by tempo variation or by the various forms of rubato which used to be acceptable. Modern flexibility is much less volatile, both in detail and across whole movements. The overall result of these changes is that performances are much less highly characterised in their rhythm than they were earlier in the century.

PART II

VIBRATO

4

String vibrato

INTRODUCTION

The development of modern vibrato on stringed instruments during the twentieth century is part of a general trend towards greater power and intensity. Vibrato is the most obvious element in the trend, and therefore the most important, but it is also closely linked to the other principal changes in string-playing – changes in the material of the strings, in styles of bowing, and in phrasing and articulation.

At the turn of the century, stringed instruments were still generally strung with gut, the lower strings overwound with metal (preferably silver). Steel E strings on the violin were becoming available by the 1890s, and according to Carl Flesch they were coming into more general use after World War I. By the 1920s Flesch was expressing the view that the difference in tone-colour between gut and metal was 'hardly noticeable', though arguments against the steel strings continued throughout the 1920s.[1] There were two reasons for adopting metal strings: greater reliability and greater power. Their reliability was uncontroversial, but the greater power which they made possible was not approved of by all players. At late as 1938 a diatribe against steel strings was published, with the title *Recovery or Ruin of the Art of Violin Playing (The Steel String, Enemy of Art)*. In it, the writer laments the deterioration of violin playing with the introduction of steel strings, particularly as they affect bowing: 'The character of the steel string requires a different, more dynamic stroke, causing a change in the bow-hold and the position of the arm. So we observe an extensive, more horizontal bowing pattern, demanded by the "modern" school, or rather necessitated by the use of the steel string . . .'[2]

The change to steel strings did coincide with the development of more forceful bowing styles, but it is much more likely that the steel strings became popular because string players were already developing more powerful bowing, and steel was better able to withstand it than gut.

Most nineteenth-century violinists had held the elbow of the bowing arm low, and violinists of the German school, led by Joachim, continued to do so into the early twentieth century. Similarly, cellists in the nineteenth century, such as Piatti, kept the elbow of their bowing arm by their side (Casals remembered being taught in the 1880s to play with a book clutched under his armpit).[3] The raising of the elbow was at first associated with French and Belgian violinists, who, according to Joachim, 'carried the use of the too high elbow, with the resultant stiffness of bowing, to [a] ... most mischievous extreme'.[4] The first use of the high elbow has been attributed to Wieniawski (a pupil of the Parisian, Massart, who also taught the highly influential Kreisler). Casals, despite his early upbringing, later advocated 'complete freedom in the movement of the right arm, including the elbow', so as to make 'the whole bow technique stronger and easier'.[5] With the raising of the elbow went a change in the grip of the hand on the bow, particularly of the violin. In the old 'German' grip, with low elbow, the fingers are close together, and roughly at right-angles to the bow. In the newer 'Franco–Belgian' grip, the hand is tilted more towards the index finger, which is therefore pushed away from the other fingers. The extreme development of this tendency is the so-called 'Russian' grip, in which the hand is further tilted, so that the index finger curls round the bow. This grip was called Russian because of its use by pupils of Leopold Auer, who taught at St Petersburg, and its most famous early advocate, Heifetz, showed the most exaggerated use of the Russian grip and raised elbow. Flesch in the 1920s declared himself in no doubt of the superiority of this grip over all others. He writes that it allows 'the most effortless method of tone production', principally because of 'the powerful outward rolling of the lower arm', and because the curled index finger allows the hand 'to take possession of the stick, control it and compel it to do its will...'[6]

The language which Flesch uses to describe this development indicates that its main purpose was powerful tone production. The strong grip on the bow, and the weight of the raised arm conveyed through the bow on to the string, became important elements in the development of violin-playing into the second half of the twentieth century. Modern styles of grip and arm position, which tend towards the 'Russian' and certainly away from the old 'German' style, have made possible not only powerful tone, but also the sharp attack and clear-cut articulation of the late twentieth-century string virtuoso. Conversely, it was not just gut strings but also the low elbow and more delicate grip which made string-playing at the beginning of the century less assertive and sharp-edged than modern playing. Here too a distinction can be drawn between German and Franco–Belgian approaches. In the nineteenth century, as Clive Brown has written (1988), it was the French and Belgians from Baillot onwards who, partly through the influence of Paganini, adopted the wider variety of bow-strokes, including various types of springing bowing, which have become standard in the late twentieth century. By contrast, the German school, from Spohr to Joachim, continued to favour a broader style of bowing.[7] The two schools remained somewhat distinct even in the late nineteenth century, and it can hardly be a coincidence that it was the Franco–Belgians, with their springing bowings, who adopted the higher elbow, and the Germans, with their broad style, who remained faithful to the old low position.

This relationship between bowing technique and articulation is a complex subject beyond the scope of this book. The reason for touching on it here is that vibrato is closely tied up with these other elements of string style. The intense and insistent quality of modern vibrato goes hand in hand with the assertive quality of modern bowing and articulation. They are all part of the same trend. Of these elements, vibrato is, to the listener, the most striking development in string-playing during the early twentieth century, and it is also the element which is most clearly audible even on recordings from the earliest years of the century.

VIBRATO

Carl Flesch (1923–8) again provides a useful summary of changing practice among violinists:

if we consider the celebrated violinists of our day, it must be admitted that in nearly every case they employ an uninterrupted (though technically unobjectionable) vibrato, while the great violinists of the middle of the last century were opposed to uninterrupted vibrato.

'Joachim's medium of expression, for instance, consisted of a very quick and close tremolo. The same holds good for *Thomson*. *Sarasate* started to use broader oscillations while *Ysaÿe*'s vibrato, which followed closely every mood of his admirable personality, became the ideal goal of the generation around 1900. But it was *Kreisler* who forty years ago, driven by an irresistible inner urge, started a revolutionary change in this regard, by vibrating not only continuously in cantilenas like *Ysaÿe*, but even in technical passages. This fundamental metamorphosis has put his indelible stamp on contemporary violin-playing, no matter whether one agrees with it, or not. In any case it seems to meet the demand of the average concert-goer of the present time to such an extent that our ears object already to the traditional gulf between the expressive theme and the unexpressive neutral passages.[8]

This distinction between expressive themes, which might have a little vibrato, and 'neutral' passages, which would not, is a fundamental feature of violin-playing in the early years of the century, and it derives from the traditional approach to vibrato in the nineteenth century, which is discussed in chapter 8. The survival of this sparing approach to vibrato into the early twentieth century is well documented on gramophone records and in the writings of the period. Joachim was the most influential player and teacher who continued to advocate this approach (1905): 'the pupil cannot be sufficiently warned against the habitual use of the tremolo, especially in the wrong place. A violinist whose taste is refined and healthy will always recognize the steady tone as the ruling one, and will use the vibrato only where the expression seems to demand it.'[9] Jelly d'Aranyi recalls Joachim's advice to her: 'Never too much *vibrato*! That's circus music.'[10]

The quality of Ysaÿe's vibrato is remembered by Flesch in his memoirs: 'the incidental, thin-flowing quiver "only on expressive notes"';[11] Szigeti quotes an anecdote from one of Ysaÿe's biographers:

Eugene's father Nicholas – who was his first teacher – admonished him at the age of five or six with a furious 'What! you already use *vibrato*? I forbid you to do so! You are all over the place like a bad tenor. *Vibrato* will come later, and you are not to deviate from the note. You'll *speak* through the violin.' This was in 1863 or 1864 approximately; and listening to the beautiful, chaste, close *vibrato* on his 1912 Columbia U.S.A. recording I feel that this paternal admonition bore fruit in Ysaÿe's *unthrobbing* lovely *cantilena* as I still remember it.[12]

Around the turn of the century vibrato was a controversial topic, and it remained so up to the 1920s. The views of many teachers are summed up by Leopold Auer (1921):

violinists who habitually make use of the device – those who are convinced that an eternal *vibrato* is the secret of soulful playing, of piquancy in performance – are pitifully misguided in their belief... No, the *vibrato* is an effect, an embellishment; it can lend a touch of divine pathos to the climax of a phrase or the course of a passage, but only if the player has cultivated a delicate sense of proportion in the use of it.[13]

Auer had studied with Joachim in the 1860s, and this cautious approach to vibrato echoes the views of Joachim himself.

Until the 1920s, most writers on the violin agree with Auer that vibrato is 'an effect, an embellishment', and with Joachim and Moser that 'the steady tone' should predominate, though Auer makes it clear that by the time he was writing vibrato was, with some players, already a habit which needed to be fought. This shift from the old to the new approach to vibrato is well illustrated by the changing tone of articles in editions of Grove's Dictionary. In *Grove I* (1879–89), under 'Vibrato', H. C. Deacon writes, 'When the vibrato is really an emotional thrill it can be highly effective... but when, as is too often the case, it degenerates into mannerism, its effect is painful, ridiculous, or nauseous, entirely opposed to good taste and common sense, and to be severely reprehended in all students whether of vocal or instrumental music.'[14] *Grove II* (1904–10) reprints this entry, but adds a further paragraph on the evidence for vibrato on stringed instruments in the seventeenth and eighteenth centuries. But under 'Fingering of Stringed Instruments' in the same edition, Alfred Gibson writes, '*The vibrato* is one of the most important embellishments used by the player... [He] should have at his command, the quick, the slow, and the gradational.'[15] Already there seems to be some conflict of opinion within the same dictionary, although even in Gibson's article the vibrato is an embellishment for selective use, and there is no suggestion that it should be used continuously. In *Grove III* (1927–8) Deacon's earlier attack on vibrato has been replaced by an entry by H. C. Colles, carefully balanced between the old and the new schools of thought: 'As an emotional effect produced by physical means it has obvious dangers, but no string-player's technique is complete without its acquirement.'[16]

By the 1920s some writers are beginning to argue that the *absence* of vibrato is a useful effect, rather than the norm. Lucien Capet (1927), one of the most respected French teachers of the period, writes, 'the omission of the left-hand vibrato (at certain moments in the musical life of a work) is a means of discovering the abstract and inexpressible beauty of universal august art. Like a vision into the hereafter, it enables us to evaluate correctly all those base expressions produced by the vibrato of the left hand.'[17]

Such a plea for abstinence implies that the use of continuous vibrato had become very common by the 1920s. Indeed, by this time writers on violin-playing were becoming generally less cautious in their attitude to vibrato. A pioneer work on violin vibrato had been published as early as 1910 by Siegfried Eberhardt, who writes that 'vibrato acts as the main function of the entire technical equipment of the violinist. The great importance of the vibrato is to give the tone individuality.'[18] One of the earliest books to advocate the extensive use of violin vibrato was written by Hans Wessely (1913), a professor of violin at the Royal Academy of Music, London, and dedicated, significantly, to Fritz Kreisler:

None will gainsay the enormous importance of this invaluable asset, without which violin playing is lifeless and void. Moderation, however, must be the invariable rule. The 'vibrato' must correspond to the various shades of the phrase in which it is being used and thus, like the painter's brush, be capable of delineating the many hues of colour which the violinist feels to be the emotion and reflection of his innermost soul.[19]

In some passages, according to Wessely, vibrato should be used all the time; elsewhere it should be applied only to long notes, as with players of the old school.

Samuel B. Grimson and Cecil Forsyth (1920) have seven pages on the mechanics of vibrato, stating that it is 'the one element in violin-playing which must be studied and understood before an adequate technique can be developed'.[20] Such a statement would have been unthinkable at the turn of the century. A number of writers in the 1920s and 1930s recommend vibrato as essential to tone or expression. The viola-player Lionel Tertis (1938) goes so far as to assert,

The vital fact about vibrato is that it should be continuous; there must be no break in it whatsoever, especially at the moment of proceeding from one note too another ... In other words, KEEP YOUR FINGERS ALIVE! ... there is nothing so deadly or ruinous to an expressive phrase as the sound of a cantabile slow passage in which one or two notes are partly or wholly devoid of vibrato.

This article, 'Beauty of Tone in String Playing', carries an approving preface by Fritz Kreisler.[21]

Cellists at the turn of the century, like violinists, describe vibrato as little more than an ornament, and some of them still use the old-fashioned term 'close shake'. Carl Schroeder (1889) writes, 'A special sign for the close shake is not in general use, its employment being left to the player's taste.'[22] E. van der Straeten (1894) advises, 'The student cannot be warned too earnestly against the abuse of vibrato, as it is quite as objectionable on an instrument as in a voice.'[23] Van der Straeten and Arthur Broadley (1899) both recommend that the vibrato should vary in speed, depending on the musical circumstances.[24]

As with violinists, the trend over the first four decades of the century was towards vibrato as an enhancement of tone, rather than the occasional ornament described by writers at the turn of the century. The most important influence on this development was, as with the violin, an outstanding individual player, Pablo Casals. Casals did not write a teaching method, but a book based on his teaching was written in collaboration with him by Diran Alexanian (1922). In contrast to the old school which 'forbade its regular use', Casals views the vibrato as 'an expressive undulation [which] allows of the singing of a phrase, with the charm and intensity of a well coloured voice ...' The quality of the vibrato should vary with the character of the music: 'For weak sounds the vibrato should be spaced and supple. For full sounds the vibrato should on the contrary be rapid and nervous.' In this varying of vibrato Alexanian agrees with Broadley and Van der Straeten. But he demonstrates Casals's fundamental opposition to the views of the old school when he discusses the frequency with which the vibrato should be used: 'As a general rule one should abstain from using the vibrato only in certain rapid virtuoso passages, where it is absolutely out of the question to give an individual color to each note, or again, in musical situations requiring, according to the taste of the player, a dull sonority ...'[25] The clear implication is that, in most musical circumstances, vibrato should be present on all notes, a practice specifically rejected by earlier writers.

The view of vibrato as an attribute of tone rather than an ornament is found in other writers on the cello from the 1920s onwards, including Suggia (1921)[26] and Hugo Becker and Dyno Rynar (1929). Becker and Rynar condemn cellists who overuse the vibrato, and attribute the modern fashion for the excessive use of vibrato to the influence of the coffee house, in which musicians 'are obliged to suit their performance to the level of their public ... they have to "lay it on thick", as they say, in order to assert themselves'. Despite this condemnation, Becker and Rynar declare that the purpose of the vibrato is 'the spiritual enlivenment of the tone', a description which distinguishes them clearly from the old school of cellists.[27]

Joachim Stutschewsky (1932–7), an influential cello teacher, gives the familiar warnings against excess, but sees vibrato as originating in 'a natural desire to intensify the tone and to throw feeling into one's play'. It will 'bring forth inner feelings set free by music, thus ennobling and intensifying the recital. It is the power of these inner feelings that modifies the intensity of the vibrato ...'[28] These modifications include a broader and slower vibrato for low notes, a shallower vibrato for higher notes, a more intense vibrato for forte, less intense for piano, and often none for pianissimo. Stutschewsky has his own approach in detail, but broadly agrees with Casals and Becker about the general use of vibrato.

The idea, widespread by the 1930s, that vibrato is a necessary constituent of beautiful string tone, shows a fundamental change of thinking compared with the views of writers at the turn of the century. It is not simply that early twentieth-century players used less vibrato and later twentieth-century players use more, but that vibrato was considered in quite different ways. The later writers came to regard it as a way of enhancing tone, but the earlier writers treated it as an ornament or embellishment, making it clear that it is to be used to decorate only selected notes or phrases.

There was also a considerable change in the early decades of the twentieth century in the technique of producing a vibrato on stringed instruments. Writers at the turn of the century describe the vibrato as being produced by the finger, the hand, or the wrist, or by combinations of them.[29] Wilhelmj and Brown (1898–1908) are unusual for their period in allowing the involvement of the forearm.[30] Writers' choice of word to describe the motion of the hand or finger is significant in itself, often 'quivering', 'trembling', or 'shaking', suggesting nothing more than a shallow tremor, a style of vibrato which is indeed heard on recordings up to the 1920s from players of the old school. Later writers increasingly tend to talk of 'rolling', 'rocking', 'oscillation', or simply 'movement', avoiding words which suggest the old-fashioned tremor, and they begin to incorporate the forearm into the mechanism of vibrato. Flesch (1923–8) gives a detailed analysis of the latest techniques, and identifies three faulty categories of vibrato:

1 The Over-Close (Finger) Vibrato
2 The Over-Broad (Wrist) Vibrato
3 The Over-Stiff (Lower Arm) Vibrato

A *perfect vibrato* is produced by the combination of the finger, hand, and arm movements. The extent to which each of these factors participates is an individual matter; yet all the joints must be loosened and prepared to take part at any moment.[31]

On the cello, Stutschewsky (1932–7) similarly describes a vibrato mechanism in which 'arm, hand, and fingers will form a swinging unit'.[32] This contrasts with earlier references to finger and hand vibrato on the cello, and Stutschewsky's 'swinging' similarly contrasts with the 'trembling' and 'shaking' of earlier writers.

One recurrent feature which is common to many writers on vibrato throughout the first half of the twentieth century is the comparison between stringed instruments and the voice, though the way they use the comparison changes as attitudes to vibrato change. William Honeyman (1892) writes, 'The close shake is an imitation of that tremulous wave which often comes unbidden into the human voice during the performance of a strained note.'[33] *Grove I* (1879–89) objects to the mannerism of vibrato 'in all students whether of vocal or instrumental music'.[34] Auer (1921) similarly complains, 'Unfortunately, both singers and players of string instruments frequently abuse the effect...'[35]

As attitudes to vibrato changed, so the comparison between stringed instruments and voice, which was previously used to restrain vibrato, was adapted to encourage it. For Alexanian (1922), vibrato 'allows of the singing of a phrase, with the charm and intensity of a well coloured voice',[36] and Becker and Rynar draw a similar analogy.[37] Conversely, by the 1930s some writers on singing use the comparison with stringed instruments to justify vocal vibrato: 'Vibrato, correctly used, is to the singer as essential to the tone colour of the voice as to the violinist is the purposeful vibrato of his finger on the string.'[38] This remained the generally accepted view of violin vibrato (and, for that matter, of vocal vibrato) into the late twentieth century.

RECORDINGS

Recordings of the earliest generation of violinists to have survived into the twentieth century – Joachim, Ysaÿe, and Sarasate – have to be treated with some caution, because they were made when the violinists were well past their prime. According to Flesch, Joachim's playing degenerated in his last years: 'Owing to the absence of any kind of vibrato, his tone had assumed a somewhat senile character, and his fingers had become gouty and stiff...' Sarasate suffered a similar decline.[39] Joachim's recordings (1903) of his own Romance in C and of Brahms's Hungarian Dance No. 1 in G minor have an occasional slight tremor on long notes, but his playing of the Adagio from Bach's unaccompanied Sonata No. 1 in G minor has virtually no vibrato of any kind. Even if Joachim's vibrato on these records cannot be taken quite at face value, an austere attitude to vibrato is strongly suggested by recordings of his pupils. Marie Soldat-Roeger, Leopold Auer, and Adela Fachiri, three of the most distinguished, can all be heard using vibrato very sparingly. Auer's use of vibrato is perhaps not quite as sparing as one might expect from his own criticism of 'violinists who habitually make use of the device'. But his vibrato is very delicate, and, even in a Romantic solo such as the 'Mélodie' from Tchaikovsky's *Souvenir d'un lieu cher* (rec. 1920) he plays many notes without vibrato at all. As to Joachim's own records, they must at least show that he regarded vibrato as one of the less important elements of violin-playing (as the advice from his *Violinschule* suggests). It would be inconceivable for a violinist of the late twentieth century to continue playing in public after he had lost his vibrato. Sarasate's recordings (1904) show a very shallow, fast vibrato. In his arrangement of Chopin's Nocturne in E flat, Op. 9 No. 2, it is audible on most long notes, and sometimes throughout entire phrases, though even in such a slow and lyrical piece of music it is often absent altogether. In faster music,

Sarasate's vibrato is heard only on the longest notes. As with Joachim, this may not show us how he played in his prime, but it must tell us something about Sarasate's attitude to vibrato. With Ysaÿe's recordings (1912) we are on safer ground. For Szigeti they reproduced Ysaÿe's playing as he remembered it, and Ysaÿe himself is reported to have approved of them.[40] They show a fast vibrato which is a little more prominent than Sarasate's, but still extremely delicate by late twentieth-century standards (Flesch's 'thin-flowing quiver' describes it very well). Even in slow melodic music, such as the 'Prize song' from Wagner's *Die Meistersinger*, Ysaÿe's vibrato is not continuous. It is used to shape the music, becoming most prominent on long or climactic notes, and often disappearing during transitional phrases.

This sparing use of vibrato continued to be the practice among many prominent violinists during the first quarter of the twentieth century. As well as Joachim's pupils, violinists with a traditional approach to vibrato include Rosé, Capet, Dushkin, Marie Hall, Betti (leader of the Flonzaley Quartet), Hauser (leader of the Budapest Quartet), and many others. Even a virtuoso like Huberman uses vibrato much more sparingly than late twentieth-century violinists. In his recording of Tchaikovsky's Concerto (rec. 1929), the lyrical second subject of the first movement has quite a warm vibrato on some notes, but many have only a touch of vibrato, and some are without any. The vibrato comes and goes with the phrasing, whereas a modern violinist would be much more likely to keep the vibrato going, to keep the fingers 'alive', as Tertis put it.

To a late twentieth-century listener, this sparing use of vibrato by earlier string-players can give an impression of somewhat tentative and inexpressive playing. But a number of players brought up before the days of universal vibrato complain on the contrary that the modern use of it imposes uniformity of expression and tone, and that the old approach was far *more* expressive. As Jelly d'Aranyi comments, 'Variety of tone! . . . It was what Joachim and all of us stood for, and is ignored by many prominent violinists, who just establish a *vibrato* and stick to it.'[41]

Of all the string-players who lived through the change from the traditional to the modern approach, the one who most succeeded in combining the virtues of the old and the new styles was the cellist Casals. Casals's view has already been quoted, that vibrato should be used most of the time, but that it should vary in character from 'spaced and supple' to 'rapid and nervous', depending on the musical circumstances. Recordings show that the variety of his vibrato was indeed one of the keys to the unique quality of his playing. In his recording of Dvořák's Concerto (rec. 1937), Casals plays the first entry of the slow movement with typically subtle changes in the character of the vibrato, warm and easy-going at first, almost vanishing at the high pianissimo passage, and then fast and passionate at the climax. Unlike most players, whose vibrato makes the tone sound homogeneous (as d'Aranyi and others complained), Casals uses vibrato to make his tone seem even more varied in character than it could have been without vibrato.

Although players and teachers of the later twentieth century came, on the whole, to agree with the 'modern' view of vibrato put forward by Flesch, Stutschewsky, and others, recordings show that the development of this consensus defies neat analysis. One might expect, for example, the pupils of a particular teacher to show a similar use of vibrato, making it possible to talk of an Auer school or Ševčík school of vibrato. However, just as the national schools of violin-playing in the nineteenth century had largely lost their identity by the beginning of the twentieth, so also the influence of teachers was inconsistent, even in so fundamental an aspect of style as the use of vibrato. The point can be illustrated by comparing Leopold Auer's views on the teaching of vibrato with the practice of his pupils. Auer writes (1921),

The excessive *vibrato* is a habit for which I have no tolerance, and I always fight against it when I observe it in my pupils – though often, I must admit, without success. As a rule I forbid my students using the *vibrato* at all on notes which are not sustained, and I earnestly advise them not to abuse it even in the case of sustained notes which succeed each other in a phrase.[42]

Auer's pupils included not only Zimbalist and Dushkin, who adhered to the traditional, selective use of vibrato as described by Auer, but also players with a more modern view of vibrato, including Elman and, especially, Heifetz, who, after Kreisler, was the most influential advocate of the continuous vibrato. Similar inconsistency is found in Ševčík's pupils. These included Jan Kubelik and Marie Hall, who used vibrato sparingly, and Rudolf Kolisch and Wolfgang Schneiderhan, who used continuous vibrato in the modern way. According to Flesch, Hubay's pupils tended to have 'too slow and broad a vibrato'.[43] But Lener's vibrato was much broader and slower than that of Szigeti or d'Aranyi, and they all studied with Hubay. To make matters even more confusing, Hubay himself studied under Joachim.

The influence of teachers on violinists at this period is often difficult to disentangle, partly because many of the leading players studied with more than one teacher. And in the early decades of the century, the continuous vibrato was spread more by example than by teaching. The single greatest influence towards its adoption was the playing of Kreisler, who, as Flesch observed, 'put his indelible stamp on contemporary violin-playing ...'[44] Through the influence of Kreisler, and later of Heifetz, there was by the 1920s a clear contrast between players of the old school, who continued to use vibrato sparingly and were predominantly of the older generation, and younger players who had adopted the continuous vibrato.

On recordings, the contrast between the old and the new school is very vivid. Sometimes the two styles can be heard side by side, for example in the famous recording of J. S. Bach's Concerto for Two Violins made in 1915 by

Kreisler and Zimbalist. This shows very clearly the difference between Kreisler's continuous vibrato, which was unusual at that date, and Zimbalist's traditional, more sparing use of it (although Zimbalist's vibrato became more prominent in Romantic solos). Records of the Budapest Quartet in the 1920s and 1930s also show the change from the old to the new approach. In the 1920s the quartet was led by Emil Hauser, a player of the old school. Josef Roismann, a violinist with continuous vibrato, joined the quartet as second violin in about 1928, and succeeded Hauser as leader in the early 1930s. The change in vibrato, though only one of the changes in the quartet's style, had a fundamental effect on the character of its performances. Records of the Budapest Quartet from the mid-1920s sound, to a late twentieth-century listener, tentative and expressively 'flat', with vibrato used only on quite long notes, and hardly at all in fast-moving passages. Recordings of the quartet from the mid-1930s, led by Roismann, have an altogether more modern character, with an almost continuous vibrato which, together with a more assertive bowing style, gives an impression of firm projection and expressive intensity – qualities which are valued in the late twentieth century. For a brief period around 1930, recordings of the Budapest Quartet have Hauser and Roismann playing together, which provides a contrast as vivid as that between Kreisler and Zimbalist.

The distinction between the old and the new approach to vibrato does not always fit neatly into a general impression of old-fashioned or modern playing. For instance, Karel Hoffmann, leader of the Bohemian Quartet, uses a rather slow vibrato which is much more prominent than that of most of his contemporaries. But he nevertheless uses it in the traditional way, as an intensifying ornament rather than a continuous effect. Jenö Lener, leader of the Lener Quartet, plays with a slow, prominent vibrato which is much more continuous than Hoffmann's (and much more prominent than Hauser's, although they both studied at the Royal High School for Music in Budapest). Reviews of the Lener Quartet from the 1920s and 1930s sometimes criticise Lener for his obtrusive vibrato. But his vibrato does not sound modern, because it is slower than that of later twentieth-century violinists, and other aspects of his playing, particularly his portamento and rhythmic style, are very much of the old school. Adolf Busch, leader of the Busch Quartet, is one of a number of players who, while adopting the modern approach to vibrato, retains some features of the old school. His vibrato is usually continuous, but in fast-moving passages, where a late twentieth-century violinist would be careful to use vibrato whenever a note is long enough for it, Busch often lets the vibrato lapse, giving his phrasing an occasional plainness of style which is reminiscent of an older generation.

Of the violinists who were already playing with continuous vibrato in the 1920s and 1930s, the majority, following the examples of Kreisler and Heifetz, played with quite a fast vibrato. This is true, for example, of Sammons, Kolisch, Roismann, Thibaud, Elman, and Onnou (leader of the Pro Arte

Quartet), Szigeti, Flesch and Busch, though Heifetz's vibrato is faster than any of these. Few violinists after about 1935 are heard playing with either a really slow vibrato or a rapid tremor.

In the general trend of violin vibrato, recordings confirm what the writings of the period suggest: that during the first three decades of the twentieth century, violinists moved away from the traditional view of vibrato as an ornament, to be used to decorate a note or to intensify a phrase, towards the modern function of vibrato to enhance tone, and therefore to be used almost all the time.

5

Woodwind vibrato

INTRODUCTION

Woodwind-playing changed as much as string-playing in the first half of the twentieth century, and the growing use of vibrato was the most important development. As on stringed instruments, woodwind vibrato was part of a wider trend, which included changes to the instruments and to general playing styles. The metal flute came to predominate over the traditional wooden flute. Differences between oboes were less important, but the style of reed changed, in many cases becoming narrower and more flexible. The German bassoon was widely adopted. Changes to the clarinet were slight, and the clarinet is the only woodwind instrument on which vibrato did not become a widespread habit by the 1940s. On all woodwind instruments, however, there was a general tendency for phrasing to become more detailed in its nuances and wider in its dynamic range, to become more 'expressive', as the word is understood in the late twentieth century. By contrast, much of the woodwind-playing from the early part of the century is relatively plain in its phrasing. The presence or absence of vibrato played a major part in this development.

This chapter is divided into four sections: flute, oboe, clarinet, and bassoon. Each section begins with documentary evidence and then moves on to recordings. Because national styles are much more distinct in woodwind- than in string-playing in the first half of the century, recordings are arranged by country, in the order France, America, Britain, Germany and Austria, and other European countries. This is roughly the order in which countries adopted the new fashion for vibrato, which was led by the French. Details of recordings are given in tables, with references to movements in which woodwind solos occur, and brief notes on the style of each player.

Writers on string-playing in the early twentieth century reveal changes in the technique of producing vibrato, with the finger, wrist, or arm. Writers on woodwind-playing, if they mention vibrato at all, rarely say anything about how to produce it, though it is clear that woodwind vibrato in the twentieth century has been, on the whole, produced by fluctuations in the supply of breath. Musicians also talk in general terms about a 'wide' or 'shallow' vibrato, though a variation in breath will obviously produce changes in both pitch and

volume. No attempt is made in this chapter to analyse vibrato beyond how it
actually sounds. For that reason, neutral terms such as 'prominent' and 'discreet' are generally used. Similarly, the speed of vibrato is described simply as
'fast', 'slow', and so on. Roughly speaking, a fast vibrato is about 8 cycles per
second, a medium-speed vibrato is about 6 c.p.s., and a slow vibrato is about 4
c.p.s.

FLUTE

The history of flute-playing in the first half of the twentieth century is to a large
extent the history of competition between the wooden and metal flutes, and of
the different styles of playing associated with them. At the turn of the century
the metal flute was already in general use in France, Belgium, Italy, and by
some (mostly French) players in America. But in Britain, Germany, and
Eastern Europe the wooden flute was still preferred.

Theobald Boehm, the inventor of the modern flute system, had made both
wooden and silver flutes. Already in the 1870s he wrote that the 'full and
pleasant quality of tone' of the wooden flute was 'valued especially in
Germany'. He acknowledged the brilliance of the silver flute, but warned that
its ease of tone-production often led to shrillness.[1] Richard Strauss in 1904
expressed the continuing German preference for the wooden flute, when he
wrote, 'wooden flutes have a finer tone than metal ones ... but the latter
respond more easily'.[2] In Britain, as in Germany, the wooden flute predominated well into the twentieth century, and most British instruction books
illustrated only the wooden flute as late as the 1930s.[3] A number of British
players remained faithful to the wooden flute even after World War II.

Even without the evidence of recordings, it is fairly clear from written
sources that twentieth-century players on the wooden flute did not inherit any
tradition of continuous vibrato. Charles Nicholson (1795–1837), regarded as
the founder of the English school, made use of 'vibration', produced either
with the breath or with a finger, but only as an occasional ornament.[4] Even this
limited effect was regarded with caution in the later nineteenth century, and
most writers in the early twentieth century, apart from the French, make no
mention of vibrato. An article in *Grove I* (1879–89) cautions against its habitual
use by singers and string-players, and says of vibrato on wind instruments only
that 'it is sometimes heard on the flute and cornet'.[5] This comment is reprinted
unchanged in *Grove II* (1904–10) and only slightly enlarged in *Grove III*
(1927–8) and *Grove IV* (1940): 'The *vibrato* is obtainable to a limited extent on
wind instruments, notably flute and cornet...'[6] *Grove* is not unusual in offering
such a restricted view of flute vibrato in Britain as late as the 1930s.[7] This in
itself suggests that in Britain, where the wooden flute still predominated,
vibrato was not widely used.

At the turn of the century the metal flute was particularly associated with the

French school of flute-playing founded at the Paris Conservatoire by Paul Taffanel (1844–1908). The teaching of Taffanel and his pupil Philippe Gaubert dominated flute-playing in France, and profoundly influenced players in America. Flautists taught by Taffanel included Georges Barrère, Georges Laurent, Louis Fleury, and Marcel Moyse, and in the early years of the century pupils of Taffanel and Gaubert became principal flautists in the orchestras of Boston, Philadelphia, Chicago, and New York.[8] Georges Barrère, principal of the New York Symphony Orchestra from 1905, taught the most influential American flautist, William Kincaid, principal of the Philadelphia Orchestra from 1921 to 1960. When the Royal Philharmonic Orchestra visited America from London in 1950, its wooden flutes caused great surprise, because the wooden instrument was by then virtually obsolete in America, and flute-playing throughout America was based on the French school.[9] In Britain the French school and its metal flute did not begin to make a serious impact until the 1930s, when Geoffrey Gilbert, principal flautist of the London Philharmonic Orchestra from 1935, took lessons from René le Roy, a pupil of Gaubert. Gilbert was the first prominent British flautist to adopt the metal instrument and the French style, and his example was followed by other British flautists in the 1940s.

The French school early in the twentieth century was distinguished from the wooden flute tradition not only by the brilliant tone of its instruments, but also by attitudes to phrasing and vibrato. As early as 1914 a British writer, Macaulay Fitzgibbon, praised the French and Belgian flautists for their 'silvery purity and sweetness of tone' and their 'exquisite' phrasing, and these qualities were the principal aims of the Taffanel school.[10] According to Louis Fleury, Taffanel stressed the importance of 'the search for tone, and the use, for this purpose, of a light, almost imperceptible *vibrato* ...'[11] Another pupil, Adolphe Hennebains, reports, 'When he spoke to us of notes with vibrato or expression, he told us with a mysterious air that these notes, forte or piano, seemed to come from within himself. One had the impression that they came directly from the heart or soul.'[12]

Contrary to these reports, Taffanel and Gaubert themselves, in their *Méthode*, argue strongly against any use of vibrato:

There should be no vibrato or any form of quaver, an artifice used by inferior instrumentalists and musicians. It is with the tone that the player conveys the music to the listener. Vibrato distorts the natural character of the instrument and spoils the interpretation, fatiguing quickly the sensitive ear. It is a serious error and shows unpardonable lack of taste to use these vulgar methods to interpret the great composers.[13]

This strict attitude was supported, in writing at least, by Georges Barrère, leading representative of the Taffanel school in America. He complained in the 1940s about the use of vibrato by modern flautists: 'For the fifty years I had been tooting on my instrument, my daily care was to *avoid* the *vibrato*.'[14] On the other hand, Marcel Moyse remembers that, in the early years of the century, some French flautists did use vibrato, and provoked a hostile reaction from traditionalists: 'Vibrato? It was worse than cholera. Young vibrato partisans were referred to as criminals. Judgements were final with no appeal. It was ruthless.'[15]

It is therefore difficult to be sure of the Taffanel school's attitude to vibrato from written evidence alone. Taffanel, Gaubert, and Barrère argue firmly against it, but Fleury and Hennebains remember its use by Taffanel, and Moyse remembers strong reaction against French vibrato early in the century. The true situation, revealed by recordings, is far from simple, but they do confirm that the growth of flute vibrato during the first half of the century really was associated with the French school, whatever Taffanel may theoretically have wished, and that players on the wooden flute generally resisted the influence of French vibrato for many years. These two traditions of flute-playing remained quite distinct for half a century.

RECORDINGS

As with violinists, recordings show that flautists did not always practise what they preached. In particular, several French flautists who argued against vibrato made use of it in their own playing. Taffanel himself made no recordings, so we shall never know whether he avoided vibrato, as his *Méthode* insists, or whether he did play with an 'almost imperceptible *vibrato*', as described by pupils. Several Taffanel pupils did make recordings, and these show that none of them played strictly without vibrato, not even Taffanel's co-author, Gaubert (see table 4).

The playing of Gaubert and Barrère contrasts strikingly with their writings. It comes as some surprise to find that, in practice, Gaubert plays with a shallow, medium-fast vibrato which, though it is lighter than that of later French flautists and varies from one note to another, is never absent for more than one or two notes at a time. His tone, even on recordings made in 1918–19, shows the brightness and richness which were associated with the French school later in the century. Barrère's vibrato, like Gaubert's, is shallow, but it is even more continuous. It is also very fast, a style of vibrato with which Barrère influenced many American flautists, as later examples will show.

The playing of Le Roy and Moyse already shows a development towards the later twentieth-century French style. Moyse in particular shows a very flexible approach to vibrato and phrasing, and his vibrato is quite moderate in speed. In the opening solo of Debussy's *Prélude à l'après-midi d'un faune*, Moyse's vibrato is sometimes inconspicuous and sometimes quite prominent, and he uses it, like Gaubert's shallower, faster vibrato, as an aid to phrasing rather than just a tonal colouring. This flexibility of phrasing and vibrato, and his

Table 4

Flautist or orchestra	Recording and date	Vibrato
P. Gaubert	Debussy, *Children's Corner*, 'The Little Shepherd' (rec. 1918–19)	shallow, medium-fast, variable prominence
P. Gaubert	Chopin, Nocturne in F sharp, Op. 15 No. 2 (rec. 1918–19)	
G. Barrère	Gluck, *Orphée et Eurydice*, 'Dance of the Blessed Spirits' (rec. c. 1916)	shallow, very fast, almost constant
G. Barrère in New York PSO	Gluck, *Orphée et Eurydice*, 'Dance of the Blessed Spirits' (rec. c. 1930)	
R. le Roy	Mozart, Flute Quartet in D, K. 285 (rec. c. 1928)	medium-prominent, fairly fast, almost constant
M. Moyse in Straram Orch.	Debussy, *Prélude à l'après-midi d'un faune* (rec. c. 1931)	variable prominence, moderate speed, very flexible phrasing

exceptionally bright and rich tone (recognisably related to Gaubert's tone), have given Moyse the highest and most long-lasting reputation of all Taffanel and Gaubert's pupils.

Pre-war recordings of French orchestras show that vibrato was in general use by French flautists in the 1920s and 1930s (table 5). It is most discreet in the Lamoureux Orchestra, and most prominent in the Paris Symphony Orchestra. In almost all examples the vibrato varies in prominence, and helps to make the phrasing flexible.

Table 6 gives examples from American orchestras. They show the influence of the Taffanel school, but they also show that by about 1930 several flautists in America had developed a style which distinguished them from most flautists in France. Taffanel's pupil Barrère played in the New York Symphony Orchestra from 1905; and an example of his playing in the Philharmonic Symphony Orchestra of New York has already been given in Table 4. Barrère's very fast vibrato was influential in America, most directly through his pupil William Kincaid who played in the Philadelphia Orchestra (1921–60). Kincaid has the fastest vibrato of any flautist in American recordings of the 1920s and 1930s, and his vibrato is prominent and almost continuous. In the Chicago Symphony Orchestra the flautist's vibrato is very fast but more discreet than Kincaid's, almost like Barrère's vibrato, and recordings of the NBC Symphony Orchestra show the very fast vibrato continuing into the 1940s. Of the four examples in Table 6, only the Boston Symphony Orchestra shows a flute vibrato which is as slow as that of most flautists in France. Marcel Moyse was active as a player and teacher in America from the 1930s onwards, but despite the great flexibility and more moderate speed of his vibrato, American flautists have continued to

Table 5

Flautist or orchestra	Recording and date	Vibrato
Paris Conservatoire Orch.	Debussy, Nocturnes, 'Nuages' (rec. c. 1929)	variable prominence, fairly fast
Paris Conservatoire Orch.	Debussy, Nocturnes, 'Nuages' (rec. c. 1939)	variable prominence, fast
Paris SO	Gluck, *Orphée et Eurydice*, 'Dance of the Blessed Spirits' (rec. 1929)	prominent, fast, almost constant
Lamoureux Orch.	Ravel, *Boléro* (rec. 1932)	very shallow, very fast, some notes none
Colonne Orch.	Beethoven, Symphony No. 6, 2nd movt. (rec. c. 1935)	variable prominence, fast

Table 6

Flautist or orchestra	Recording and date	Vibrato
Chicago SO	J. S. Bach, Suite No. 2 in B minor, Sarabande (rec. c. 1929)	shallow, very fast
Philadelphia Orch. (W. Kincaid)	Debussy, *Prélude à l'après-midi d'un faune* (rec. c. 1930)	prominent, exceptionally fast, constant
Boston SO	Tchaikovsky, Symphony No. 6, 1st movt. (rec. c. 1931)	medium-prominent, fairly fast
NBC SO	Brahms, Symphony No. 1, 4th movt. (rec. 1941)	variable prominence, very fast

favour a faster and more constant vibrato than European flautists of the French school.

A number of Taffanel's pupils visited Britain early in the century, but the flautists heard in recordings of British orchestras up to the 1920s show that the wooden flute tradition was still predominant, with its less brilliant tone, little or no vibrato, and with none of the French flexibility of phrasing. Not one of the flautists in table 7 uses a real vibrato. The flautist in the Royal Philharmonic Orchestra comes nearest to it (probably Albert Fransella, a Dutchman). In his performance of Debussy's *Prélude* several long notes have a slight tremor, and the two highest notes have a more prominent vibrato. But any impression of flexibility which this might have created is destroyed by a clumsy breath in the middle of the solo. None of the other examples show more than an occasional tremor, and most have no vibrato of any kind.

Table 7

Flautist or orchestra	Recording and date	Vibrato
London SO (Gordon Walker)	Delius, *Brigg Fair* (rec. c. 1928)	occasional slight tremor, plain phrasing
Royal Albert Hall Orch. (Gilbert Barton)	Debussy, *Prélude à l'après-midi d'un faune* (rec. c. 1926)	occasional slight tremor, plain phrasing
Royal PO (Albert Fransella)	Debussy, *Prélude à l'après-midi d'un faune* (rec. c. 1926)	variable tremor, most notes none, clumsy breathing
Hallé Orch.	Dvořák, Symphony No. 9, 1st movt. (rec. c. 1928)	no vibrato, unshaped
New Queen's Hall Orch.	Schubert, Symphony No. 8, 1st movt. (rec. c. 1927)	no vibrato, unshaped
Royal Opera House Orch.	Rossini, 'Tancredi' Overture (rec. c. 1930)	no vibrato, unshaped

Table 8

Flautist or orchestra	Recording and date	Vibrato
BBC SO (Robert Murchie)	Brahms, Symphony No. 4, 4th movt. (rec. 1934)	very shallow, slightly variable, very fast
London SO (Gordon Walker)	Brahms, Symphony No. 1, 4th movt. (rec. 1939)	very fast, medium-prominent in loud solo
London PO (Geoffrey Gilbert)	Debussy, *Prélude à l'après-midi d'un faune* (rec. 1939)	slightly variable, medium speed, very flexible phrasing
BBC SO (Gerald Jackson)	Beethoven, Symphony No. 4, 2nd movt. (rec. 1939)	very shallow, quite slow
Hallé Orch.	Berlioz, *Symphonie fantastique*, 3rd movt. (rec. c. 1947)	shallow, fairly slow on some notes
Royal Opera House Orch.	Tchaikovsky, *Sleeping Beauty*, Act I (rec. c. 1946)	prominent, very fast
Philharmonia Orch.	Walton, Viola Concerto, 3rd movt. (rec. 1946)	very prominent, quite slow
Philharmonia Orch. (Gareth Morris)	Beethoven, Symphony No. 7, 1st movt. (rec. c. 1950)	variable, shallow, medium speed
Royal PO (Gerald Jackson)	Delius, *Summer Evening* (rec. 1949)	variable, shallow, fairly slow, flexible phrasing

British recordings from the 1930s and 1940s show a gradual spreading of French influence in flute-playing (table 8). But the change of style was much slower and much less complete than in America. In America the French school became so predominant that the wooden flute and the style of playing associated with it were virtually obsolete by 1920. In Britain, one prominent player, Geoffrey Gilbert, was taught by Le Roy and played on a metal flute from the mid-1930s. In Debussy's *Prélude* Gilbert's tone is bright and rich, in the French style, and his phrasing is very flexible. But his vibrato is much slower than Le Roy's, suggesting the influence of the oboist Leon Goossens, with whom Gilbert played in the London Philharmonic Orchestra. Other flautists in Britain continued in the traditional English style on the wooden flute. These included Robert Murchie (BBC Symphony Orchestra) and Gordon Walker (London Symphony Orchestra), though in prominent solos their use of the tremor is more noticeable than in recordings of the 1920s, and Murchie's phrasing is quite flexible. Even in the 1940s and later, some British players such as Gerald Jackson (Royal Philharmonic) and Gareth Morris (Philharmonia) continued to play on the wooden flute, but by now even these flautists were influenced by the French school to the extent that they used a discreet medium-speed vibrato, unlike earlier players on the wooden flute who had played with a rapid tremor or with no vibrato at all.

The history of British flute-playing from the 1920s to the 1940s does not therefore show a simple change from the English to the French style, but rather an amalgamation of the two styles, with a number of players continuing to play on the wooden flute, but with most players showing some influence of French vibrato and phrasing. Like the Americans, the British developed a style of vibrato which was somewhat distinct from that of other countries, tending to be slower and more subtle than in France, and much slower than in America. These differences between French, American, and British vibrato continued to characterise flute-playing in these countries later in the century.

In Berlin and Vienna, the tradition of playing the wooden flute with almost no vibrato persisted even longer than in Britain (table 9). Very little vibrato is heard in recordings of the Berlin Philharmonic and the Vienna Philharmonic until after World War II. As in Britain in the 1920s, the style of phrasing in Berlin and Vienna was quite plain, without the detailed nuances of the French school, though not quite as abrupt as in some British playing. Even in the long solo in Mahler's *Das Lied von der Erde* the flautist of the Vienna Philharmonic plays almost without vibrato, though by the date of this recording (1936) the vibrato heard on a few long notes is a delicate medium-speed vibrato, rather than the tremor heard a few years earlier. The Vienna Symphony Orchestra is unusual among the orchestras of Vienna and Berlin in showing the use of quite a constant, fast flute vibrato in the early 1930s. By the late 1940s the flautists of the Vienna Philharmonic and the Berlin Philharmonic had adopted a gentle medium-speed vibrato similar to that used by some British players on the

Table 9

Flautist or orchestra	*Recording and date*	*Vibrato*
Berlin PO	J. S. Bach, Brandenburg Concerto No. 4, 2nd movt. (rec. c. 1933)	flute 1: occasional tremor; flute 2: none
Berlin PO	Beethoven, Symphony No. 7, 1st movt. (rec. 1943)	little or none
Berlin PO	Brahms, Symphony No. 3, 2nd movt. (rec. 1949)	shallow, medium speed, flexible phrasing
Berlin State Opera	R. Strauss, *Don Juan* (rec. 1929)	shallow, fast, on some long notes
Vienna PO	Brahms, Symphony No. 3, 2nd movt. (rec. c. 1931)	slight trace of fast, some shading
Vienna PO	Mahler, *Das Lied von der Erde*, 'Das Abschied' (rec. 1936)	very shallow, medium speed, on some long notes; long diminuendo
Vienna PO	Brahms, Symphony No. 1, 4th movt. (rec. 1947)	medium-prominent, medium speed, some shading (loud solo)
Vienna SO	Grieg, *Peer Gynt*, Act IV, Prelude (rec. c. 1934)	fast, quite constant, flexible phrasing

Table 10

Flautist or orchestra	*Recording and date*	*Vibrato*
Concertgebouw Orch.	Ravel, *Boléro* (rec. c. 1930)	variable, fairly fast
Dresden State Opera	R. Strauss, *Don Juan* (rec. 1938)	prominent, fast, almost constant
Czech PO	Dvořák, Cello Concerto, 1st movt. (rec. 1937)	none, long-term phrasing
Budapest PO	Mozart, Piano Concerto in G, K. 453, 2nd movt. (rec. c. 1928)	occasional tremor
Milan SO	Cimarosa, *Matrimonio Segreto*, Overture (rec. c. 1929)	occasional tremor
Accademia di Santa Cecilia, Rome	Beethoven, Symphony No. 6, 2nd movt. (rec. c. 1947)	none

wooden flute at this date, but much more discreet than the vibrato used in France and America.

Other European orchestras varied considerably in their styles of flute-playing in the 1920s and 1930s (table 10). The principal flautist of the Concertgebouw Orchestra approaches closest to the French style, with a definite, fairly fast, flexible vibrato which is heard in this orchestra from the late 1920s through to the late 1940s. The flautist of the Dresden State Opera Orchestra plays in the late 1930s with a more conspicuous and continuous vibrato than in Berlin and Vienna, though it is faster than in the Concertgebouw Orchestra. The orchestras of Prague, Budapest, and Milan show a style of flute-playing closer to those of the Berlin Philharmonic and Vienna Philharmonic, with little or no vibrato, and the Accademia di Santa Cecilia provides an example of an Italian flautist playing with absolutely no vibrato in the late 1940s, at a time when even the Vienna Philharmonic and Berlin Philharmonic were beginning to use it.

OBOE

Like flute-playing, oboe-playing in the early twentieth century was divided between French and German traditions and, as with the flute, these schools were associated with the different instruments developed in the nineteenth century. The oboes favoured in France, America, and Britain were based on the French instruments developed by the Triebert family in the mid-nineteenth century.[16] German and Viennese oboists continued to use instruments derived from earlier nineteenth-century models which had a wider bell than the French oboes. The Viennese oboe was based on J. Sellner's early nineteenth-century instrument, and Sellner's *Oboe School* of 1825 was still in use, in a revised edition, in the early twentieth century.[17]

Players on the French oboe generally used a narrower reed than the traditional reed of the German and Viennese instruments. James McDonagh (1924), one of the most distinguished early twentieth-century British oboists, writes of the 'coarser, trumpet-like quality produced in the older instrs. by a wide reed'.[18] Ulric Daubeny (1920) confirms that the 'fine attenuated timbre peculiar to the modern oboe, and the delight of all musicians, is dependent far more on the adoption of the small narrow reed than on any mere mechanical improvements in manufacture and construction.'[19] In contrast to his preference for the German flute, Richard Strauss (1904) favours the French oboe:

The French instruments are of finer workmanship, their registers are more even, they respond more easily in the treble and allow a softer pp on low tones. Correspondingly, the style of playing and the tone of French oboists is by far preferable to that of the German players. Some German 'methods' try to produce a tone as thick and trumpet-like as possible, which does not blend in at all with the flutes and is often unpleasantly prominent.

The French tone, though thinner and frequently tremulant, is much more flexible and adaptable; yet, when it is necessary, its forte can be penetrating and also much more resonant.[20]

It is significant that Strauss complains of German methods which actively encourage a thick tone. This raises the important point that differences between individual players, and between national schools of playing, are the result not just of different instruments and reeds, but of different aims in tone production. Strauss approves of the flexible French tone, but seems to dislike its 'tremulant' quality. Quite how frequently French playing was tremulant is one of the main topics of this section, though as with the flute, it is a subject about which written documents are frustratingly unrevealing.

The point about varying aims in tone production is illustrated by a noted English teacher of composition, Frederick Corder (1895), who advises students, 'The tone of the Oboe is thin, penetrating and exceedingly nasal. It . . . should not be heard for too long together.'[21] The French oboe was already widely used in England by the time Corder was writing, but as his caution implies, the English style on the French oboe retained much of the character of the German tradition to which Strauss objected. The most celebrated player and teacher in England at the turn of the century, William Malsch (1855–1924), who was principal oboist in the Queen's Hall Orchestra until 1904, played on a French instrument from 1897, and yet was described as having a 'broad powerful tone' rather than the more delicate and flexible tone of the French school.[22]

The French school of oboe-playing derived principally from the teaching of Georges Gillet, Taffanel's contemporary at the Paris Conservatoire. A French writer described Gillet as 'the most extraordinary virtuoso oboist who ever lived. The quality of his tone was exquisite, delicate and clear, but at the same time capable of power.'[23] Gillet's influence, like Taffanel's, was strong not only in France but also in America. Pupils of Gillet were the principal oboists of the Boston Symphony Orchestra from the turn of the century (Georges Longy 1898–1925, Fernand Gillet from 1925), and Gillet's pupil Marcel Tabuteau became the best-known oboist and teacher in America as principal of the Philadelphia Orchestra 1915–54.

In Britain the French style was introduced by a Belgian, Henri de Busccher, who succeeded Malsch as principal in the Queen's Hall Orchestra in 1904. The conductor of the orchestra, Henry Wood, called de Busccher 'incomparable', though he also had some reservations about the increasing refinement of English oboe tone through French influence:

Our woodwind players have refined their tone-quality to such an extent, and the tone of the strings has been so much enlarged, that it has become difficult to make woodwind solos tell . . . Hence, when we go to Germany, the first thing which strikes us is the 'bite' of the oboes and bassoons, even while we dislike their 'throaty' quality.[24]

To some extent Wood seems to have valued the penetrating qualities of German oboists to which Strauss objected.

De Busccher left Britain in 1913 to become principal of the New York Symphony Orchestra (1913–20) and later of the Los Angeles Philharmonic (1920–48). He was succeeded in the Queen's Hall Orchestra by Leon Goossens who, though taught by Malsch, was greatly influenced by de Busccher. Goossens was later to become the most influential oboist in Britain, not only because of his adoption of the refined French style in general, but specifically because of his pioneering use of vibrato. Writing about the early part of his career, Goossens remembers,

the fashionable woodwind sound in the early days of this century was more wooden. *Vibrato* was rarely, if ever used, and certainly not as a fundamental aspect of tone production. Those first days at the Queen's Hall Orchestra represented for me a period of isolation from the prevalent style of sound reproduction. I suffered a great deal of abuse and jibing from other players at this time for persisting with my own concept of a beautiful oboe sound incorporating *vibrato* as an essential aspect of its singing quality.[25]

As was mentioned in the section on flute-playing, few writers outside France make any mention of woodwind vibrato in the early part of the century, and the comment in *Grove I* and *II* that vibrato 'is sometimes heard on the flute and cornet' suggests that it was even less used by British oboists than by flautists. Richard Strauss's observation that French oboe tone was 'frequently tremulant' in the early years of the century seems to imply that German oboists did not habitually use vibrato. But there are few such clues to the habits of oboists in the written evidence of the early twentieth century. Only recordings show the complex pattern of different styles, and the changing attitude to vibrato over the first half of the century.

RECORDINGS

As with flute-playing, recordings confirm that the most important development in oboe-playing during the first half of the twentieth century was the spread of the French style, with its flexible tone and phrasing and the use of vibrato. Table 11 gives examples of Georges Gillet, the founder of the modern French style, and of his pupils who spread his influence in America. Like the Taffanel school of flautists the Gillet school of oboists is characterised by a light and bright tone quality, but the phrasing and use of vibrato vary considerably from player to player. Taffanel did not teach the use of vibrato on the flute, and, on the evidence of a 1905 recording, Gillet himself used little or no vibrato in his playing. It is possible that he uses a slight tremor, but irregularities in the recording make this difficult to assess. As with the Taffanel school, it was the pupils rather than the teacher who fully exploited the possibilities of vibrato, though in various ways.

In the Prelude to Act III of *Lohengrin* (the earliest recording of the Boston Symphony Orchestra), Georges Longy plays with virtually no vibrato in the first half of the solo, but with distinct traces of vibrato in the second half.

Table 11

Oboist or orchestra	Recording and date	Vibrato
Georges Gillet	Rossini, 'Ah! Mathilde' (rec. 1905)	little or none
Boston SO (Georges Longy)	Wagner, *Lohengrin*, Act III, Prelude (rec. 1917)	slight traces
Boston SO (Fernand Gillet)	Sibelius, Symphony No. 2, 1st and 3rd movts. (rec. 1935)	shallow, very fast on some notes
Philadelphia Orch. (Marcel Tabuteau)	Brahms, Symphony No. 1, 2nd movt. (rec. c. 1928)	very variable, fast, very flexible phrasing

Table 12

Oboist or orchestra	Recording and date	Vibrato
Paris Conservatoire Orch.	Debussy, Nocturnes, 'Nuages' (cor anglais), 'Fêtes' (oboe) (rec. c. 1929)	very variable, shallow, fairly fast, detailed phrasing
Paris SO	Weber, Konzertstück in F minor (rec. c. 1936)	very shallow, fairly fast
Lamoureux Orch.	D'Indy, Symphonie sur un chant montagnard, 1st movt. (cor anglais) (rec. c. 1932)	shallow, fairly fast on most notes
Lamoureux Orch.	Franck, *Psyché* (rec. c. 1935)	variable, medium speed
Colonne Orch.	Berlioz, *Romeo and Juliet*, Feast of the Capulets (rec. c. 1930)	prominent, fairly fast
Colonne Orch.	D'Indy, Symphonie sur un chant montagnard, 1st movt. (cor anglais) (rec. c. 1935)	none, very flexible phrasing
Straram Orch.	Debussy, *Prélude à l'après-midi d'un faune* (rec. c. 1931)	variable, medium speed, very flexible and detailed phrasing

Longy's successor, Fernand Gillet, plays with a slight, very fast vibrato on some notes, but others, even some long notes, have little or none. Marcel Tabuteau in the Philadelphia Orchestra uses a fast vibrato much more prominently than either Longy or F. Gillet, and his vibrato and phrasing are very flexible, like those of some French flautists.

While the pupils of Georges Gillet were spreading the French oboe style in America, French oboists in French orchestras had similarly established a tradition by 1930 of playing the oboe and cor anglais with vibrato, often with great flexibility of phrasing, and with a bright and reedy tone. Of the examples in

Table 13

Oboist or orchestra	Recording and date	Vibrato
Philharmonic SO of New York	Beethoven, Symphony No. 7, 1st movt. (rec. 1936)	very variable, shallow, fairly fast
Philadelphia Orch. (Marcel Tabuteau)	Sibelius, *Swan of Tuonela* (cor anglais) (rec. 1929)	very sparing, fast
Philadelphia Orch.	Sibelius, *Swan of Tuonela* (cor anglais) (rec. c. 1941)	very sparing, medium speed
Boston SO	Tchaikovsky, *Romeo and Juliet* (cor anglais) (rec. 1936)	none
Boston SO	Berlioz, *Harold in Italy*, 3rd movt. (cor anglais) (rec. 1944)	variable, shallow, very fast
Chicago SO	Wagner, *Lohengrin*, Act III, Prelude (rec. 1930)	virtually none
Chicago SO	Beethoven, Piano Concerto No. 4, 1st movt. (rec. 1942)	virtually none
Los Angeles PO (de Busccher)	Debussy, *Prélude à l'après-midi d'un faune* (rec. 1937)	variable, very shallow, medium speed, very flexible phrasing
NBC SO	Brahms, Symphony No. 1, 2nd movt. (rec. 1941)	prominent, constant, fast

table 12, only one is played without vibrato, the cor anglais of the Colonne Orchestra. A fairly fast vibrato is used by most of the other players, most delicately in the Paris Symphony Orchestra, and most prominently by the oboist of the Colonne Orchestra. The Lamoureux and Straram Orchestras use a medium-speed vibrato, and the oboist of the Straram Orchestra has the most supple phrasing of all French players, with the vibrato varying greatly in prominence, and a wide dynamic range being used to shape the melodic line.

Apart from the pupils of Georges Gillet, there was a general influence of the French oboe style in American orchestras (table 13). As with flute-playing, the vibrato tends to be faster in America than in France, but its prominence and speed vary greatly from one player to another. Of these examples, only the oboist of the Chicago Symphony Orchestra and the cor anglais of the Boston Symphony Orchestra are heard playing without noticeable vibrato. In the Boston and Philadelphia Orchestras the cor anglais in the 1930s is played with less prominent vibrato than the oboe (as in the Colonne Orchestra). The 1931 Philadelphia recording of *The Swan of Tuonela* is particularly interesting, because the cor anglais solo is played by the principal oboist, Tabuteau, with a much more restrained vibrato than in his oboe-playing. The playing of Henri de Busscher in the Los Angeles Philharmonic is of particular significance for British oboe-playing because of his influence on Leon Goossens. His phrasing is

Table 14

Oboist or orchestra	Recording and date	Vibrato
London SO	Brahms, Symphony No. 1, 2nd movt. (rec. 1924)	none, no shaping
Royal Albert Hall Orch.	J. S. Bach orch. Elgar, Fantasia in C minor, BWV 537 (rec. 1926)	none, no shaping
New Queen's Hall Orch.	Franck, Symphony, 2nd movt. (cor anglais) (rec. c. 1924)	none, no shaping
Hallé Orch.	Dvořák, Symphony No. 9, 2nd movt. (cor anglais) (rec. c. 1924)	none, no shaping
Hallé Orch.	Brahms, Violin Concerto, 2nd movt. (rec. 1928)	tremor on some notes, some shaping, uneven line
Royal Opera House Orch.	Rossini, *Tancredi*, Overture, (rec. 1930)	none
James McDonagh	Wagner, *Tristan and Isolde*, Act III, Prelude (cor anglais) (rec. c. 1923)	none, flexible phrasing, sustained legato
Royal PO (Leon Goossens)	Beethoven, Symphony No. 5, 1st movt. (rec. 1927)	prominent, fairly slow, very flexible phrasing, wide dynamic range

exceptionally flexible in its dynamic shaping, and the delicate, reedy tone is unmistakably French in style. The vibrato, however, is very subtle, moderate in speed, but never very prominent and sometimes absent altogether. As later examples will show, it was the tone and the dynamic phrasing, rather than the vibrato, which were the principal influences on Goossens.

In Britain, although the French oboe was in general use in the early twentieth century, the influence of French style was not widespread until the mid-1930s (table 14). In most of the examples from the 1920s, the oboe and cor anglais are played with no vibrato at all, and with virtually no shaping of phrases. This lack of shaping is particularly striking in long solos such as those in Brahms's Symphony No. 1 (London Symphony Orchestra), Franck's Symphony (New Queen's Hall Orchestra, cor anglais) and Dvořák's Symphony No. 9 (Hallé Orchestra, cor anglais). They give an impression of the inflexibility of tone of which Richard Strauss complained in German oboists. An exception is the most admired cor anglais player of the early 1920s, James McDonagh, who played in the Queen's Hall Orchestra. His playing in the solo from *Tristan* is without vibrato, but the tone is more flexible, and the phrases are more legato, and more carefully shaped and sustained, than in most other examples from the 1920s. Of the examples from the 1920s, only Leon Goossens in the Royal Philharmonic shows the use of a real vibrato. The influence of de Busscher's phrasing and tone is clear, but the prominent, rather slow vibrato is unique to Goossens at this date.

Table 15

Oboist or orchestra	Recording and date	Vibrato
London PO (Leon Goossens)	Bizet, Symphony in C, 2nd movt. (rec. c. 1938)	very variable, fairly slow vibrato, very flexible phrasing and rubato; 2nd oboe no vibrato
London PO	Bizet, Symphony in C, 2nd movt. (rec. c. 1948)	fairly prominent, medium speed; 2nd oboe trace of medium-speed vibrato
Busch Chamber Players (Evelyn Rothwell)	Bach, Brandenburg Concerto No. 1, 2nd movt. (rec. 1935)	variable, medium speed, flexible phrasing
London SO	Brahms, Symphony No. 1, 2nd movt. (rec. 1939)	medium speed, several notes without, flexible phrasing
London SO	Vaughan Williams, Symphony No. 6, 2nd movt. (cor anglais); 4th movt. (oboe) (rec. 1949)	oboe very variable, fairly slow; cor anglais none
BBC SO	Schubert, Symphony No. 9, 1st movt. (rec. c. 1935)	slightly variable, fairly fast
BBC SO	Brahms, Violin Concerto, 2nd movt. (rec. 1943)	almost constant, medium speed, flexible phrasing
BBC SO (Terence McDonagh)	Warlock, *The Curlew*, (rec. c. 1931)	occasional, shallow, medium speed, flexible phrasing
Royal PO	Delius, *Irmelin*, Prelude (rec. 1946)	variable, fairly slow
Philharmonia Orch.	Brahms, Violin Concerto, 2nd movt. (rec. 1946)	fairly constant, prominent, fairly fast, flexible phrasing; 2nd oboe similar, medium speed
Hallé Orch.	Mozart, Divertimento in D, K. 251, 3rd movt. (rec. c. 1943)	none
Hallé Orch.	Berlioz, Symphonie Fantastique, 3rd movt. (oboe and cor anglais) (rec. c. 1947)	variable, medium speed on both instruments
Royal Opera House Orch.	Adam, *Giselle*, Act II, Pas de deux (rec. c. 1946)	none

Table 15 shows the spread of the French oboe style, largely through the influence of Goossens, to other British players in the 1930s and 1940s. Goossens's playing achieved greatest fame in Beecham's London Philharmonic in the 1930s. The solo in Bizet's Symphony in C shows the great flexibility of his vibrato and the warm reediness of his tone, as well as his extraordinary rhythmic freedom and wide dynamic range. At the beginning of each phrase the vibrato is almost absent, but it increases towards each climax, so that it becomes an integral part of the phrasing. The second oboist, who plays at the end of the first section of the solo, imitates Goossens's style of rubato, and, to some extent, his dynamic shaping, but uses almost no vibrato.

The influence of Goossens on other British oboists was considerable. By the mid-1930s it was becoming increasingly unusual for oboists to play without vibrato (though less so for cor anglais players), and the predominant oboe tone was softer and reedier than in the 1920s. Partly as a result of the spread of vibrato, the unshaped phrasing often found in the 1920s gave way to greater flexibility. The playing of Goossens's pupil Evelyn Rothwell in the 1930s shows the unmistakable influence of Goossens in vibrato, tone, phrasing, and rubato. A few British oboists and cor anglais players are still heard playing without vibrato into the 1940s, but by the mid-1940s the fairly slow and flexible vibrato derived from Goossens had become the norm in British oboe-playing.

The change in oboe-playing was greater in Britain than in any other country. In France and America vibrato was already established quite early in the century, and the changes in style over the first half of the century were slight. But in Britain most oboists played without vibrato, with hard tone, and with plain, unshaped melodic lines, as late as the 1920s. The change to the style of the 1940s, with its confident vibrato and flexible phrasing, was therefore very great.

In other European countries, with the exception of France and Holland, the tradition of playing without vibrato persisted much longer than in Britain. Almost all recordings of oboists from Vienna, Berlin, and Dresden have little or no vibrato throughout the 1920s and 1930s (table 16). The cor anglais of the Berlin State Opera is unusual in having a slight, fast vibrato on long notes in the early 1930s. The oboist of the same orchestra comes closest to the bald British style of the 1920s, playing the solo from *Don Juan* not only without vibrato but also with an almost unchanging dynamic level. By contrast the oboist of the Dresden State Opera plays the same solo with long-term dynamic shading and a carefully sustained legato line. This broad, smooth style of phrasing is characteristic of German and Viennese oboe-players. The tone quality varies from player to player, the Viennese oboe having a particular plangency of its own, but the predominant tone is darker and mellower than that of French and British oboists. The pre-war German tone and phrasing are heard at their best

Table 16

Oboist or orchestra	Recording and date	Vibrato
Vienna PO	Beethoven, Symphony No. 3, 2nd movt. (rec. 1936)	none, broad phrasing
Vienna PO	Wagner, *Flying Dutchman*, Overture (oboe and cor anglais) (rec. 1949)	oboe very sparing, very shallow, broad phrasing; cor anglais almost none
Vienna SO	Haydn, Symphony No. 39, 3rd movt. (rec. c. 1952)	none, broad phrasing
Berlin PO	Mozart, Sinfonia Concertante, K. 297b, 2nd movt. (rec. c. 1937)	occasional trace, fast, broad phrasing
Berlin PO	Brahms, Symphony No. 3, 3rd movt. (rec. 1949)	none, broad phrasing
Berlin State Opera	R. Strauss, *Don Juan* (rec. 1929)	none, plain phrasing
Berlin State Opera	Rossini, *William Tell*, Overture (cor anglais) (rec. c. 1933)	sparing, shallow, very fast
Dresden State Opera	R. Strauss, *Don Juan* (rec. 1938)	none, broad phrasing
Bayreuth Festival Orch.	Wagner, *Tristan and Isolde*, Act III, Prelude (cor anglais) (rec. 1928)	very occasional tremor, broad phrasing

in the examples of the Berlin Philharmonic and the Bayreuth Festival Orchestra (cor anglais), which are both played with the most beautifully sustained legato phrasing, a simple but refined style which is quite different from the more detailed phrasing (and vibrato) of the French school. Oboists in the Berlin Philharmonic are heard playing in this broad style, without vibrato, into the late 1940s, and in the Vienna Symphony Orchestra the oboe is still played without vibrato even in the early 1950s. In the Vienna Philharmonic the principal oboist had adopted a very delicate fast vibrato by the late 1940s, but he uses it very sparingly, and even in the same recording the cor anglais is still played without any vibrato.

Table 17 shows examples from Holland, Czechoslovakia, Hungary, Spain, and Italy. Of these, only the Concertgebouw Orchestra of Amsterdam shows the use of a real vibrato on the oboe, similar to the flute vibrato in this orchestra (see table 10), together with detailed flexibility of phrasing. This style has more in common with the French than the German, though the Concertgebouw oboe-playing in the 1920s and 1930s has an unusual pungency of tone. By the late 1940s the tone has become smoother and more rounded, and the vibrato slower and more constant, like that of some post-war British players. Of the other orchestras in table 17, the Czech Philharmonic in the 1930s comes closest to the German style, with little or no vibrato and broad, legato phrasing. Unusually, the cor anglais in the Czech Philharmonic in the late 1930s uses

Table 17

Oboist or orchestra	Recording and date	Vibrato
Concertgebouw Orch.	J. C. Bach, Symphony in B flat, Op. 18 No. 2, 2nd movt. (rec. c. 1928)	variable, prominent, fast, flexible phrasing
Concertgebouw Orch.	Tchaikovsky, *Romeo and Juliet* (cor anglais) (rec. 1930)	occasional tremor, plain phrasing
Concertgebouw Orch.	Bartók, Concerto for Orchestra, 3rd movt. (rec. c. 1949)	fairly constant, fairly slow
Czech PO	Dvořák, Symphony No. 7, 2nd movt. (rec. 1938)	none, broad phrasing
Czech PO	Dvořák, Symphony No. 9, 2nd movt. (cor anglais) (rec. c. 1937)	sparing, shallow, medium speed
Budapest PO	Mozart, Piano Concerto in G, K. 453, 2nd movt. (rec. c. 1928)	occasional slight tremor
La Scala, Milan	Bizet, *Carmen*, Aragonaise (rec. 1921)	none
Accademia di Santa Cecilia, Rome	Beethoven, Symphony No. 6, 1st movt. (rec. c. 1947)	occasional slight tremor

more vibrato than the oboist, the reverse of the comparison found elsewhere in Europe and America. The remaining examples show little use of vibrato, and the style of phrasing is generally quite plain, without either the detailed nuances of the French school or the broad phrasing of the Germans and Viennese.

CLARINET

The history of clarinet-playing in the early twentieth century is much simpler than that of oboe- or flute-playing. Differences between the clarinets used in different countries were slight, compared with those between the various flutes and oboes. More important in determining the quality of tone was the style and arrangement of the reed. According to Anthony Baines the French (also the Italians and Americans) used a short lay and soft reed, the Germans (also the Austrians, Russians, and Dutch) used a small, hard reed, producing a broad, creamy sound and superb forte (epitomised by the playing of Leopold Wlach in the Vienna Philharmonic from 1930 to 1953), and the English used a medium length of lay and a medium-hard reed, producing a firm and clear tone, a tradition set by Charles Draper and continued by his pupil Frederick Thurston.[26]

As with the flute and oboe, French clarinet-playing exerted a strong influence in America. The most influential clarinettist in America in the early twentieth century was the Frenchman Daniel Bonade, who joined the Philadelphia Orchestra in 1917. Bonade is reported to have enlarged his French tone for use in the Philadelphia Orchestra in large American concert halls.[27]

Table 18

Clarinettist or orchestra	Recording and date	Vibrato
Paris Conservatoire Orch.	Borodin, *In the Steppes of Central Asia* (rec. c. 1929)	variable rapid tremor, slight nuances
Paris Conservatoire Orch.	Roussel, *Petite Suite*, 'Pastorale' (rec. c. 1948)	variable rapid tremor, very flexible phrasing
Paris SO	Weber, Konzertstück in F minor (rec. c. 1936)	very fast tremor on long notes, some shaping
Lamoureux Orch.	Franck, *Psyché*, 'Le Sommeil de Psyché' (rec. c. 1935)	occasional slight very fast tremor, some shaping
Straram Orch.	Debussy, *Prélude à l'après-midi d'un faune* (rec. c. 1931)	occasional very slight tremor, slight shaping
Colonne Orch.	Beethoven, Symphony No. 6, 2nd movt. (rec. c. 1935)	none, little shaping

Vibrato, which is an important factor in the history of oboe- and flute-playing in the first half of the twentieth century, is rarely mentioned by writers on the clarinet during this period. F. G. Rendall (1931) states that a sustained vibrato 'is quite impossible on the clarinet', an assertion which is ill-founded, but which certainly does not suggest the widespread use of vibrato on the clarinet at that time.[28] Charles Koechlin (1948), describing the middle register of the clarinet (from a French point of view), writes that 'It has, in its tone, vibrant emotion and passionate tenderness', a description which might or might not suggest the use of vibrato.[29] The American clarinettist Robert Willaman (1949) writes strongly against clarinet vibrato, despite the universal acceptance of vibrato on the other woodwind instruments in America by this date. He describes the habit as originating in saxophone vibrato in dance bands around 1920, as a palliative for crude tone production. 'It may be that vibrato is a real improvement. Some people put sugar on ice cream. A great many do not and never will.'[30]

RECORDINGS

The impression given by Koechlin that vibrato might have been used by French clarinettists in the first half of the century is confirmed by recordings (table 18). Like French oboe tone, French clarinet tone in recordings from the 1920s and 1930s is bright and reedy. But the vibrato on the clarinet is usually a very rapid tremor, much faster than the oboe vibrato of the period, and most clarinettists use it more sparingly than most oboists. The most prominent tremor is heard in the Paris Conservatoire Orchestra, both in the 1920s and in

Table 19

Clarinettist or orchestra	Recording and date	Vibrato
Philharmonic SO of New York	Beethoven, Symphony No. 7, 2nd movt. (rec. 1936)	none, broad phrasing
Philharmonic SO of New York	Tchaikovsky, Symphony No. 6, 1st movt. (rec. 1944)	none, broad phrasing, wide dynamic range
Philadelphia Orch.	Brahms, Symphony No. 3, 2nd movt. (rec. 1928)	none, broad phrasing, wide dynamic range
Philadelphia Orch.	Schubert, Symphony No. 9 (rec. 1941)	none, detailed phrasing, wide dynamic range
Boston SO	Tchaikovsky, Symphony No. 6, 1st movt. (rec. c. 1931)	none, little shaping
Boston SO	Brahms, Violin Concerto, 2nd movt. (rec. 1939)	none, some shaping
Chicago SO	Beethoven, Piano Concerto No. 4, 1st movt. (rec. 1942)	none
NBC SO	Beethoven, Violin Concerto, 2nd movt. (rec. 1940)	none, broad phrasing, wide dynamic range

the 1940s. Of the other examples, only the Colonne Orchestra has no clarinet vibrato at all, and this clarinettist also plays with little dynamic variation. Other French clarinettists show some flexibility of phrasing, but only in the Paris Conservatoire Orchestra in the 1940s is the clarinet phrasing as flexible as the phrasing of French oboists and flautists. French clarinet-playing, therefore, was generally more restrained than oboe- and flute-playing, both in its vibrato and in its style of phrasing.

French woodwind influence was widespread in America from the turn of the century, and American oboists and flautists quickly adopted the vibrato. But despite the tremor used by French clarinettists, the clarinet was played without any vibrato in America even as late as the 1940s (table 19). To this day the clarinet in America is usually played without vibrato, except by jazz-players. The style in these examples is generally broad in phrasing, more in the German than in the French manner, and the tone of most players is between the mellow tone of the German school and the reedier, brighter tone of the French. The only development between the 1920s and the 1940s is a tendency to use a greater dynamic range for phrasing in the later examples, sometimes with more detailed nuancing than in the 1920s (this is particularly noticeable in the two examples of the Philadelphia Orchestra).

The most influential British clarinettists of the early part of the century were Charles Draper and his pupil Frederick Thurston. They both played without any vibrato, with a predominantly broad style of phrasing, and with a clear,

Table 20

Clarinettist or orchestra	Recording and date	Vibrato
Charles Draper	Mozart, Clarinet Quintet (rec. 1928)	none, broad phrasing
BBC SO (Frederick Thurston)	Beethoven, Symphony No. 4, 2nd movt. (rec. 1939)	none, broad phrasing
Reginald Kell	Brahms, Clarinet Quintet (rec. 1937)	very variable prominence, fairly slow, detailed phrasing, wide dynamic range
London PO (Reginald Kell)	Beethoven, Violin Concerto, 2nd movt. (rec. 1936)	occasional, fairly slow, flexible phrasing
London SO	Brahms, Symphony No. 4, 2nd movt. (rec. c. 1927)	none, little shading
London SO	Vaughan Williams, Symphony No. 6, 4th movt. (rec. 1949)	none
Royal Albert Hall Orch.	Elgar, Enigma Variations, Variation 13 (rec. 1926)	none, wide dynamic range
New Queen's Hall Orch.	Schubert, Symphony No. 8 (rec. c. 1927)	none, broad phrasing, wide dynamic range
Hallé Orch.	Beethoven, Symphony No. 4, 2nd movt. (rec. c. 1927)	none, broad phrasing
Hallé Orch.	Berlioz, *Symphonie fantastique*, 3rd movt. (rec. c. 1947)	none, little shaping
Royal Opera House Orch.	Adam, *Giselle*, final scene (rec. c. 1946)	none, marked shaping
Royal PO (Jack Brymer)	Delius, *Summer Evening* (rec. 1949)	fairly prominent, fairly slow, on long notes, detailed phrasing
London PO	Stravinsky, *Firebird*, Scherzo (rec. c. 1947)	none, slight shaping
Philharmonia Orch.	Balakirev, Symphony, 3rd movt. (rec. 1949)	none, broad phrasing

bright tone which (like the American tone) was intermediate between the French and the German. This remained the model for most British clarinettists from the 1920s to the 1940s (table 20). As with oboists, there was one British clarinettist who pioneered the use of vibrato from about 1930 onwards, Reginald Kell. Kell was a pupil of Haydn Draper (Charles Draper's nephew), who used no vibrato. In the 1930s, Kell's vibrato was unique, and so was his smooth and creamy quality of tone. His vibrato is not the tremor of the French, but quite a slow vibrato like that of the oboist Leon Goossens, with whom Kell played in the London Philharmonic (1932–6), and by whom he was strongly influenced. Kell's style contrasts vividly with the traditional British clarinet style. His phrasing is extremely flexible, with detailed dynamic nuances, a wide dynamic range, and a vibrato which varies in prominence from one note to another, very much in the mould of Goossens's oboe-playing. The slow movement of Brahms's Quintet shows that in a really dominant solo his vibrato becomes very prominent. In more subdued solos, as in Beethoven's Violin Concerto, it is audible only on occasional long notes. Kell played in orchestras throughout the 1930s and 1940s (London Philharmonic 1932–6, London Symphony Orchestra 1936–9, Royal Philharmonic and Philharmonia 1945–8), but most other British orchestral recordings of the period show no influence of Kell's style. Frederick Thurston remained principal clarinettist of the BBC Symphony Orchestra until 1946, and most other players continued to follow the tradition of Thurston and Draper. Of the clarinettists in Table 20, only one uses vibrato, Jack Brymer in the Royal Philharmonic (1949). Like Kell, he uses quite a slow vibrato which is present on most long notes, his tone is smooth, and his phrasing is more detailed than that of the traditional British clarinet style.

Table 21 shows that neither the tremor of the French clarinettists nor the slower vibrato of Reginald Kell exerted any influence in the orchestras of Vienna, Berlin, Dresden, Amsterdam, Prague, Milan, Rome, or Barcelona. None of these examples shows the use of any vibrato, and a broad style of phrasing predominates. The most detailed phrasing is heard in the Casals Orchestra of Barcelona and the Milan Symphony Orchestra, and the plainest phrasing in the Berlin State Opera, the Concertgebouw Orchestra (whose clarinets also have the reediest tone) and the Czech Philharmonic. Leopold Wlach, the best-known clarinettist of the Austro–German school, is heard in recordings of the Vienna Philharmonic (1930–53). His broad and creamy tone is at the far extreme from the bright reediness of the French, and he plays with carefully sustained long-term shading, and with subtle dynamic nuances which never disturb the overall breadth of the phrases.

BASSOON

Bassoon-playing in the early twentieth century, like flute- and oboe-playing, was divided between two different instruments, the French and the German, which tended to be played in different styles. The German Heckel bassoon was already in general use in Germany and Austria before the turn of the century, and the first tutor for the Heckel bassoon had been published in 1887.[31] Elsewhere in Europe the French Buffet-system bassoon, based on earlier models, was still preferred in the early twentieth century. The French instrument was more flexible and subtle in tone than the German, while the German instrument was bolder and more even in tone quality, and easier to play in tune. The usual difference in tone between the two instruments was partly to do with

Table 21

Clarinettist or orchestra	Recording and date	Vibrato
Vienna PO (Leopold Wlach)	Beethoven, Violin Concerto, 2nd movt. (rec. 1936)	none, broad phrasing
Vienna PO (Leopold Wlach)	Brahms, Symphony No. 1, 2nd movt. (rec. 1947)	none, broad phrasing, some detailed nuances
Members of Berlin PO	Beethoven, Quintet for Piano and Wind (rec. c. 1933)	none, little shaping
Berlin PO	Brahms, Symphony No. 3, 2nd movt. (rec. 1949)	none, broad phrasing
Berlin State Opera	Beethoven, Violin Concerto, 2nd movt. (rec. 1926)	none, little shaping
Dresden State Opera	R. Strauss, *Don Juan* (rec. 1938)	none, broad phrasing
Concertgebouw Orch.	Ravel, *Boléro* (rec. c. 1930)	none, little shaping
Concertgebouw Orch.	Bartók, Concerto for Orchestra, 1st movt. (rec. c. 1949)	none, slight shaping
Czech PO	Dvořák, Cello Concerto, 2nd movt. (rec. 1937)	none, little shaping
Casals Orch. Barcelona	Beethoven, Symphony No. 4, 2nd movt. (rec. 1932)	none, detailed phrasing, wide dynamic range
Milan SO	Respighi, *Pines of Rome* (rec. c. 1929)	none, subtle nuances
Accademia di Santa Cecilia, Rome	Beethoven, Symphony No. 6, 2nd movt. (rec. c. 1947)	none, broad phrasing

their reeds, the French bassoon, particularly in France, generally being played with a softer reed than the German. In France, the French bassoon was considered by far the superior of the two, as Lavignac's *Encyclopédie* noted in the late 1920s: 'it is rare [in Germany] to find musicians playing as well on their instrument as the French: first, because they do not know how to arrange their reeds perfectly ... secondly, because the bore of their bassoon produces a sonority greatly inferior to ours'.[32] The French continued to ignore the German bassoon throughout the first half of the century. As late as 1948 Koechlin writes of the improvements to the bassoon made by Buffet, Evette, and Schaeffer, but makes no mention of the German bassoon. Koechlin values the French bassoon particularly for its tone-quality in the upper register, which is unobtainable on the bolder-toned Heckel bassoon: '3rd octave: Dreamy poetry, discreet and restrained emotion, inward, almost timid: like a horn or a very soft saxophone.'[33]

In Britain, most bassoonists used the French instrument until the 1930s, and a number of writers, like Koechlin, particularly admire the upper register: 'The tone is hoarse and harsh in the low notes, but capable of considerable expression and pathos in the high notes.'[34] 'The upper register is perhaps the most beautiful of all ... Besides its resemblance to a high tenor voice, it has somewhat the same quality as the 'cello.'[35] The German bassoon had been in use in the Hallé Orchestra since the early years of the century. Hans Richter, who conducted the Hallé from 1900 to 1911, brought two Viennese bassoonists to Manchester, one of whom, Otto Schieder, taught Archie Camden, the first celebrated British player on the German bassoon. Camden was principal bassoonist of the Hallé Orchestra from 1914, and of the BBC Symphony Orchestra from 1933 to 1946. When the Hallé visited London in 1924–5, its bassoons were described by Eric Blom as 'quite out of the ordinary'.[36] Camden's use of the German instrument was not widely followed by other British players until the 1930s, when what Baines calls 'a sweeping German invasion' took place, partly as a result of the visit of Toscanini's Philharmonic Symphony Orchestra of New York in 1930.[37] A number of British players, however, notably Cecil James, continued to play on the French bassoon after World War II.

In America, French bassoons were still in use in some orchestras in the 1920s, including the New York Symphony Orchestra, but the German bassoon replaced the French instrument in Toscanini's combined Philharmonic Symphony Orchestra of New York in the late 1920s. The German bassoon was already in use in the 1920s in the Philadelphia Orchestra, whose principal bassoonist from 1922 to 1937, Walter Guetter, was influential as a player and teacher.[38] Despite the widespread use of the German bassoon, American styles of phrasing and tone were in general a compromise between German and French styles, as recordings show.

RECORDINGS

The tone of the French bassoon is heard at its most reedy and flexible in French recordings (table 22). Several French bassoonists use some vibrato by the 1930s, but it is nearer to the French clarinet vibrato than to their flute or oboe vibrato. Usually it is very fast, often it is very sparing, and some players do not use it at all. A much slower vibrato, more like some French oboe-vibrato, is first heard in the late 1930s in the Paris Conservatoire Orchestra. By the late 1940s this slower vibrato has become more prominent.

In America many players were using the German bassoon by the 1930s. But their flexible phrasing, warm tone, and use of vibrato make their bassoon-playing closer to the French than to the Germans in style (table 23). Few American recordings of bassoonists show a complete lack of vibrato, and those that do are from the 1920s and early 1930s. In the New York Symphony Orchestra, before its amalgamation with the New York Philharmonic, the bassoonist plays on a French bassoon in a very French style, with a warm, reedy tone, and a fairly fast, subtle vibrato which gives flexibility to the phrasing. All the other examples, including those of the amalgamated Philharmonic Symphony

Table 22

Bassoonist or orchestra	Recording and date	Vibrato
Paris Conservatoire Orch.	Debussy, Nocturnes, 'Fêtes' (rec. c. 1929)	none, flexible phrasing
Paris Conservatoire Orch.	Debussy, Nocturnes, 'Fêtes' (rec. c. 1939)	shallow, medium speed, flexible phrasing
Paris Conservatoire Orch.	Fauré, *Pavane* (rec. c. 1948)	variable, fairly prominent, medium speed
Paris SO	Weber, Konzertstück in F minor (rec. c. 1936)	slight tremor on one note, some shaping
Lamoureux Orch.	Ravel, *Boléro* (rec. 1932)	tremor on one note, unshaped
Lamoureux Orch.	Albéniz-Arbós, *Iberia*, 'El Corpus en Sevilla' (rec. c. 1950)	fairly constant, prominent, fairly slow, flexible phrasing
Colonne Orchestra	Beethoven, Symphony No. 6, 2nd movt. (rec. c. 1935)	very shallow, sparing, very fast, no dynamic shaping
Straram Orch.	Stravinsky, *Rite of Spring* (rec. 1929)	very fast tremor on long notes

Table 23

Bassoonist or orchestra	Recording and date	Vibrato
New York SO	Ravel, *Ma mère l'oye*, 'Petit Poucet' (rec. c. 1928)	slightly variable prominence, fairly fast, shallow.
Philharmonic SO of New York	Beethoven, Symphony No. 1, 2nd movt. (rec. c. 1931)	none
Philharmonic SO of New York	Tchaikovsky, Symphony No. 6, 1st movt. (rec. 1944)	variable prominence, fast, subtle nuances
Philadelphia Orch. (Walter Guetter)	Rachmaninoff, Piano Concerto No. 2, 2nd movt. (rec. 1929)	slightly variable, shallow, fast
Philadelphia Orch. (Sol Schoenbach)	Stravinsky, *Petrushka* (rec. 1937)	almost constant, very fast
Boston SO	Tchaikovsky, Symphony No. 6, 1st movt. (rec. c. 1931)	almost none, subtle nuances
Boston SO	Sibelius, Symphony No. 2, 1st and 2nd movts. (rec. 1935)	very shallow, fast, on some notes, flexible phrasing
Boston SO	Sibelius, Symphony No. 2, 1st and 2nd movts. (rec. 1950)	sometimes quite prominent, medium speed, flexible phrasing, wide dynamic range
NBC SO	Beethoven, Violin Concerto, 1st movt. (rec. 1940)	variable prominence, fast, subtle nuances

Table 24

Bassoonist or orchestra	Recording and date	Vibrato
London SO	Chopin, Piano Concerto No. 2, 1st movt. (rec. 1931)	none, slight shaping
Royal Albert Hall Orch.	Beethoven, Symphony No. 5, 2nd movt. (rec. c. 1923)	occasional slight tremor, slight dynamic variation
Royal Albert Hall Orch.	Debussy, Nocturnes, 'Fêtes' (rec. c. 1925)	none, some shaping
New Queen's Hall Orch.	Tchaikovsky, Symphony No. 6, 1st movt. (rec. c. 1924)	none
Archie Camden	Mozart, Bassoon Concerto (rec. c. 1927)	none, plain phrasing
Royal PO	R. Strauss, *Don Juan* (rec. c. 1928)	none, some shaping
BBC SO (Archie Camden)	Beethoven, Symphony No. 6, 2nd movt. (rec. 1937)	none, plain phrasing
Hallé Orch.	Beethoven, Symphony No. 5, 2nd movt. (rec. 1947)	variable, shallow, fairly fast, subtle phrasing
Royal Opera House Orch.	Tchaikovsky, *Swan Lake*, Act III, Pas de deux (rec. c. 1949)	none, plain phrasing
Royal PO	Mozart, *Magic Flute*, Overture (rec. c. 1950)	fairly prominent, medium speed, subtle phrasing
London PO	Stravinsky, *Firebird*, Berceuse (rec. c. 1947)	occasional, shallow, fairly fast, some shaping
Philharmonia Orch.	Tchaikovsky, Symphony No. 5, 1st movt. (rec. c. 1946)	none, plain phrasing

Orchestra of New York, sound as if they are played on the German bassoon. The most celebrated bassoonist of the pre-war period, Walter Guetter, played in the Philadelphia Orchestra (1922–37). Although his instrument is German, his tone retains some of the warmth of the French style, and his fast, shallow, slightly variable vibrato also sounds quite French, rather like the flute vibrato of William Kincaid in the same orchestra. Like Kincaid, Guetter was influential as a player and teacher, and his compromise between French and German styles remained characteristic of American bassoon-playing later in the century.

In Britain, most bassoonists in the 1920s still played on the French instrument, with the exception of Archie Camden who was the pioneer on the German instrument (table 24). British bassoonists in recordings from the 1920s play the French bassoon in quite a different style from the French, with a harder and less flexible tone, and with no vibrato. In most instances the style of phrasing is very plain and unshaped. This is still true in the playing of Archie Camden, despite the change to the German instrument. His tone is slightly fuller and more rounded than that of other players in the 1920s, who still played

Table 25

Bassoonist or orchestra	Recording and date	Vibrato
Vienna PO	Beethoven, Violin Concerto, 2nd movt. (rec. 1936)	none, broad phrasing
Vienna PO	Beethoven, Symphony No. 6, 2nd movt. (rec. 1952)	none, plain phrasing
Members of Berlin PO	Beethoven, Quintet for Piano and Wind (rec. c. 1933)	none, broad phrasing
Berlin State Opera Orch.	Beethoven, Violin Concerto, 2nd movt. (rec. 1926)	tremor on one note, broad phrasing
Dresden State Opera Orch.	R. Strauss, *Don Juan* (rec. 1938)	occasional trace, broad phrasing
Concertgebouw Orch.	Tchaikovsky, Symphony No. 5, 1st movt. (rec. 1928)	shallow, fast, on long notes, flexible phrasing, wide dynamic range
Concertgebouw Orch.	Bartók, Concerto for Orchestra, 2nd movt. (rec. c. 1949)	fairly prominent, variable, medium speed, flexible phrasing
Czech PO	Dvořák, Symphony No. 7, 2nd movt. (rec. 1938)	none
Budapest PO	Mozart, Piano Concerto in G, K. 453, 2nd movt. (rec. c. 1928)	none, plain phrasing
Casals Orch. Barcelona	Beethoven, Overture, 'Ruins of Athens' (rec. 1932)	none, plain phrasing
Accademia di Santa Cecilia, Rome	Beethoven, Symphony No. 6, 2nd movt. (rec. c. 1947)	none, broad phrasing

on French instruments. But his recording of Mozart's Bassoon Concerto, made in the late 1920s while he was principal bassoonist of the Hallé Orchestra, is, by late twentieth-century standards, sometimes plain to the point of abruptness. Nor is there any noticeable dynamic shaping in his solo in Beethoven's Symphony No. 6, made ten years later. This style gives his playing a continuity with earlier British players which is more striking than any differences in tone quality. Many other British players changed to the German bassoon during the 1930s, but the change was at first undramatic because they too continued to play in much the same style. The main effect of the German instrument was a slight improvement in the general standard of tuning. It is only in recordings from the 1940s that the style of British bassoon-playing begins to change to any great extent, with the introduction of vibrato and a more flexible manner of phrasing by some players. Two of the five post-war examples are still played in the plain old British style, but the other three show the use of vibrato and some subtlety of phrasing. Ironically, although most players had by now changed from the French to the German instrument, this development in style was derived from French and French-influenced examples, such as Goossens on the oboe and Gilbert on the flute.

Bassoonists in other European countries were mostly sparing in the use of vibrato, with the exception of the Concertgebouw Orchestra (table 25). Recordings from Vienna and Berlin show virtually no bassoon vibrato up to the 1950s, and their style of phrasing, like that of their oboists and clarinettists, tends to be broad and sustained, rather than detailed, like the French, or plain, like the British. This breadth of phrasing shows off the rounded tone of the German bassoon particularly well. The difference between Austro–German and British styles is demonstrated by recordings of the slow movement of Beethoven's Violin Concerto. The bassoonists of the Vienna Philharmonic (1936) and Berlin State Opera Orchestra (1926) shape each phrase with quite marked crescendos and diminuendos. The bassoonist of the London Philharmonic (1937) restricts himself to slight taperings at the ends of phrases. This is typical of comparisons between Austro–German and British bassoonists in the 1920s and 1930s.

The examples of the Concertgebouw Orchestra are exceptional in the use of a flexible vibrato and detailed shaping of phrases, which brings them closer to the French than the Germans in style. Between the 1920s and the 1940s the vibrato became slower and more prominent, as it did on the oboe in this orchestra.

CONCLUSION

As with string-playing, the broad trend in woodwind vibrato over the first half of the twentieth century is very clear. In the early years of the century, most woodwind-players played without vibrato, and by the 1940s almost all flautists and oboists, some bassoonists, and a few clarinettists, played with vibrato. It was adopted first in France, and by French players in America, was spreading to many British players by the 1930s, and only in the late 1940s became accepted in Berlin and Vienna.

The pioneering of the French, and the reluctance of the Germans and Viennese, seems to link string and woodwind vibrato. The violinist who first made the continuous vibrato popular, Kreisler, was taught in Paris by Massart, and Massart had earlier taught Wieniawski who is supposed, according to Kreisler, to have 'intensified' the vibrato (a claim which is discussed in Chapter 8). Ysaÿe, a Belgian who certainly did use a delicate vibrato, was also taught for a time by Massart and Wieniawski, and Sarasate, whose vibrato was less prominent than Ysaÿe's, was taught in Paris by Alard. The continuous vibrato may or may not have been a Franco–Belgian invention, but it seems very likely that French taste was a significant factor in its development. French influence was certainly by far the most important element in the spread of woodwind vibrato, beginning with Taffanel, Gillet, and their pupils. The comparative reluctance of German and Viennese woodwind-players to adopt vibrato was paralleled by the opposition to violin vibrato of the German school, led by Joachim and his pupils.

The development of both woodwind and string vibrato went with other changes in tone and phrasing. Flute tone in many countries became not only more vibrant but also more penetrating and brilliant, partly through the widespread adoption of the metal flute. Again, the parallel with string-playing is obvious, with the adoption of steel strings and more powerful bowing techniques. Styles of phrasing on all woodwind instruments tended to become more assertive, with more detailed nuances and a wider dynamic range used to shape melodic lines. A modern musician might say that phrasing became more 'musical'. The less varied shaping of early twentieth-century phrasing now often seems bald and 'unmusical', just as much early twentieth-century string-playing, with its unassertive phrasing and sparing vibrato, now sounds expressively thin and tentative.

Clarinettists, like other woodwind-players, were affected by the changing approach to phrasing, but surprisingly few of them adopted the vibrato. The slow vibrato of Kell had a limited influence in Britain from the 1940s onwards, but the tremor of French clarinettists was virtually ignored outside France, even in America, where other woodwind-players adopted French vibrato enthusiastically. There seems to be no really satisfactory explanation for this. It goes against not only the fashion for vibrato, but also the trend towards homogeneity of tone and ensemble in the modern orchestra. The vibratoless sound of the woodwind section in the early years of the century was sometimes described as 'organ-like', and the clarinet was a natural part of it. Since the general adoption of vibrato, the clarinet often stands out as the only survivor from the old days. The modern listener is accustomed to it, but the contrast with the other woodwind instruments can be most odd, particularly when a solo line passes from flute or oboe to clarinet, and the vibrato suddenly seems to have been switched off. Perhaps the resistance of most clarinettists to vibrato originated as a reaction against the vibrato of jazz clarinettists and saxophonists. The remark of an American clarinettist, quoted earlier, that using vibrato is like putting sugar on ice-cream, could hardly have been made by a flautist or oboist. It suggests that clarinet vibrato was considered uniquely vulgar and, by implication, that it should be left to players of vulgar music. The flute, oboe, and bassoon have not been widely used in jazz, so comparisons with jazz vibrato have not had the same inhibiting effect.

The general adoption of almost continuous vibrato on strings and most woodwind has had a profound impact on musical expression. Flesch wrote that the ears of the 1920s were already beginning to object to the 'traditional gulf between the expressive theme and the unexpressive neutral passages'. Hans

Keller used to recall walking out of a pre-war performance by the Busch Quartet as they began Schubert's Quartet in A minor, as a protest against their 'expressive' vibrato in the 'non-expressive' accompanying figure of the opening bars. But what Keller was objecting to was part of a general trend. In the late twentieth century, the vibrato of most string-players, flautists, and oboists is rarely absent for more than a note or two in succession, except in fast-moving passages where there is no time for it. Vibrato has come to impose a uniform heightened expression on most playing (and singing). The effect is to deny that any passages are 'unexpressive' or 'neutral'. The idea that 'the steady tone' should predominate, and that vibrato should be used only to intensify carefully selected notes or phrases, as Joachim, Auer, and others insisted less than a century ago, is quite alien to most late twentieth-century string-players and many woodwind-players. Of course the finest string- and woodwind-players still use vibrato in a genuinely expressive way, making it faster or slower, deeper or shallower, depending on the musical circumstances. But in general, vibrato has come to dominate modern playing.

It is only performers on period instruments who nowadays take a more selective view of vibrato, though as part of a historical reconstruction of much earlier performance practice. It might come as a surprise to many of them to learn that one only has to step back to the 1920s to find oboists and flautists playing without vibrato, and string players who use vibrato as 'an effect, an embellishment', rather than as a perpetual tone-intensifier. It will be interesting to see whether the historically-inspired restraint in vibrato will begin to influence other string- and woodwind-playing. It is possible to imagine a general return to something more like the 'old-fashioned' attitude to vibrato of the early twentieth century. If this were to happen, the perpetual vibrato of the late twentieth century might itself come to be seen as old-fashioned.

PART III

PORTAMENTO

6

Solo portamento

While the use of vibrato by string-players was gradually increasing over the first half of the twentieth century, the use of portamento, or audible sliding, was becoming less frequent and more subtle. In the early years of the century the portamento was used very frequently by violinists, often routinely at any change of position. On the cello, with its greater distances and more frequent changes of position, the portamento tended to be even more frequent and more prominent than on the violin. On both instruments by the 1930s it was coming to be viewed as an ornament requiring delicate treatment.

In *Grove I* (1879–89) J. A. Fuller-Maitland defines portamento as 'A gradual *carrying* of the sound or voice with extreme smoothness from one note to another ... It is of frequent occurrence as a musical direction in vocal music or in that for stringed instruments ...'[1] In *Grove II* (1904–10) this definition is reprinted, and under 'slide' there is also the following comment by Olga Racster: 'To violinists the "slide" is one of the principle vehicles of expression, at the same time affording a means of passing from one note to another at a distance. The rules governing the "slide" are not restricted, as its use and effect depend upon the judgement of the player.'[2] Many writers in the early years of the twentieth century recommend the portamento as essential to fine violin-playing, and, as with vibrato, several stress the link between string-playing and singing. For Joachim and Moser (1905) the entire raison d'être of portamento derives from singing:

As a means borrowed from the human voice ... the means and manner of executing the portamento must come naturally under the same rules as those which hold good in vocal art. The portamento used on the violin between two notes played with one bow-stroke corresponds, therefore, to what takes place in singing when the slur is placed over two notes which are meant to be sung on one syllable.[3]

Leopold Auer (1921) advises, 'In order to develop your judgement as to the proper and improper use of the *portamento*, observe the manner in which it is used by good singers and by poor ones.'[4]

Interpreting these recommendations of portamento is not as easy as it might appear. Even late twentieth-century string-players use some portamento, and although these quotations seem to imply much more frequent use of the effect in the early years of the century, they do not define how often portamento was used in practice, or how audible it should be. Similar difficulty applies to words of caution which at first seem straightforward. Auer writes, 'the portamento becomes objectionable and inartistic – resembling more than anything else, it seems to me, the mewing of a cat – when it is executed in a languishing manner, and used continually'. According to the cellist Van der Straeten, abuse of the portamento 'gives a whining effect which becomes irritating, and even intolerable'.[5] There are many similar cautions in writings from the turn of the century to the 1920s,[6] but they do not mean very much to a reader of a later generation. If a writer instructs violinists to use vibrato 'only on occasional long notes', at least this indicates that it is not to be used continuously. But advice to use portamento 'sparingly' or 'with good taste', to avoid using it 'frequently' or executing it 'in a languishing manner', could just as well be given by a writer of the 1990s as a writer of the 1900s. To understand what these recommendations really meant in the early years of the century, we must turn to technical descriptions, editions, and recordings.

As with the history of vibrato, Carl Flesch (1923–8) provides a useful starting point. He examines the methods of achieving a portamento, and distinguishes between three basic types:

1 An uninterrupted slide on one finger (example 6.1a).
2 A slide in which one finger slides from the starting note to an intermediate note, and a second finger stops the destination note (example 6.1b).
3 A slide in which one finger plays the starting note, and a second finger stops an intermediate note and slides to the destination note (example 6.1c).

Flesch calls the second method the 'B-portamento' and the third method the 'L-portamento', after the 'beginning' and 'last' finger, and for convenience these terms will be used throughout this chapter. In none of these slides is the intermediate note, or the join between the two fingers, intended to be audible. Flesch writes that earlier teachers accepted the single-finger and B-portamento, but rejected the L-portamento: 'When we consult the best-known violin methods with regard to this point, we are obliged to admit that all their authors, without exception, recognize the *B-portamento* as the only road to salvation, while the *L-portamento*, on the other hand, is excommunicated as a devilish invention of bad taste.' But, he adds,

a gulf which cannot be bridged yawns between theory and practice. It is a fact that among the great violinists of our day there is *not one* who does not more or less frequently use the *L-portamento*. A refusal to accept it, therefore, amounts to a condemnation of all modern violin playing and its representatives, beginning with Ysaÿe, and it is questionable whether there are any who would go so far.[7]

The principal reason for this 'gulf between theory and practice' is that, at the time Flesch was writing, the best-known violin methods were still those from the turn of the century or earlier. As with vibrato, Joachim and Moser (1905)

Ex.6.1 (a)–(c)   The three main methods of fingering a portamento, from Flesch, *The Art of Violin Playing*, I, 30.

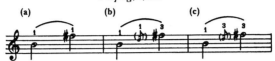

base their discussion of the slide involving two fingers on a quotation from Spohr, which states that the starting finger must slide (as in Flesch's B-portamento), and that a slide with the second of the two fingers (Flesch's L-portamento) 'must be rejected as faulty', except when sliding to a harmonic. Joachim and Moser, again quoting Spohr, stress that the intermediate note in a two-finger slide should not be heard.[8]

On the cello, Broadley (1899) recommends the single-finger portamento for most situations, or the B-portamento to cover large distances. Van der Straeten (1898) describes the same types of slide as Flesch on the violin. In the case of the single-finger slide he warns, 'great care must be taken to guard against weak sentimentality accruing from letting the finger travel too slowly'.[9]

A number of writers on the violin stress, like Joachim and Moser, that the slide should appear continuous and that the intermediate note should not be heard.[10] But William Honeyman (c. 1891) admits that 'as a matter of fact, this injunction is quietly ignored by many of our greatest players. The leading note in their slides is heard; and though the effect, like that of the close shake, may be much abused and overdone, very powerful and thrilling is the weird intensity of expression so produced.'[11] This admission is rare in instruction books, but Flesch states that Ysaÿe cultivated a B-portamento 'with a clearly audible intermediary note', and remembers hearing a specific example (example 6.2).[12]

Few writers from the turn of the century admit the acceptability of the L-portamento. Van der Straeten (1898) recommends on the cello a rapid upward L-portamento 'if the upper note is very short, the time quick, and the end note has to be sounded with great force'.[13] John Dunn (1898) writes that such a slide after a change of string is 'a striking mannerism common to many, but not all, players of the modern French school ... To violinists taught in the strictly German school such a mannerism is at first disagreeably striking, but to a certain extent wears off with custom.'[14] According to Flesch it was Sarasate who introduced a 'discreet' L-portamento;[15] Kreisler reintroduced it, 'making it more emphatic', and his example was followed by many violinists later in the century. Heifetz made a particular speciality of it, to the extent that it produced 'a certain monotony'.[16] It is perhaps significant that both Sarasate and Kreisler were taught by Frenchmen, Sarasate by Alard and Kreisler by Massart. This, however, takes us into the subject of nineteenth-century portamento, which is discussed in Chapter 8.

Hans Wessely (1913), in his book dedicated to Kreisler, describes an L-portamento after a change of bow.[17] Kreisler's own most characteristic

Ex.6.2   An example of Ysaÿe's portamento, from Flesch, *Violin Fingering*, 365.

portamento, described as an L-portamento by Flesch, is analysed quite differently by Yampolsky (1933). He describes it as a single-finger slide, 'with a particular kind of accent with the bow on the *final point of the slide*'.[18] This disagreement between Flesch and Yampolsky acts as a useful warning. It is not always possible to judge by ear exactly how a particular portamento is achieved. A single-finger portamento, with the end of the slide emphasised, can sound very similar to an L-portamento. It is quite probable that Kreisler, and later Heifetz, used both methods. Recordings show that Flesch and Yampolsky were both right to say that Kreisler tended to emphasise the end of the slide, and the same effect was used more frequently by Heifetz.

Contemporary writings, therefore, make it clear that, in the early years of the twentieth century, a smooth portamento (either the B-portamento with an inaudible join, or the single-finger portamento) was regarded as the norm. The L-portamento was generally discouraged, except to a harmonic, but was already used by some players, particularly in the French tradition. A B-portamento with an audible intermediate note, though most often disapproved of in instruction books, was sometimes used in practice, notably by Ysaÿe. Writers frequently praise the portamento as a device which brings the violin closer to the ideal of the human voice, but equally frequently warn against excessive use of it. But the question remains: what did writers mean by 'excessive use', and how frequently did early twentieth-century violinists use the portamento?

Flesch draws an important distinction between portamentos which are deliberately contrived for expressive effect, and those which are merely convenient: 'In practical teaching I usually stigmatize the kind of audible portamento which is aesthetically inexcusable but technically convenient as "bus-portamento" – the cheapest and most comfortable way, to move between positions by taking the portamento-bus.'[19] In *Violin Fingering* (1944), Flesch gives many examples from violin music illustrating the use of portamento, in many cases comparing fingerings which he recommends with late nineteenth- and early twentieth-century fingerings which he considers old-fashioned. The earlier fingerings are usually criticised by Flesch because they result in portamentos which are too frequent, which create false accents, or which are for the player's convenience rather than the expressive shaping of the passage. The fingerings which he recommends are much closer to the taste of the late twentieth century than the earlier fingerings, and comparison between them gives an indication of how the use of portamento became more sparing and selective over the first four decades of the century.

Joachim and Moser's edition of Beethoven's string quartets (1904) supplies

Ex.6.3   Beethoven, String Quartet in E flat, Op. 74, fourth movement, bars 8–12, fingered by
Joachim and Moser (below), and Flesch (above). *Violin Fingering*, ex. 630.

Ex.6.4   Brahms, Violin Concerto, first movement, bars 538–42, fingered by Ševčík. *Violin
Fingering*, ex. 479.

Flesch with several examples of undesirable portamentos. He writes that this
edition, 'despite its virtues, pays very little attention to the unjustified accents
on weak beats that are produced by changes of Position'. Example 6.3 shows a
fingering which weakens a strong beat, and Flesch comments, 'The unattractive glissando [marked by a cross] must absolutely be avoided.' Late twentieth-
century violinists would agree with this judgement, so it is worth remembering
that the Joachim Quartet was famous for its performances of the Beethoven
Quartets. Similarly, example 6.4 from Brahms's Violin Concerto shows the
fingering recommended by one of the most prominent teachers of the turn of
the century, Ševčík – 'a horrible example of what not to do', according to
Flesch. In example 6.5 Flesch objects to Ysaÿe's fingering in his own music, on
the grounds that it produces repetitive descending portamentos. Again, a late
twentieth-century violinist would tend to agree with Flesch, though in Ysaÿe's
recording of this music (1912) the passage passes very quickly and the portamentos are barely noticeable.

Example 6.6, from Sarasate, 'produces no less than four highly questionable
portamenti'. Here too there is a conflict between the edition and a recording. In
Sarasate's recorded performance (1904) he seems to have used an alternative
fingering which results in a different placing of the portamentos (see example
6.13).

The great majority of the old-fashioned portamentos to which Flesch
objects, in these and other examples in his book, are slides on a single finger.
Many of Flesch's examples date from the turn of the century or before, but
editions from this period often remained in print for many years, and frequent
one-finger portamentos continued to be a feature of new editions of violin
music until the 1920s.

Editions of the standard violin repertoire from the turn of the century show
that Flesch's examples of old-fashioned portamentos were typical of the period.
This is illustrated by example 6.7, which shows an extract from the second
movement of Mendelssohn's Violin Concerto, as fingered by Joachim and
Moser (in the *Violinschule* (1905)), J. Becker (c. 1893) and Guido Papini (1893).

Ex.6.5 Ysaÿe, *Lointain passé*, fingered by Ysaÿe (below) and Flesch (above). *Violin Fingering*, ex. 500.

Ex.6.6 Chopin-Sarasate, Nocturne in E flat Op. 9 No. 2, bars 4 and 27–28, fingered by Sarasate (below) and Flesch (above). *Violin Fingering*, ex. 1539.

Ex.6.7 Mendelssohn, Violin Concerto, second movement, bars 563–9, fingered by Joachim, Papini, and Becker.

The fingering at bar 37 is particularly striking, where all three editions have three consecutive slides on the first finger.

At the turn of the century little distinction was made between the fingerings for music of different periods. Most of the examples given so far in this chapter have been from nineteenth-century music. In earlier music there are generally fewer necessary changes of position, but nevertheless editions from around 1900 suggest portamentos almost as frequently in J. S. Bach and Mozart as in Mendelssohn, Brahms, or Tchaikovsky.

Example 6.8 shows extracts from two editions of J. S. Bach's Concerto in D minor for two violins, by Wilhelmj (1901) and Joachim and Moser (1905). Wilhelmj's edition remained in print for many years, and it includes the repeated slides over rising thirds shown in example 6.8a. Joachim and Moser give far fewer fingerings, but certainly do not imply these portamentos. This

Ex.6.8 J. S. Bach, Concerto in D minor for 2 Violins, second movement, fingered by Joachim and Moser (below) and Wilhelmj (above). (a) bars 4–6, solo violin I; (b) bar 9, solo violin I.

(a)

(b)

difference of approach is indicated even more clearly by example 6.8b from the same movement. This phrase occurs several times during the movement, and each time Wilhelmj places a single-finger slide at the rising third. Joachim avoids a portamento with a staccato note. Joachim and Moser's restraint in Bach, compared with their frequent indications of portamento in their editions of Beethoven, Mendelssohn, and Brahms, suggests a historical sensitivity which was unusual at the turn of the century.

Over the period 1900–30, editions of violin music began to show a divergence between the traditional style, with frequent portamentos, and the later style, with fewer portamentos. Editions of Beethoven's violin sonatas provide many illustrations. An extract from the Sonata in F, Op. 24 ('Spring') is given in example 6.9 with fingerings by Fritz Kreisler (1911), Arnold Rosé (c. 1917), and Hans Wessely (1923). Of the three, the fingering by Rosé, although not the earliest, is the most old-fashioned, with five one-finger slides which are not in the other two editions, and a portamento indicated by a line (to the A flat at the beginning of bar 42). Kreisler and Wessely give altogether fewer fingerings than Rosé, and the frequency of portamento is therefore left more open. But there are clear implications that fewer portamentos are intended than in the Rosé edition. Wessely gives one one-finger slide over a semitone in bar 40, but he specifically avoids three of Rosé's longer slides: at bar 39 (by using the fourth finger), bar 42 (by a change of string), and bar 52 (by a change of finger). Kreisler's fingering is even sparser than Wessely's, containing no indications of one-finger slides. Later editions of Beethoven's Violin Sonatas are very sparing in the use of portamento.

Although the editions by Kreisler and Wessely are more sparing of portamento than editions by players of the old school, such as Rosé, their use of the portamento can nevertheless seem excessive by late twentieth-century standards. Wessely's fingering for a passage in Tchaikovsky's Violin Concerto is shown in example 6.10. Admittedly he cautions that two consecutive slides should be exceptional, and 'as a rule this habit should not be contracted'.[20]

Ex.6.9 Beethoven, Violin Sonata in F, Op. 24, second movement, bars 38–54, fingered by
Kreisler, Rosé, and Wessely.

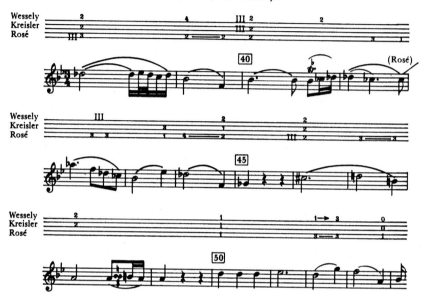

Ex.6.10 Tchaikovsky, Violin Concerto, first movement, bars 71–2, fingered by Wessely.

Even in editions of late nineteenth-century music, however, by the 1920s a
clear divergence of style was emerging between the old school and the modern
school. The slow movement of Brahms's Violin Sonata No. 3 in D minor
provides a typical comparison. Fingerings are shown from two editions published
within a year of each other (example 6.11). The fingering from the edition by
Schultze-Biesantz and Kähler (1929) has many single-finger portamentos in the
style of the 1900s. The fingering by Carl Flesch (1928) preserves some portamentos, at bars 4, 6, and 8, but avoids others, at bar 2 and, in particular, at bar
10, where the repeated slides on the first finger in the Schultze-Biesantz edition
are very characteristic of the old approach which Flesch helped to refine.
Editions of Brahms's sonatas later in the century have been 'cleaned up' even
more thoroughly.

The change in approach to portamento during the early decades of the
twentieth century was as great on the cello as on the violin, but as with the
change in vibrato, it was largely due to the influence of one pioneer, Casals.
Emanuel Feuermann, one of the leading cellists of a later generation, wrote of
Casals,

Ex.6.11   Brahms, Violin Sonata in D minor, Op. 108, second movement, bars 1–17, fingered by Schultze-Biesantz and Flesch.

Nobody who ever heard him play can doubt that with him a new period for the 'cello began. He has shown that the 'cello can sing without becoming overly sentimental, that phrasing on the 'cello can be of highest quality. He adopted a technique according to the musical requirements. The enormous reaches seem to have disappeared; so have the ugly noises theretofore considered an integral part of 'cello playing. He has set an example for the younger 'cellists and demonstrated what can be done on it.[21]

One of the keys to Casals's quality of phrasing and lack of sentimentality was the avoidance of the 'ugly noises' previously associated with long shifts, in other words the portamentos of the old school. Casals achieved this by the increased use of stretching, or extension, in order to avoid changes of position. Casals recalled in the 1950s that this new technique met resistance from teachers of traditional methods:

Some of these technical ideas of mine are already widespread, but it does not mean that, at first, they did not shock many players of the old school. One of these modifications consists of using the extension of the fingers in a general way; this makes the playing easier and avoids a lot of shifts which are often detrimental to the music played.[22]

Alexanian (1922), in his book based on Casals's methods, gives exercises for practising the use of 'irregular' extensions.[23] He stresses that, in practice, fingerings, even those of scale passages, depend on the rhythm of a passage, and that one must try to avoid 'the disagreeable effect caused by certain fingerings that are contrary to the rhythm', in other words, the portamentos creating false accents which Flesch was anxious to avoid.[24] Although players of the old school continued to use traditional fingerings, the technical and musical advantages of

Casals's fingering technique were becoming widely accepted by the late 1920s.[25]

Becker and Rynar (1929), while rejecting some of the new finger extensions, nevertheless show a more refined attitude to portamento than the writers of the old school. They distinguish between the usual three types of portamento, the slide with a single finger, and Flesch's B-portamento and L-portamento. The first two types are more suitable 'for the lyrical'; the third is more 'for the heroic'. This represents a substantially less cautious advocacy of the L-portamento than by most earlier cellists. Becker and Rynar also identify four general rules for the portamento:

1 One should perform ... every portamento with a diminuendo;
2 The further apart the notes which are to be joined lie, and the slower the sliding movement carried out, the more essential the diminuendo;
3 One should never follow a portamento in one direction immediately with one in the opposite direction.
4 One should accompany portamento with a vibrato when great passion, grief, deep emotion or the extinguishing of vital energy is to be depicted. However, this nuance should be executed only from a higher to a lower note.

Becker and Rynar warn that 'Constant audible sliding during shifting has an obtrusive and repulsive effect', and their rules for the portamento, particularly the insistence that every portamento should be accompanied by a diminuendo, imply greater refinement in the character of the sliding compared with most earlier writers. However, Becker did not go as far as Casals in the avoidance of portamento, and opposed the general use of extended fingerings, considering that they stretched the fingers in a way which went against 'the principle of letting the left hand take an unconstrained, natural attitude.'[26]

Becker's chief opponent on this subject was not Casals himself, but Joachim Stutschewsky, the teacher who most systematically analysed the new stretching technique in his book *Das Violoncellspiel/ The Art of Playing the Violoncello* (1932–7). Stutschewsky states the principles of the new fingering as follows: 'The best fingering is the one restricting the changes of position to a minimum ... When choosing a fingering, the composer's intention will have to be decisive and not the personal ease.'[27] Stutschewsky's intention of making fingering subservient to musical considerations is very similar to Flesch's approach to violin fingering, and he gives a number of examples to show how the stretching of a finger can avoid a change of position and hence a portamento. Stutschewsky comments that such fingerings 'only seem insurmountable to an inexperienced player who in the beginning, is not familiar with it ... Students with a sense for musical style will appreciate this fingering also from the musical point of view and will give up unjust misgivings and old prejudices.' Stutschewsky singles out as a holder of 'old prejudices' Hugo Becker, whose attack on the new stretching technique he regards as 'little justifiable'.[28]

Apart from the portamentos implied by fingering, it is not uncommon to find portamentos specifically indicated by early twentieth-century composers, either by a word ('portamento' or 'glissando') or by a connecting line. These portamentos fall into at least two distinct categories. For composers whose string-writing is broadly in the nineteenth-century tradition, such as Elgar and Mahler, requests for portamento fall within the late nineteenth- and early twentieth-century convention which has been discussed in this chapter. It is perhaps significant that such indications of portamento, which occur occasionally in Elgar and frequently in Mahler, are rarely given by composers of the late nineteenth century, such as Brahms, Wagner, Tchaikovsky or Verdi. Perhaps this suggests that the habitual use of portamento was perceived by Elgar and Mahler as being already in decline by the turn of the century, so that they needed to indicate a portamento if they wanted to be sure of hearing one. Examples are much more common in orchestral than in solo writing.

Composers writing in a less conventional string style, such as Bartók and Ravel, began to use portamento in a new way, as a special effect. Flesch coined the term 'fantasy portamento' for this use of portamento, which he saw as deriving from Hungarian gypsy music and from jazz. Examples of the former are very frequent in Bartók's violin writing, and Ravel uses both gypsy-inspired and jazz-inspired portamentos. The second movement of his Violin Sonata (1920) makes the origin of its portamentos explicit in the title, 'Blues'.

Schoenberg and Berg make frequent use of the portamento, but not usually in a way which suggests the influence of jazz or gypsy music. As the style of their string-writing is, in general, closer to the conventions of the late nineteenth century than the writing of Bartók or Ravel, their use of the portamento also suggests a closer link to nineteenth-century tradition. Where the melodic style is at its most conventional, suggesting a nostalgic reminiscence of earlier Viennese string-writing, the portamento increases the impression of nostalgia, at least to a late twentieth-century audience. The second movement of Berg's String Quartet Op. 3 (1910) contains writing of this kind. But it is open to question whether portamento would have sounded particularly nostalgic to Berg's contemporaries in the early years of the century, because it was still a present-day habit. Nor is it clear whether, by indicating portamentos, Berg intended to increase their overall frequency, or to emphasise them at particular points, or simply to identify the preferred position of portamentos, leaving the choice of others to the performers. It is certainly difficult to imagine the players at the first performance of the quartet in 1911 avoiding portamento elsewhere in Berg's melodic line simply because he specifies it at particular points.

Editions give some indication of how frequently portamento may have occurred in the early years of the twentieth century, and provide instances where composers specifically ask for it. Writings on string-playing give advice on methods of sliding. But what is missing from the documentary evidence is any clear idea of the usual *manner* of playing portamentos, their prominence,

Ex.6.12   Schubert, String Quartet in D minor, D. 810 ('Death and the Maiden'), second movement, bars 22–4, as played by Joachim. *Violin Fingering*, ex. 1559.

shaping, and speed. More often than not, early twentieth-century sources give instructions which can only be interpreted by a reader who is already familiar with the prevailing taste of the time. Thus Joachim and Moser (1905) write, 'It will depend entirely on the character of the passage in question whether the portamento is to be executed slowly or quickly, with tenderness or with passion.'[29] A late twentieth-century writer might well give similar advice, but would certainly mean something quite different by it. Flesch sheds some light on a specific aspect of Joachim's portamento, and on a mannerism of the late nineteenth century: 'Whoever remembers Joachim's quartet playing, when he was at his best, will never forget the poetic quality he achieved by the portamento in the following example [example 6.12]. Unfortunately the *crescendo* and *decrescendo* on the *portamento* ... a favourite mannerism of that period, detracted somewhat from the beauty of the passage.'[30] Flesch states that these swells during portamentos continued to be taught at the Berlin Hochschule after Joachim's death in 1907.[31]

Few early twentieth-century sources give such detailed descriptions of the shaping of portamentos. Most restrict themselves to generalised calls for taste and discretion, and assume that the contemporary reader will know what is meant. What written evidence there is about the use of portamento is often vague or even contradictory. For example, Bachmann (1925) writes, 'Sarasate had one great quality amid a number of others; he practised the *glissando* with circumspection.'[32] John Dunn (1898) confirms this description:

Almost unique in striking contrast to [Joachim] is Sarasate. There seems to be an almost total absence of gliding; an effort to hide the interval between one note and another by leaving out all gliding and substituting most electric leaps ... Of course Sarasate *does* glide, as also does Joachim make electric leaps, but what I have noted as above is the leading characteristic about the gliding of these two artists.[33]

And yet Flesch remembers Sarasate's pioneering use of the L-portamento, and quotes an edition by Sarasate which includes many single-finger portamentos (see example 6.6). What is one to make of such contradictions? It is possible to conjecture that, although Sarasate used the portamento frequently by late twentieth-century standards, he used it discreetly by the standards of c. 1900. But without the recordings, the written evidence would give little idea of what Sarasate's portamento sounded like. Herman Klein (1923) writes that singers at the turn of the century, after a period of excessive portamento, learnt to imitate 'the grace, perception and restraint of players of the violin ... like Joachim, Sarasate, Ysaÿe ... who were the right models from whom to acquire them'.[34]

This suggests that, to a contemporary singer, Joachim, Sarasate, and Ysaÿe appeared to use portamento in a similar way, and all three used it with restraint. This contradicts the view that Joachim and Sarasate had different approaches, and an examination of these violinists' fingerings leaves a late twentieth-century reader wondering exactly what Klein means by 'restraint'.

Leopold Auer (1921) not only objects to the continual use of a languishing portamento, but also gives a specific piece of advice: 'The *portamento* should be employed only when the melody is descending, save for certain very exceptional cases of ascending melody.'[35] But in the examples given in this chapter, and elsewhere in the editions of the period, ascending portamentos are at least as common as descending ones. Did Auer really play as he taught, and did his pupils follow his advice?

As with many other aspects of early twentieth-century performance practice the problem can only be clarified by recordings. The picture which they reveal is, however, complicated. In some cases recordings support the written evidence, in other cases they contradict it.

RECORDINGS

Early twentieth-century writings on portamento, and the fingerings given in editions of the period, have already suggested that notions of 'grace, perception, and restraint' in the use of portamento have radically changed in the last hundred years. Recordings vividly confirm this impression. They also confirm the implication of early twentieth-century writings that the single-finger and B-portamento were the usual methods of sliding in the early years of the century, although the L-portamento, not widely accepted in writings until the 1930s, was certainly used by some players from the earliest years of the century. The first two examples in this section include two of the most admired players from the turn of the century, Sarasate and Ysaÿe, whose portamentos were particularly varied (and frequent), and who both used the L-portamento.

Chopin, Nocturne in E flat, Op. 9 No. 2 (example 6.13)

Sarasate   (rec. 1904)
Drdla   (rec. 1903)

Within these six bars, Sarasate plays twelve portamentos, and Drdla plays ten. In Sarasate's performance the 'forbidden' L-portamento occurs five times (at the points marked 'L'), which is nearly half the total number. This confirms Flesch's statement that Sarasate used this style of portamento. The last quaver of bar 2 has a slide up to it after a change of string. The remaining portamentos are single-finger or B-portamentos. Sarasate's use of the device is therefore very varied. Drdla also seems to use the L-portamento, particularly at the first interval of the melody, where Sarasate uses one too. This contradicts Dunn's

Ex.6.13 Chopin, Nocturne in E flat, Op. 9 No. 2, bars 1–6, Sarasate (solid line) and Drdla (dotted line).

Ex.6.14 Wagner, *Die Meistersinger*, 'Prize Song', bars 1–11, Ysaÿe.

statement that the L-portamento was a speciality of the French at this time. Sarasate was taught by a Frenchman, but Drdla, a Hungarian, was taught by the Austrian, Hellmesberger at the Vienna Conservatoire.

Wagner, *Die Meistersinger*, Prize Song (example 6.14)

Ysaÿe (rec. 1912)

Ysaÿe plays twelve portamentos within the first ten bars of this piece, even more frequently than Sarasate in the previous example. Sarasate averages one portamento every six intervals, and Ysaÿe averages more than one every four intervals. Such frequent sliding is not unusual in recordings from the first quarter of the century, though it would be considered grotesque in a late twentieth-century violinist (except in jazz-playing). Again, this recording confirms Flesch's testimony. Flesch reports that Ysaÿe cultivated a B-portamento with an audible intermediate note, against the prevailing orthodoxy of the period, and this extract contains several clear examples (marked with a 'B'). There is also one example of what sounds like an L-portamento (into bar 2). Most of the remaining slides sound like single-finger portamentos. Ysaÿe's portamentos are therefore, like Sarasate's, very varied in character.

Ex.6.15 Joachim, Romance in C, bars 9–32, Joachim.

Joachim, Romance in C (example 6.15)

Joachim   (rec. 1903)

Joachim's use of the portamento is as striking as Sarasate's and Ysaÿe's, but it illustrates the point that portamento does not have to be very frequent to sound excessive to a modern listener. In the opening of his Romance, Joachim plays nine portamentos, an average of one every seven intervals. Although this is less frequent than Sarasate's sliding and much less frequent than Ysaÿe's, Joachim's sliding sounds the most old-fashioned of the three. This is partly because he uses less vibrato than Sarasate or Ysaÿe, and therefore already sounds more old-fashioned even before he slides. But it is also because of the manner of his sliding. Flesch remembered Joachim's crescendo and diminuendo during a portamento, 'a favourite mannerism of that period' (as in example 6.12). In example 6.15, it is not clear that the volume actually swells during the portamento, but in many cases the sliding is certainly at least as loud as the notes before and after it, as well as being slow. To modern ears this gives an obtrusive and lugubrious character to Joachim's portamentos, and makes them seem repetitive, particularly the descending portamentos at bars 14, 18, 24, and 30. This is not to say that all Joachim's portamentos sound exactly the same. Some are more prominent than others, because of differences in volume or speed. But they are not as varied in shaping as Sarasate's or Ysaÿe's, and there is certainly no impression that Joachim ever uses the L-portamento.

Spohr, Violin Concerto No. 9 in D minor, second movement (example 6.16)

Marie Soldat-Roeger   (rec. c. 1920)

As with vibrato, one might think that Joachim's generally slow and unshaped portamento could be the result of his decline in old age. Again, however, recordings of his pupils show a similar style, suggesting that this was a genuine

Ex.6.16   Spohr, Violin Concerto No. 9 in D minor, second movement, bars 5–20,
Soldat–Roeger.

part of Joachim's practice. One of his most distinguished pupils, Marie Soldat-
Roeger, plays this movement by Spohr much as Joachim plays his Romance,
though with more frequent portamentos (an average of one every four
intervals), and with several instances where portamentos follow each other
consecutively.

J. S. Bach, Sonata in G minor for Unaccompanied Violin, Adagio

Joachim   (rec. 1903)
Kreisler   (rec. 1926)

One implication of Joachim's editions which is borne out by his few recordings
is that he played with much less frequent portamentos in Bach than in
nineteenth-century music. This is the only aspect of Joachim's playing which
now sounds more modern in style than most other violinists of the early
twentieth century. The point is illustrated by comparison between Joachim and
Kreisler. Kreisler plays occasional portamentos throughout the movement.
They become frequent at bars 11–12, where he uses a succession of portamentos
over large intervals to create a climax of expressive intensity, much as he might
in Brahms or Grieg. Joachim plays no portamento in these bars, and in the
entire movement he plays only two noticeable portamentos, compared with
Kreisler's 23. This is despite the fact that in all other ways – phrasing, rhythm,
vibrato – Joachim's playing marks him as a player of an earlier generation than
Kreisler. Joachim's sparing use of portamento in Bach was not generally
followed by other violinists of the early twentieth century, not even by his own
pupils. Soldat-Roeger is much less restrained in her performance of the Adagio
from the unaccompanied Sonata in C.

Ex.6.17 Tchaikovsky, *Souvenir d'un lieu cher*, 'Mélodie', arr. Wilhelmj, bars 1–17, Auer.

Tchaikovsky, *Souvenir d'un lieu cher*, Mélodie (arr. Wilhelmj) (example 6.17)

Auer   (rec. 1920)

Leopold Auer is one of the writers who, while praising the portamento as 'one of the great violin effects', warns that it becomes objectionable when it is 'executed in a languishing manner, and used continually'. By the standards of the late twentieth century, Sarasate, Ysaÿe, Joachim, and Soldat-Roeger all use the portamento continually, and in a languishing manner. Auer himself was taught by Joachim, and his approach to portamento, as shown in his recordings, is nearer to that of his teacher than one might suppose from his writings. In the opening of Tchaikovsky's 'Mélodie', Auer averages one portamento for every six intervals (discounting the staccato scale in the ninth bar), and most of the portamentos are quite slow and prominent. They are, however, a little more varied than Joachim's portamentos. For example, at bar 7 there is a portamento after a change of string, at bar 13 the emphasis is on the end of the slide, and at bar 15 Auer plays a B-portamento with an audible intermediate note. Auer's instruction that 'the *portamento* should be employed only when the melody is descending, save for certain very exceptional cases of ascending melody', is not borne out by his own playing. Admittedly in this extract he plays only four ascending portamentos, compared with six descending, but the circumstances in which he plays them are hardly 'very exceptional'.

Frequent, slow, prominent portamento is the rule rather than the exception in recordings of violin-playing from the first quarter of the century. It demonstrates that what early twentieth-century writers meant by restraint, discretion, and taste in the use of portamento was quite different from their meaning in the late twentieth century. A gradual change in attitude to portamento is clearly audible on recordings from the 1920s and 1930s. A new generation of players introduced a more sparing and discreet use of portamento, and the continual, heavy portamentos of the older generation fell into disuse. Recordings of any standard work in the violin repertoire can be used to show how the style changed. One work by J. S. Bach and one by Elgar will demonstrate the point.

J. S. Bach, Concerto in D minor for two violins, second movement (example 6.18)

Kreisler and Zimbalist   (rec. 1915)
A. and A. Rosé   (rec. c. 1930)
Busch and Magnes   (rec. 1945)

Editions by Wilhelmj and by Joachim and Moser of Bach's Concerto in D minor for two violins have been discussed earlier in this chapter (example 6.8). In the slow movement, the fingerings by Wilhelmj suggest frequent portamentos, often at the same point in a phrase each time it occurs. Recordings show that violinists of the old school do play this movement with frequent portamentos, sometimes placing them according to Wilhelmj's suggestions, and sometimes not. Violinists of the more modern school play it with fewer and more discreet portamentos.

Zimbalist and Arnold Rosé represent the old approach to portamento (Flesch described Arnold Rosé's style as 'that of the [eighteen] 'seventies, with no concession to modern tendencies in our art').[36] Busch and Magnes show the more sparing use of portamento which was widespread by the 1930s, and Kreisler shows an intermediate stage between these two styles. Even the most modern of these performances, by Busch and Magnes, is still some way from the very sparing approach to portamento found in Bach-playing of the late twentieth century. Though not the earliest of the three, the performance by Arnold Rosé shows the most consistently old-fashioned view of the first violin part. At bars 4–6, he slides slowly up and down in a manner very characteristic of the old style. His repeated portamentos over rising thirds are consistent with Wilhelmj's fingering, but those over descending sixths are not necessarily implied by Wilhelmj (Wilhelmj suggests a harmonic at the A in bar 5, which would discourage a slide down from it). Rosé plays this passage in exactly the same way when it is repeated at the end of the movement (bars 44–6). Similarly, in both violin parts, at bars 8–9 the Rosés mark the climax of each phrase with a portamento at the rising third, and the same applies when these phrases recur at bars 25–8. This consistent repetition of portamento contrasts with Arnold Rosé's treatment of the semiquavers in bars 13–15. Here his placing of portamentos is quite inconsistent, creating the kind of apparently random rhythmic emphases to which Flesch objected in many old-fashioned

Ex.6.18 J. S. Bach, Concerto in D minor for 2 Violins, second movement, bars 1–16, A. and A. Rosé (on the line), Kreisler and Zimbalist (above the line), and Busch and Magnes (below the line).

fingerings. Rosé repeats this pattern of portamentos almost exactly at bars 48–9, but where the passage occurs transposed down a fourth, at bars 19–20, Rosé plays only one portamento, probably because at this pitch the passage lies conveniently across three strings. Alma Rosé's use of the portamento is a little less old-fashioned than Arnold's. At bars 14–15 she avoids the portamentos over rising thirds, which Arnold plays at bars 5–6, though she does play the descending portamentos. Where this passage is repeated at the end of the movement (bars 47–50) she plays both ascending and descending portamentos, but slides very quietly, unlike Arnold Rosé, so the effect is not quite as old-fashioned as it looks on paper. Alma Rosé is also very sparing of incidental portamentos in semiquaver passages. At bars 4–6 she plays none of the portamentos which Arnold plays in the equivalent passage at bars 13–15.

If Arnold Rosé gives the most old-fashioned performance of the first violin part, Zimbalist certainly gives the most old-fashioned performance of the second part. At bars 13–15 he plays slow, prominent portamentos up and down, as Rosé does at bars 4–6, and he does the same at the end of the movement, without any attempt to soften the sliding. Zimbalist's passing portamentos in the semiquaver passage at bars 4–6 seem as haphazard as Rosé's at bars 13–15. Unlike Rosé, Zimbalist changes the placing of the portamentos slightly when this passage is repeated at bars 44–6. There is another example of inconsistency at bars 8–9. In the Rosés' performance, each of the semiquaver phrases is played with a portamento at the rising third, but Kreisler and Zimbalist place their portamentos differently each time. Zimbalist introduces yet another variation where this passage is repeated at bars 35–6. (Bars 25–8, which would have provided an interesting comparison with the Rosés, are cut in the Kreisler/Zimbalist recording.) Zimbalist's portamentos are, however, a little more varied in type than Rosé's (for example, the second portamento in bar 2 sounds like an L-portamento). In general, Kreisler's portamentos are much less frequent than Zimbalist's. At bars 5–6, although Kreisler plays portamentos up and down, he avoids the repetitiveness of Rosé and Zimbalist by carefully not sliding over the penultimate phrase (second half of bar 5). Where this passage is repeated (bars 45–6) Kreisler reduces the number of portamentos still further. From a late twentieth-century standpoint, Kreisler's choice of portamentos seems more discriminating than that of Rosé or Zimbalist. Kreisler still introduces a number of passing portamentos in the semiquaver passage at bar 13–15, but fewer than Rosé and Zimbalist in equivalent passages. Kreisler plays bars 48–9 with exactly the same portamentos as bars 14–15. (Bars 19–20 are cut in this recording.)

Busch and Magnes represent a further step towards the modern approach to portamento. In particular, there is much less impression of portamentos occurring casually or at random than in the earlier recordings. There is only an occasional portamento in the semiquaver passages at bars 4–6, 13–15, and equivalent passages later in the movement (bars 19–21, 44–6, and 47–9). This is partly accounted for by the use of staccato and semi-staccato bowings at the ends of phrases. The sliding up and down at bars 4–6 is still quite frequent by late twentieth-century standards, but the slides are faster and lighter than in the earlier recordings, so that the end of one note and the beginning of the next are always clearly defined. Bars 25–6 and 28 stand out as more old-fashioned in style. Here there are rather casual-sounding portamentos within semiquaver groups, creating an accent which divides the six semiquavers into two groups of three, instead of the usual three groups of two. Flesch would no doubt have regarded this as false accentuation created by portamento, an effect which a late twentieth-century violinist would tend to avoid.

Music of the late Romantic period presents many more opportunities for a violinist to use portamento than eighteenth-century music. Whereas late twentieth-century performances of Bach tend to be very sparing of portamento, it is still a frequently used device in Brahms, Tchaikovsky or Elgar, though its frequency varies considerably from one player to another. This continued acceptance of portamento in late Romantic music means that the changing attitudes over the century tend not to produce such clear contrasts between earlier and later styles. Nevertheless, the same underlying trend, from frequent, prominent portamentos to less frequent, lighter portamentos, can be heard in recordings made in the first half of the century.

Elgar, Violin Concerto, second movement, fig. 45 to fig. 47

Hall   (rec. 1916)
Sammons   (rec. 1929)
Menuhin   (rec. 1932)

Recordings of Elgar's Violin Concerto show that, in this type of music, changes in the character of the portamento are much more striking than changes in its frequency. By the time of Elgar's death in 1934, the work had been recorded by three violinists who, despite a wide variety of styles, were all approved by the composer. Marie Hall, a pupil of Wilhelmj and Ševčík, uses portamento in the old manner. Albert Sammons was virtually self-taught, and, although he was an almost exact contemporary of Marie Hall, he shows a much more refined use of portamento. Yehudi Menuhin, a pupil of Enescu, represents a younger generation of players, with an even more discreet use of portamento than Sammons.

The first violin entry in the slow movement of the concerto shows that the difference between the frequency of these three players' portamento was not very great, at least in the first eight bars of the entry (Hall's recording has a cut from the end of the second bar after fig. 46). To the ear, however, the difference between Hall and the other two is substantial. Almost all of Hall's portamentos are slow, prominent, and unshaped, in the manner of Joachim and his pupils. A high proportion of them seem to be single-finger portamentos, and several of them end with an emphatic change of bow, giving a gulping effect characteristic of the old school. Most of Sammons's portamentos are much faster and lighter than Hall's, and a high proportion of them are B-portamentos, which therefore slide over a shorter distance and provide a more definite start to the second note. Some of Sammons's portamentos have an audible intermediate note. Menuhin's portamentos are even more discreet than Sammons's, because they are, in general, played much more quietly than the notes before and after them.

These three recordings demonstrate that there is no simple answer to the question of what style of portamento Elgar expected in his music. When he wrote the concerto in 1907–10, the predominant approach to portamento in England was set by Joachim and his pupils, a style exemplified by Marie Hall. And yet the concerto was written for Kreisler, and for many years championed by Sammons, and both Sammons and Kreisler used portamento with greater discretion, and with greater variety of shaping, than most players in the early years of the century. Elgar's score provides further potential confusion for later generations. The first four bars of this solo are marked to be played on the G-string, but only one interval is fingered – the octave leap, marked to be played with the first finger. A violinist of a later generation might take that to mean that *only* that interval should have a portamento. For a player of Elgar's day, the predominant style would have ruled out that interpretation.

Cellists recorded over the first four decades of the century demonstrate the changing approach to portamento as clearly as violinists. Recordings of cellists of the old school, like those of violinists, illustrate once again the impossibility of judging performance practice accurately from written sources. Writers on cello portamento from the turn of the century caution against exaggeration (Schroeder), sentimentality (Van der Straeten), and the marring of phrasing (Broadley). As with violin-playing, it would be impossible to deduce from such cautions that most cellists until the 1920s used frequent and prominent portamentos in a manner which seems indiscriminate to a listener of the late twentieth century.

Elgar, Cello Concerto, second movement (example 6.19)

Squire   (rec. 1930)
Harrison   (rec. 1928)
Casals   (rec. 1945)

W. H. Squire was an admired player of the old school, taught by Piatti, and Beatrice Harrison was a pupil of Hugo Becker. These three players there-fore represent stages in the development from the old to the new approach

Ex.6.19 Elgar, Cello Concerto, second movement, bars 1–26, Squire (solid line), Harrison (dotted below), and Casals (dotted above).

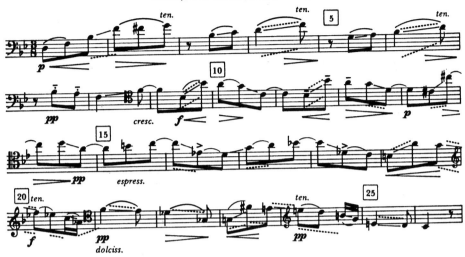

to portamento, and their playing shows great differences in the frequency and character of their portamento. In this passage, Squire plays 23 portamentos, Harrison plays sixteen, and Casals plays ten. Squire's portamentos are mostly slow and unsoftened by a diminuendo, and sound as if they are played on a single finger. Those of Harrison, and especially of Casals, are generally faster, and much more varied in type. Some are single-finger slides, some are clearly on two fingers, and many are softened by a diminuendo. Casals's portamento, like his vibrato, is very selective and subtle. His first two portamentos, in bars 4 and 6, are very smooth and soft. The first octave leap, at bar 9, is a delicate B-portamento with only a trace of the intermediate note. But at bar 11 he gives the identical interval a really emphatic intermediate note. The big leap at the beginning of bar 19 also has a clear intermediate note, but the portamento to the climax, from bar 19 to bar 20, is firm and smooth. Nowhere do these different effects seem contrived. Casals uses the portamento to underline the progress of the melody in a way which seems entirely natural, though no other cellist has ever used the device in quite the same way.

Chopin, Nocturne in E flat, Op. 9 No. 2, arr. for cello and piano (example 6.20)

Weist Hill   (rec. c. 1915)
Casals   (rec. 1926)
Feuermann   (rec. c. 1938)

Casals and Feuermann play the arrangement by Popper, which is shown here (example 20a). Weist Hill plays the arrangement by Servais, which is transposed

Ex.6.20 Chopin, Nocturne in E flat, Op. 9 No. 2, arr. Popper; Weist Hill (solid line), Casals (dotted above), and Feuermann (dotted below). (a) bars 1–8; (b) bar 4, fingered by Servais; (c) bar 4, as probably fingered by Weist Hill.

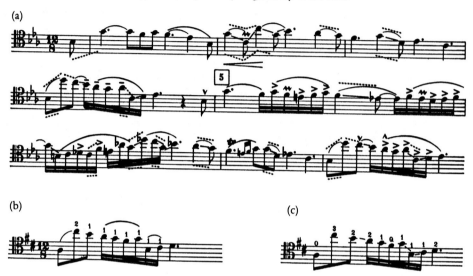

to D, but his portamentos are shown on Popper's arrangement for ease of comparison. Of the three players, Weist Hill is of the old school, both in his vibrato, which is always very delicate and sometimes almost absent even on long notes, and in his use of portamento. He plays eighteen portamentos during this passage. In the longer slides he uses B-portamentos, and the join between the sliding of the first finger and the stopping of the second finger is sometimes audible, for example in the first three slides of bar 2. Most of the shorter slides are continuous, and seem to be played on a single finger. However, all the sliding, whether continuous or not, is slow and prominent, and without any noticeable dynamic shaping. The overall effect is therefore unvaried, even though at least two types of slide are used. At bar 2, Weist Hill plays four slow slides in succession, producing exactly the sort of lugubrious effect which Casals's innovative fingerings were designed to avoid. At the beginning of bars 4 and 8, Weist Hill is the only one of the three players who does *not* slide up the leap of a tenth. This might seem surprising, but the reason is probably convenience rather than taste. In Servais's arrangement the leap is from A to C sharp, and the A is most easily played as an open string. The continuation of the same phrase does raise a point of early twentieth-century taste. In Servais's arrangement seven notes, from the third to the ninth note of the bar, are fingered to be played entirely on the first finger, as shown in example 6.20b. Weist Hill clearly does not play this fingering. At bar 4, he slides three times (Casals and Feuermann slide only once), and the long descending portamento is audibly a B-portamento, not a single-finger slide. The intervals without sliding seem to be separately fingered. A likely fingering for Weist Hill's performance of this bar is therefore as shown in example 6.20c. This example suggests that, although Weist Hill's portamentos are frequent, even he considered the continuous sliding implied by Servais's fingering of this passage excessive. Whether this can be taken to suggest that taste in cello portamento became more refined between the mid-nineteenth century (when Servais's arrangement was published) and the early twentieth century is an open question.

Both Casals and Feuermann slide less frequently than Weist Hill. Compared with Weist Hill's eighteen portamentos, Casals plays sixteen and Feuermann plays thirteen. This might seem a surprisingly small difference between the old and the new approach, but the differences in the style of their portamento are far greater than the difference in frequency. Of the three players, Casals most varies the speed and shape of the sliding. Only two of his slides are slow, the leaps of a tenth at bars 4 and 8, and even these are not as slow as Weist Hill's slides. At the beginning of bar 2 Casals's first two portamentos are very firm and prominent, underlining the sudden large intervals after the even progression of the preceding bar. By contrast, the interval of a semitone at the end of bar 2 is played with a very smooth single-finger slide (Casals does the same at the end of bar 6). The portamento at bar 3 (and at bar 7) is a B-portamento with a clearly audible intermediate note, giving a plaintive character to the falling fourth. This very varied use of portamento is characteristic of Casals's playing, and he uses it in a masterly way, together with carefully controlled dynamics and vibrato, to shape the progress of the melodic line.

Feuermann's performance contains the fewest number of portamentos. They are all lighter and faster than Weist Hill's, but they are not quite as varied in type as Casals's. Most of Feuermann's portamentos fall into two types: one for ascending, the other for descending. All but one of the descending portamentos are B-portamentos with an audible intermediate note (the exception being a single-finger slide over a semitone at the end of bar 6). In most instances the intermediate note is barely noticeable – far less prominent than in Casals's portamento at bar 3 – but it is enough to give a slight hint of plaintiveness to almost all of Feuermann's descending slides. In most cases the descending slide is accompanied by a diminuendo (as in Becker's instructions), and this prevents the effect becoming monotonous. The sliding is heaviest, and the intermediate note is most prominent, at bar 7. Feuermann changes the notation of bar 3, making it identical to bar 7, but the additional weight of the portamento at bar 7, and the more prominent intermediate note, give emphasis to the repetition. By contrast, Feuermann's ascending portamentos are not noticeably interrupted. Although some of the slides over the larger intervals presumably involve two fingers, the effect is of a continuous slide towards the second note. Occasionally, in particular at the leap of a tenth in bars 4 and 8, there is a suggestion of emphasis on the end of the slide, though it is not clear whether this is caused by the use of an L-portamento. As with the descending slides Feuermann softens all of these ascents by playing them lightly. But because the ascending slides appear continuous, and the descending slides are interrupted, Feuermann creates the strong impression that the upward slides rise *to* a note and the downward slides fall *from* a note. In bar 2 this varied shaping prevents the three adjacent portamentos from sounding excessive. Weist Hill's four slow portamentos in this bar are simply a slide followed by a slide followed by a slide followed by another slide. Feuermann creates more the effect of a falling sigh, followed by an upward reach, another falling sigh, and then a firm arrival (without a slide) on the B flat. Feuermann's portamentos seem, therefore, to have a clear expressive purpose compared with the sliding of the old school, although they do tend to fall into a more predictable pattern than the more varied portamentos of Casals.

Smetana, String Quartet No. 1 in E minor, third movement (example 6.21)

Bohemian Quartet   (rec. 1928)

The cellist of the Bohemian Quartet, Ladislav Zelenka, uses portamento in a similar way to W. H. Squire, Weist Hill, and other cellists of the old school. He plays eight portamentos in the opening six bars of the movement, and almost all of them are slow. Two of the longer slides are audibly B-portamentos, in bars 3 and 4, but the intermediate note is barely detectable and the overall impression is that all the portamentos in the passage are continuous. There is, however, some expressive variety in the way they are used. The first interval in bar 1, from F to B flat, is played with quite a fast slide, giving a firm start to the passage. By contrast, the descending slide from G to D flat at the end of bar 4 is exceptionally slow, which intensifies the arrival at the lowest point of the passage, and underlines the end of the cadenza-like flourish in bar 4. The slow single-finger slides in bar 6 are accompanied by a very marked ritenuto. They have the effect of softening the beginning of each trill, creating a very plaintive lead-in to the principal theme at bar 7.

Bars 7–14 illustrate the point that the use of portamento can affect both melody and texture. The first violin (Karel Hoffmann) plays without noticeable sliding, but the second violin (Josef Suk) and viola (Jiři Herold) play seven portamentos between them. This has the general effect of highlighting the contrapuntal texture of the writing, an effect which is very often found in recordings of string quartets at this period (and of orchestras, as chapter 7 will show). In this example, all the portamentos are single-finger slides over a tone or semitone. Each emphasises a move of particular harmonic significance, in five cases a chromatic shift of a semitone, and in two cases a contradiction of a preceding harmony (in bar 10 the move to F natural which contradicts the F flat of the previous bar, and in bar 13 the move to D flat which contradicts the preceding D natural).

Ex.6.21 Smetana, String Quartet No. 1 in E minor, third movement, bars 1–14, Bohemian Quartet.

Beethoven, String Quartet in C sharp minor, Op. 131, first movement (example 6.22)

Busch Quartet (rec. 1936)

The Bohemian Quartet (established 1892) was the oldest of the prominent quartets playing in the 1920s. The Busch Quartet (established 1919) was one of a younger generation of quartets which, in general, played with fewer and less prominent portamentos than the Bohemian Quartet. Nevertheless the effect of

Ex.6.22   Beethoven, String Quartet in C sharp minor, Op. 131, first movement, bars 1–20, Busch Quartet.

portamento, particularly in the inner parts of the texture, is striking in recordings of the Busch, Lener, and Flonzaley Quartets (the best-known quartets recording in the 1920s and 1930s).

This example, the opening of a fugal section, again illustrates the effect of portamento in contrapuntal writing. Represented on paper, it might not seem frequent enough to make much difference to the texture of the music. The first violin (Adolf Busch) plays the greatest number, six, the viola (Doktor) plays four, the second violin (Andreasson) plays two, and the cello (Hermann Busch) plays none (though he does slide later in the movement). But even these quite infrequent portamentos are enough to give a particular feeling of independence to the four lines. It is not only the sliding in the inner parts which creates this effect. The second entry of the fugue subject is played by the second violin without any sliding (bars 4ff), but the portamentos in the first violin's counter-melody at this point enhance the separate identity of the two parts. It is difficult to imagine that the quartet's use of portamento was pre-planned in any detail; the impression is rather of spontaneity, or at least of an expressive effect which was left to the taste of the individual player. Thus the viola is the only one of the four players to play the fugue subject itself with portamentos (at bars 8–9). He does the same where the subject recurs in the viola part a fifth higher (at bars 34–5). This gives the viola's entries a different emphasis from those of the other players. It is partly this varied use of portamento by the Busch Quartet which conveys the impression of an ensemble of individuals, rather than an ensemble in which individuality is suppressed. In different ways, this impression is characteristic of all the leading quartets of the early twentieth century.

Mozart, String Quartet in G, K. 387, fourth movement

Lener Quartet   (rec. c. 1930)

The fugal passages of this movement show the extent to which the use of portamento in the same phrase could vary from player to player, and from one occurrence of the phrase to another, within the same performance. During bars 1–17 and 143–59, the five notes of the fugue subject are played with a portamento at the following points of the phrase: between the first and second notes (first violin at bars 143–4 and at bars 151–2), between the second and third notes (first violin at bars 6–7, up to a harmonic, and cello at bars 156–7), and between the third and fourth notes (cello at bars 11–12 and at bars 149–50). At bars 1–5 and 13–17 the second violin and viola play the subject without portamento. At no time in the two passages is the subject played the same way twice in succession. It is a matter of opinion whether this gives an impression of spontaneity, and individual freedom within the ensemble, or whether it simply shows a haphazard approach to portamento. The Lener Quartet's portamento is often slower and more prominent than the Busch Quartet's, and its apparently random placing can therefore seem more obtrusive to a late twentieth-century listener. However, there is no reason to assume that its playing would have struck a listener of the early twentieth century in this way. Contemporary reviews sometimes criticised Lener for his unusually prominent vibrato, but not for the quartet's portamento.

Ex.6.23   Dvořák, *Songs My Mother Taught Me*, Tauber, Ponselle, Teyte, Kreisler, Sammons, Squire, Harrison, and Kennedy. (a) singers; (b) strings.

(a)

Ex.6.23(b)

Dvořák, *Songs My Mother Taught Me* (example 6.23)

Tauber   (rec. 1938)
Ponselle (rec. 1928)
Teyte   (rec. 1932)

Violin arrangements (in E flat)

Kreisler (rec. 1928)
Sammons   (rec. c. 1926)

Cello arrangements

Squire   (in E flat, rec. c. 1928)
Harrison (in D, rec. c. 1928)
Kennedy   (in E flat, rec. c. 1929)

Leopold Auer (1921) writes, 'In order to develop your judgement as to the proper and improper use of the *portamento*, observe the manner in which it is used by good singers and by poor ones.'[37] The last two examples in this chapter show that, in practice, singers and string-players used portamento in rather different ways.

In Dvořák's *Songs my mother taught me*, Tauber is the most sparing of the three singers in his use of portamento. In the first verse it occurs only at the five large intervals; in the second verse it occurs at the two descending octaves, and over two smaller intervals. Tauber's portamentos are quite fast and gentle, and the impression, even to a late twentieth-century listener, is of tasteful restraint. Ponselle and Teyte sing twice as many portamentos as Tauber, and in the second verse Teyte sings even more. The main difference between these two singers and Tauber is that Ponselle and Teyte slide not only over the large intervals, but over several of the smaller intervals, particularly the slurred pairs of descending seconds. This gives a more overtly sorrowful character to the phrasing. In Teyte's performance, this sorrowful emphasis is intensified towards the end of the song. At the descent from the high G, she sings a succession of six falling portamentos over small intervals, which are slower than her portamentos in the first verse. Similarly, her portamentos over large intervals are more prominent in the second than in the first verse.

The two violinists play arrangements in E flat, in which the two verses are played at different octaves: the first verse is played a seventh lower than the original, on the G-string, and the second verse is played a second higher than the original (they also play a third verse which is not shown here). Of the cellists, Squire and Kennedy also play the song in E flat. Harrison, in the famous recording played out of doors with nightingales, plays in D major as in the original, but without piano accompaniment. Despite the diversity of these arrangements, a clear distinction emerges between the five string-players and the three singers. The main difference is not in the number of portamentos, but in their placing and character. There are particular places where string-players often slide and singers rarely do. In the three performances by singers, there are only two instances of a slide to the first beat of the bar. These are at bars 18–19, where Ponselle slides to the high G, anticipating the accented syllable, and at bars 39–40, where Teyte's portamento from G to F sharp intensifies the legato, and removes any feeling of an accent on the first beat of bar 40. Elsewhere, the singers avoid sliding to first beats. By contrast, the string-players often slide to the first beat of the bar. Kreisler does it seven times (more than a third of his total number of slides), Sammons does it four times, Squire and Harrison do it three times each, and Kennedy, who has the smallest overall number of slides, does it once. Kreisler in the first two instances (at bars 10–11 and bars 14–15) pushes towards the beat with what might be an L-portamento – a style of portamento which Flesch and Yampolsky describe as characteristic of Kreisler – but he defines the first beat of bar 18 by the change of bow rather than a push of the slide. Kreisler adopts a similar pattern for the slides to first beats at the beginning of the second verse (into bars 31, 35, and 38). Sammons similarly pushes towards the beat with an L-portamento into bars 11 and 31, and again into bar 38 (in contrast to the first verse). Even where a slide to the first beat is not an L-portamento (as in most of the cellist's examples), the effect is very much a modification of the accent rather than an intensification of legato. Such an effect is used much less frequently by singers than by string-players. The only use of a similar effect in the three singers' recordings occurs at bars 18–19, where Ponselle anticipates the syllable with a slide, in a manner which is not unlike the string-player's L-portamento. In general, however, the singers avoid slides from a weak to a strong beat. Conversely, two of the singers, Ponselle and Teyte, use the slide between slurred pairs of descending seconds more frequently than any of the string-players. The slide with a single finger over a small interval is particularly praised by some writers on string-playing, as a way of imitating 'the matchless *legato* which the human voice alone can attain'.[38] But the effect which Ponselle and Teyte employ is used only occasionally by the string-players. Singers and string-players coincide most nearly in their treatment of the large intervals (at bar 11 and similar phrases). But even here the string-players vary the portamentos much more than the singers. Kreisler plays the large portamentos quite slowly and prominently in the first verse (on the G-string), but more delicately in the second verse (an octave up). Sammons plays each of the three large descending intervals in the first verse with a portamento, and at bar 19 he plays a B-portamento with a clearly audible intermediate note. This gives a plaintive emphasis to the climax of the melody, and contrasts with the smooth single-finger slides which he plays either side of it at bars 18 and 22. In the second verse Sammons plays the large descending intervals without portamento. Of the cellists, Squire plays with predominantly quite slow and prominent portamentos. Harrison's portamentos over the large intervals in the first verse are softened by diminuendos, and become slower as the verse progresses; the descent from G to C sharp in bar 19 is particularly languishing, though it is questionable whether Harrison would have played it quite like that in a normal performance with piano. She seems to play all the long portamentos in the first verse with a single finger, but in the second verse Harrison plays the descending octaves with shorter B-portamentos with audible intermediate notes. Kennedy has the most discreet and infrequent portamentos of all five string-players, but he too varies the character of the sliding at the large intervals. At the descending octave at bar 11 he plays quite a short B-portamento, at bar 15 he plays a very fast portamento, and at bar 19 he plays a single-finger portamento. In the second verse he plays both octave descents audibly as B-portamentos, though with only the discreetest of intermediate notes.

This comparison suggests that string-players use a much greater variety of portamento than singers, both in its character and in its placing. The three singers use portamento almost exclusively to enhance the legato between one note and another. Although this is often the effect with the string-players' portamento, they also use it to modify accents, as a kind of ornament, particularly when a portamento pushes towards a strong beat. Even when the placing of a slide coincides with those of the singers, as at the descending octaves, the effect is not always simply an enhancement of the legato. The B-portamento with an audible intermediate note has rather the effect of a deliberate interruption, somewhat like a gulp or sob. Singers rarely use such a device except in moments of extreme passion, but for string-players it is a regular part of the expressive stock-in-trade.

Schubert, *Ave Maria* (example 6.24)

McCormack and Kreisler (in English)   (rec. 1914)
Schumann (in German)   (rec. 1934)
Gigli (in Latin)   (rec. 1947)

Violin arrangement by Wilhelmj

Heifetz   (rec. 1926)
Menges   (rec. c. 1927)
Huberman   (rec. c. 1929)
Zimbalist   (rec. c. 1931)

The difference between singers and string-players is even more striking in Schubert's *Ave Maria* than in the previous example. By comparison with the violinists, the three singers perform the extract with few portamentos, and in all cases they slide from an accented to an unaccented note, never to an accented note. McCormack sings three portamentos, and each of them is over a descending tone or semitone where there is no change of syllable. Schumann

Ex.6.24 (a) and (b)   Schubert, *Ave Maria*, bars 3–8, McCormack/Kreisler, Schumann, Gigli, Heifetz, Menges, Huberman, and Zimbalist. (*Note*: Pitch as in Wilhelmj's arrangement. Schubert's original is a 7th higher.)

sings only two very delicate portamentos, over rising and falling thirds. Gigli, in a performance which is grotesquely disjointed by aspirates, sings three portamentos. The first, at the beginning of bar 6, occurs long before the change of syllable on the second beat, so that the portamento (like the aspirates elsewhere) is as much a rhythmic interruption as a join between the first and second beats. The effect is somewhat like the string-players' B-portamento with an audible intermediate note. Gigli's second portamento in bar 6 is a more conventional slide close to the change of syllable. His third portamento, in bar 7, again occurs early, though not as early as the first portamento.

The difference between singers and string-players in their use of portamento is vividly illustrated by McCormack's recording, in which Kreisler plays the melody in unison with the singer (apart from some double-stopping in bar 8). Kreisler and McCormack slide over the same interval in bar 3, but Kreisler slides later than McCormack, so that the two portamentos are separately audible. At the two other points where McCormack slides, Kreisler does not, but he slides in several other places, to a total of nine portamentos compared with McCormack's three. Several of them are single-finger portamentos from accented to unaccented notes, like the most usual singer's portamento, but three of them (two in bar 5 and the first in bar 6) are emphatic slides to accents. The first portamento in bar 5 consists of a slide *up* to the note during a descending interval, an effect usually produced at a change to a lower string – another example of a device which is quite different to a singer's portamento. It might seem strange that two musicians should perform the same melody in unison in so apparently unco-ordinated a way. But this juxtaposition of two quite different approaches is presumably the point of the exercise. If the two performers had co-ordinated their portamentos, the violin would have been much less clearly audible. As it is, the violin creates a counterpoint to the voice, even though it is playing the same notes.

Wilhelmj's arrangement is pitched a seventh lower than Schubert's original, and is played on the G-string. Like Kreisler, the four other violinists play with many more portamentos than the three singers. Menges plays thirteen, Heifetz plays twelve, Zimbalist plays ten, and Huberman plays eight (the same number as Kreisler). Huberman, Heifetz, and Zimbalist all play examples of slides to accents. Huberman plays what sounds like an L-portamento from C to E in bar 3 and bar 7. In bar 4, Heifetz plays a single-finger portamento up to D, but with the emphasis towards the accent as in an L-portamento. Zimbalist also gives a push towards this D, by sliding to it after a change of bow. At bar 7, Heifetz is the only violinist who slides to the climax of the phrase on G. All four violinists vary the speed of their portamentos considerably. Huberman and Menges have the slowest slides, over the descending intervals in bars 3, 6, and 7. Menges has two examples of slides with audible intermediate notes, at the two rising intervals in bar 5.

These two examples, Schubert's *Ave Maria* and Dvořák's *Songs my mother taught me*, perhaps show the difference between singers' and string-players' use of portamento at its most extreme. In particular, Wilhelmj's arrangement of *Ave Maria*, transposed down and played on the G-string, seems intended to encourage frequent portamento (like the well-known 'Air on the G-String'). String-players do tend to use the portamento more sparingly in more restrained styles of writing, but their general approach to portamento, and the comparison with singers' portamento, is, in less exaggerated form, broadly as in these two examples. Some singers use more frequent and more prominent portamentos than others, but string-players use a greater variety of portamento than singers, including not only single-finger slides and uninterrupted B-portamentos, but also B-portamentos with an audible intermediate note, and portamentos with the emphasis on the end of the slide. String-players also frequently use a portamento as an approach to an accent, rather than simply as a smooth join between two notes. The result of all these differences is that singers on the whole use portamento as a way of intensifying legato, whereas string-players use it not only in this way, but also as an ornament.

7

Orchestral portamento

INTRODUCTION

In many ways orchestral string-players of the early twentieth century shared the style and technique of soloists and chamber musicians. In fact it is not really possible to separate string-players into these different categories. Then as now, most players led a varied professional life. All except the most renowned soloists spent much of their time playing in orchestras (including not only symphony orchestras but also theatres and hotels), and many orchestral players spent part of their time playing solo or chamber music. Again, then as now, students simply learned the violin or cello in the style of the day, whether they were in the end destined for a career as soloists or in orchestras.

Soloists and orchestral players therefore shared broad characteristics and trends. Presumably almost all orchestral players at the turn of the century played with gut strings, as recommended in the writings of the time, but by the 1930s most violinists would have adopted steel E strings. One would expect orchestral players at the turn of the century to play with frequent portamento and sparing vibrato, but by the 1930s with more vibrato and less portamento. That much is obvious. But orchestral playing is different from solo playing. Performing with a large number of string-players means, to some extent, sacrificing one's own tastes and characteristics to a corporate effect. How far this process goes will depend on the amount and quality of rehearsal, and on the general habits of the time. With a modern, highly-drilled orchestra, all the violinists play in much the same way, and that way is the late twentieth-century way. In the orchestras of the early twentieth century, violinists played in the style of the period, but their co-ordination was a good deal more haphazard than in the modern orchestra, partly because of the shortage of rehearsal time and the prevalence of the deputy system. There was little opportunity to develop the unanimity of style and approach which is expected of an orchestral string section in the late twentieth century.

The problem was particularly acute in Britain and France. One of the principal qualities required of a British string-player at the turn of the century was therefore quick thinking. Arthur Broadley (1899) advises cellists, 'The orchestral player requires the ability to quickly divine the most suitable positions in which to play any given passage, when seen expressed in musical notation.'[1] This is still true of sight-reading, but in Broadley's day it applied to deputies turning up to play in the concert. Oscar Cremer (1924) takes the same point further: 'Don't pencil your own fingering over certain passages that are awkward to play; remember that other violinists have to play from these parts at some time, and what fingering suits one may not suit another; as a rule violinists do not like to come across parts with fingerings marked.'[2] By contrast, Adrian Boult witnessed the exceptionally thorough rehearsals of Casals's orchestra in Barcelona in 1923, and commented, 'Matters of bowing, and sometimes, too, of fingering, were often discussed, and in all important passages the strings bowed together.'[3] This contrasted vividly with the British practice of the time, to which Boult was accustomed. John Dunn (1898) hopes for 'leaders capable of doing what little is now-a-days required of them, such as marking the bowings in all the parts alike so as to obtain a correct and uniform phrasing and bowing throughout', but he makes it clear that few leaders actually do this.[4] In the 1920s, concert-goers in Manchester 'were so startled with the stark discipline of the strings of the Berlin Philharmonic when they visited the City under Furtwängler that they could not hear the music for watching the up-and-down-altogether of the bows'.[5] The unanimity of bowing in the Vienna Philharmonic Orchestra was also remarked upon when it visited London in 1931.[6]

These comments, and others like them, suggest that in British orchestras until about 1930, individual players generally bowed and fingered as they thought fit. Players in Vienna, Berlin, and Barcelona in the 1920s were subjected to more rigorous discipline, at least in bowing, and the same is reported of Toscanini's Philharmonic Symphony Orchestra of New York. But written information about orchestral string practice is scattered, usually consisting of little more than such comments made in passing. Violin and cello methods usually make no mention of orchestral playing. Orchestral string parts from the early twentieth century might perhaps yield more detailed information, but parts are re-used, and old fingerings and bowings do not often survive.

Because written information is so fragmentary, recordings are even more vital than with solo string-playing. Orchestras were not recorded in the earliest years of the century, but from about 1915 onwards recordings of orchestras began to be made, and after the introduction of electrical recording in 1925 records of the principal orchestras of Europe and America quickly became available. They provide clear and detailed evidence that the greatest change in orchestral string practice in the early twentieth century was in the use of portamento.

In some ways orchestral portamento is easier to deal with than solo por-tamento. The attitude of a soloist to portamento depends on various factors – teachers, the influence of other soloists, personal taste and idiosyncrasy. Soloists use a variety of different types of portamento, and no two players use them in quite the same way. With orchestral playing, these factors are to a large extent ironed out. The vast majority of orchestral portamentos from the early part of the century sound like the traditional single-finger or B-portamento, and the main difference between orchestras, and between different periods, is in its heaviness and frequency.

To put it negatively, what one gets from orchestral recordings is the lowest common denominator of portamento. Orchestras show what everyone does, not what exceptional individuals do. But the positive side of this is that one gains a broad picture of general habits, not only of particular orchestras, but also of different countries, and of the way styles change over time. This makes it possible to organise the subject more systematically than solo portamento, by dividing the recordings into different countries, and treating each country chronologically.

RECORDINGS: BRITAIN

British orchestras of the 1920s generally played with very frequent portamento. The practice varied slightly from one orchestra to another, and the most consistent users of frequent portamento were the Royal Albert Hall Orchestra and the Hallé Orchestra. Example 7.1a is typical of the playing of these two orchestras in the early 1920s, in the period immediately before the introduction of electrical recordings.

Brahms, Symphony No. 2, second movement (example 7.1a)

Royal Albert Hall Orchestra, cond. Ronald   (rec. c. 1925)

Example 7.1a gives a useful indication of what can and cannot be deduced about the practice of orchestral portamento from pre-electric recordings. As usual at this period, the string section of the orchestra was drastically reduced in size, and the players performed in cramped conditions, grouped as closely as possible to the recording horn or horns. Survival for the four minutes of each side must have taken precedence over any subtleties of performance, so it would be unwise to draw too many conclusions from these recordings. Nevertheless, two distinctive features stand out. The first is the astonishing frequency of the portamentos: 26 in these sixteen bars, an average frequency of approximately one every four intervals. This is as great a frequency as in any examples of solo violin- and cello-playing from the early years of the century. The second feature is the unvarying character of the portamentos. They are all slow, prominent, continuous, and unshaped by a crescendo or diminuendo, giving the impression that the players are sliding monotonously and routinely at every change of position, in the manner characterised by Flesch as 'bus-portamento'.

Ex.7.1 Brahms, Symphony No. 2, second movement, bars 1–17. (a) RAH Orch., Ronald; (b) London PO, Beecham; (c) Berlin PO, Fiedler; (d) Philadelphia Orch., Stokowski; (e) New York SO, Damrosch.

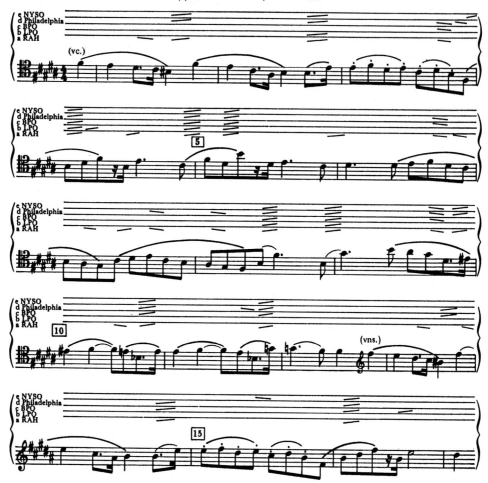

However, in the under-rehearsed British orchestras of the 1920s, it is very likely that this effect of almost continuous sliding is created by different players changing position at different places. In electrical recordings (after 1925), in which the full string section is used, the effect of only a small proportion of the players sliding over a particular interval is to create a quieter, more discreet portamento than if all the players are sliding together. In a pre-electrical recording, with perhaps four first violins, a portamento by one or two violinists is almost as prominent as a portamento played by all of them. But even though portamento in the complete string section might therefore have sounded less monotonous than in the reduced ensemble of the recording studio, recordings such as this give clear evidence that the Hallé and Royal Albert Hall Orchestras played in the early 1920s with very frequent, slow, and unshaped portamento.

These two orchestras continued to play in a similar style into the late 1920s, and in the case of the Hallé Orchestra until the early 1930s (the Royal Albert Hall Orchestra did not make records after 1930).

Elgar, Variations on an Original Theme ('Enigma'), theme (examples 7.2a and b)

Royal Albert Hall Orchestra, cond. Elgar   (rec. 1926)

Hallé Orchestra, cond. Harty   (rec. 1932)

These are electrical recordings, and therefore a full string section is playing. For this reason the melodic line sounds smoother and more coherent than in example 7.1a and the portamentos seem less obtrusive, although they are still slow, prominent, and frequent. The Hallé plays even more portamentos than the Royal Albert Hall Orchestra (21 compared with 18), but the Hallé's portamentos tend to be played a little faster, probably because of the quicker tempo. The Royal Albert Hall Orchestra is conducted by the composer, and Elgar's flexible tempo, lingering tenutos, and careful dynamic shaping make the portamentos seem a more natural part of the legato line than in example 7.1a, quite apart from the differences in recording technique and size of orchestra. The portamentos themselves, however, are generally slow and largely unshaped, and placed with an inconsistency which is characteristic of British orchestras in the 1920s. This is particularly clear in bars 7–10, where the same melodic shape is played four times. The falling quavers at the end of each bar have a portamento between them each time, but the earlier part of the bar is played in three different ways: without portamento (bars 7 and 9), with a portamento between the first pair of quavers (bar 8), and with a portamento to the third crotchet beat (bar 10). The Hallé performance shows similar inconsistencies in these bars. This variation in the placing of portamentos can hardly have been a planned effect. It is more likely that players are simply changing position at the most convenient points in the melodic line. Late twentieth-century orchestras generally disguise such inconsistencies by making changes of position unobtrusive, or arrange fingerings which allow greater consistency of phrasing, but British orchestras of the 1920s made no attempt to disguise this variation in the placing of portamento. From the viewpoint of the late twentieth century, it is debatable whether routine portamento of this kind serves a deliberately expressive purpose, or whether it occurs simply through mechanical convenience. Even if one takes the latter view, as Flesch certainly would, it cannot be denied that inconsistently placed portamentos were an accepted part of British orchestral performance practice in the 1920s.

Ex.7.2   Elgar, Variations on an Original Theme ('Enigma'), theme. (a) RAH Orch., Elgar; (b) Hallé Orch., Harty; (c) BBC SO, Boult; (d) Hallé Orch., Barbirolli.

Most other British orchestras of the 1920s used portamento almost as frequently and prominently as the Hallé and Royal Albert Hall Orchestras. One characteristic which they all shared was that they made little distinction between music of different periods. Works of the eighteenth and early nineteenth centuries present generally fewer opportunities for portamento than Elgar; but quite frequent and prominent portamentos are nevertheless heard in British recordings of Beethoven, Mozart, Haydn, and J. S. Bach from the 1920s.

Ex.7.3 Haydn, Symphony No. 101 ('The Clock'), second movement, bars 2–10. (a) Hallé Orch.,
Harty; (b) New York PSO, Toscanini; (c) NBC SO, Toscanini.

Haydn, Symphony No. 101 ('The Clock'), second movement (example 7.3)

Hallé Orchestra, cond. Harty   (rec. c. 1928)

J. S. Bach, Mass in B minor, 'Agnus Dei'

London Symphony Orchestra, cond. Coates   (rec. c. 1929)

These performances present the modern listener with a greater problem than
the previous examples. Quite noticeable portamento is still an accepted
expressive device in Elgar and Brahms, but in eighteenth-century music
discretion in shifting is now the general rule. The result is that, whereas in Elgar
the portamento of the 1920s sounds like old-fashioned over-use of an expressive
device, the same style in eighteenth-century music now sounds quite inappro-
priate. The violin line which opens Bach's 'Agnus Dei' sounds particularly
grotesque, even though the actual number of portamentos is not very great
(seven in the first eight bars). In the 1920s slow, undisguised portamento was
accepted in Bach and Haydn as it was in Elgar.

Two British orchestras in the 1920s tended to use portamento more
sparingly than the orchestras considered so far. These were the Royal Philharmonic Orchestra, who, under Sir Thomas Beecham, could be quite subtle
in their portamento, and the New Queen's Hall Orchestra, whose conductor,
Sir Henry Wood, had strong views on the subject. In 1927 he wrote, 'String
players have been sliding about their fingerboards in a barbarous manner

Ex.7.4   Elgar, Violin Concerto, first movement, bars 1-2, LSO, Elgar.

during the past few years, having acquired the habit, I fancy, in restaurant orchestras where the public seems to enjoy the wobble and the slide with certain dishes, possibly because tasteless and nauseating playing is suitable to similar kinds of food.'[7] Wood's orchestra was in the 1920s the only London orchestra in which deputies were not allowed, and this stability must have enabled him to influence the string style to an extent unusual at the time. His dislike of excessive portamento is certainly reflected in the recordings of the New Queen's Hall Orchestra.

Elgar, Violin Concerto, first movement (example 7.4)

New Queen's Hall Orchestra, cond. Wood   (rec. 1929)
London Symphony Orchestra, cond. Elgar   (rec. 1932)

Elgar's recording has a warm portamento up and down each time this motif occurs. Wood's performance is brisker in tempo and phrasing, and has no noticeable portamento in the opening bars (though perhaps a trace of it before the soloists's first entry, two bars before figure 9).

By the 1930s, the trend towards more discreet use of portamento by soloists was beginning to influence British orchestral playing. The fashion was led by two newly established orchestras, the BBC Symphony Orchestra (formed 1929) and the London Philharmonic Orchestra (formed 1932). They had direct links with the two orchestras which had shown unusual discretion in the use of portamento in the 1920s, the New Queen's Hall Orchestra and the Royal Philharmonic Orchestra. Members of the New Queen's Hall Orchestra formed the nucleus of the BBC Symphony Orchestra, and the London Philharmonic Orchestra incorporated a number of the regular players from the Royal Philharmonic Orchestra. Albert Sammons, a violinist of the modern school who played with restrained portamento, and who had led the Royal Philharmonic Orchestra, now became the leader of the London Philharmonic Orchestra. The conductor of the London Philharmonic Orchestra was Sir Thomas Beecham, under whom the old Royal Philharmonic Orchestra had shown unusual subtlety. The conductor of the new BBC Symphony Orchestra was Adrian Boult, a conductor noted for his straightforwardness and orderliness, who would have encouraged the more refined approach to portamento which members of his orchestra brought with them from Wood's New Queen's Hall Orchestra. Both of the new orchestras received substantially more regular rehearsal than the orchestras of the 1920s, and this would have made possible the development of a more uniform approach to string style in general.[8] The difference in the use of portamento between the two new orchestras and those of the 1920s is very striking.

Elgar, Variations on an Original Theme ('Enigma'), theme (example 7.2c)

BBC Symphony Orchestra, cond. Boult   (rec. 1936)

The BBC Symphony Orchestra plays fifteen portamentos, compared with eighteen in the Royal Albert Hall Orchestra and 21 in the Hallé Orchestra. The difference in effect is far greater than this comparison might suggest, because of the manner in which the portamentos are played. In the Hallé and Royal Albert Hall Orchestras, most of the portamentos are slow and prominent. In the BBC performance none of the portamentos are very slow, and many of them are very discreet, because they are fast or disguised by being played quietly. They are also spaced very carefully. Only in four bars do two portamentos occur within a single bar, compared with six bars in the Royal Albert Hall and seven bars in the Hallé. This is a substantial difference in a passage only seventeen bars long. In bar 13, where the Royal Albert Hall has three heavy slides within a single bar, and the Hallé has four, the BBC Symphony Orchestra has only one delicate portamento and avoids the portamento up a seventh (A to G) which is heard even in some late twentieth-century performances.

Brahms, Symphony No. 2, second movement (example 7.1b)

London Philharmonic Orchestra, cond. Beecham   (rec. 1936)

The London Philharmonic plays seven portamentos compared with 26 in the Royal Albert Hall Orchestra (example 7.1a). In the Royal Albert Hall Orchestra the sliding is slow, prominent and unshaped, but in the London Philharmonic it is generally faster, and forms part of a carefully shaped melodic line. Admittedly some of the portamentos are a little slower than would be considered usual in a late twentieth-century performance, though some audible sliding is still accepted in a late Romantic cello line which covers such large intervals. The avoidance of portamento in the continuous quavers of bars 6–8 is striking in example 7.1b, compared with the six slides in this passage in example 7.1a. Similarly, example 7.1b has no portamentos in bars 12–16, where example 7.1a has four. Example 7.1b comes nearest to the old style of the 1920s in bar 4. Here there are two portamentos in succession, a procedure which was acceptable in solo playing at the turn of the century, but which was discouraged by the 1930s. Perhaps these two successive portamentos are caused by some players sliding at the first interval and others at the second.

Ex.7.5   Brahms, Tragic Overture, 23rd to 30th bar of E, BBC SO, Toscanini.

Ex.7.6   Beethoven, Symphony No. 4, second movement, bars 2–9, BBC SO, Toscanini.

Comparison between British orchestras of the 1920s and the late 1930s invariably shows a substantial decrease in the frequency and prominence of portamento in the later recordings. Another development in Britain in the 1930s was a growing tendency to distinguish in style between Romantic and pre-Romantic music. In the 1920s, eighteenth-century music was already sometimes performed by chamber ensembles, such as the London Chamber Orchestra, instead of the full strings of the symphony orchestra, but their style of playing, and in particular their approach to portamento, was much the same in Bach and Mozart as in Brahms and Elgar. In the 1930s several orchestras began to distinguish between a Romantic style, in which warm portamento was still used (though not the routine slow sliding of the 1920s), and a Classical style which was more sparing of portamento. Recordings of the London Philharmonic Orchestra illustrate this distinction, and it is particularly clear in Toscanini's recordings with the BBC Symphony Orchestra.

Brahms, Tragic Overture (example 7.5)

BBC Symphony Orchestra, cond. Toscanini   (rec. 1937)

Beethoven, Symphony No. 4, second movement (example 7.6)

BBC Symphony Orchestra, cond. Toscanini   (rec. 1939)

The warm portamentos in example 7.5 (Brahms) are comparable with those in performances of late Romantic music by the London Philharmonic Orchestra. In the last bar of the example, it is doubtful whether all the violinists play two portamentos in such quick succession. Judging by its greater prominence, more violinists play the second than the first. By contrast, Toscanini's performances of Beethoven are as free of portamento as any recorded performances of this period. Example 7.6 has only three very discreet portamentos.

Not all British performances of Classical and pre-Classical music in the 1930s were as restrained in their use of portamento as example 7.6. Unusually frequent portamentos can be heard in one of the most admired chamber orchestras of the period, the Busch Chamber Players, which was led by the Busch Quartet but otherwise consisted of British players at this period.

J. S. Bach, Brandenburg Concerto No. 1, fourth movement, Polonaise

Busch Chamber Players   (rec. 1935)

The portamentos are quite frequent, and at the repeats of each half of the Polonaise, although the most prominent portamentos are often played at the same points as in the first playing (for example, a slide up a tenth to B flat at bars 19–20), subsidiary portamentos occur inconsistently. Bars 1–4, for instance, are played with seven portamentos the first time but only four when repeated. Bars 9–12 are played with five portamentos the first time but only two at the repeat. At bars 17–20, where the music of bars 1–4 is transposed up a fifth, the first playing has only one portamento (up a tenth into bar 20), and the repeat has three. The general pattern over the Polonaise is that the first half has fewer portamentos when repeated than at the first playing (fifteen compared with 22), and the second half has more frequent portamentos when repeated than at the first playing (ten compared with six). As in earlier examples, it is difficult to judge how much of this pattern is the result of detailed planning and rehearsal, but some of the portamentos suggest a free approach to fingering. Bar 5, for example, has two consecutive portamentos at each playing. The first time they occur over the first two intervals of the bar, but in the repeat they occur over the second two intervals. If all the violinists play all of these portamentos, they must be using a fingering with two consecutive changes of position, an old-fashioned procedure by the 1930s. Furthermore, they must either be using a different fingering at the repeat, or a fingering with three consecutive changes of position, of which two are audible as portamentos at each playing. It is very much more likely that different players are using different fingerings, and that the overall pattern of portamentos in the Polonaise is a composite of different portamentos resulting from various fingerings used simultaneously. This might seem rather like the routine and somewhat random portamento of the 1920s. But the result sounds very different, because most of the portamentos are fast and discreet. They give an impression of spontaneous exploration of the melodic line, by subtle variation in the shaping of the phrases, a style which reflects that of Busch's own solo playing and of his quartet.

Ex.7.7 Brahms, Piano Concerto No. 2, first movement, bars 48–55. (a) Philharmonia Orch.,
Dobrowen (solid line); (b) Philadelphia Orch., Ormandy (dotted line).

By the late 1940s, British orchestras had moved even further towards the
very sparing use of portamento familiar in the late twentieth century. This is
true even in music of the late Romantic period, and the two examples which
follow are typical of the years immediately following World War II.

Elgar, Variations on an Original Theme ('Enigma'), theme (example 7.2d)

Hallé Orchestra, cond. Barbirolli   (rec. 1947)

Brahms, Piano Concerto No. 2, first movement (example 7.7)

Philharmonia Orchestra, cond. Dobrowen   (rec. 1947)

In example 7.2d, the Hallé Orchestra plays only seven portamentos, of which
three are very inconspicuous. This compares with 21 portamentos in the Hallé
Orchestra (1932), eighteen in the Royal Albert Hall Orchestra (1926), and
fifteen in the BBC Symphony Orchestra (1936). In example 7.7a the Philharmonia Orchestra plays only four discreet portamentos.

A similarly 'clean' orchestral string style is found in most recordings of
British orchestras from the late 1940s. For example, Beecham's newly formed
Royal Philharmonic Orchestra plays Delius with much more subtle portamento in the 1940s than his London Philharmonic Orchestra did in the
1930s, illustrating the point that contemporary fashion in orchestral style is a
more powerful influence than the individual character of a particular conductor. Occasional instances of prominent portamento can still be found in the
1940s, but by this date they are unusual. The tendency in the 1950s and 1960s
was for British orchestras to become yet more sparing in their use of
portamento, often resisting it even in Brahms and Elgar. But the change in the
post-war period has been very slight compared with the radical change of style
from the 1920s to the 1940s, and to a large extent the late twentieth-century
British attitude to orchestral portamento was fully formed by the late 1940s. In
recent years some conductors have reintroduced the occasional portamento

into performances of late Romantic music. But the modern selected and carefully rehearsed portamento is far removed from the habitual use of it in the 1920s and 1930s.

RECORDINGS: BERLIN AND VIENNA

Compared with British orchestras, continental orchestras do not show quite such an extreme change in the use of portamento between the 1920s and the 1940s, but there is nevertheless a clear general trend from quite frequent and prominent portamento in the 1920s to infrequent and discreet portamento by the late 1940s. Fewer recordings of continental orchestras than of British orchestras were made before the late 1920s, but it is clear that prominent portamento was still part of the string style of Berlin and Vienna around 1930.

Brahms, Symphony No. 2, second movement (example 7.1c)

Berlin Philharmonic Orchestra, cond. Fiedler   (rec. c. 1931)

Haydn, Symphony No. 88, second movement

Vienna Philharmonic Orchestra, cond. Krauss   (rec. c. 1931)

The Berlin Philharmonic Orchestra plays with quite frequent portamentos in the late 1920s and early 1930s, but the sliding is never as frequent, nor as unvaried, as the most extreme British examples of the period. Example 7.1c is much nearer in style to example 7.1b (London Philharmonic Orchestra 1936) than to example 7.1a (Royal Albert Hall Orchestra 1925). Example 7.1c has fourteen portamentos, compared with 26 in example 7.1a and seven in example 7.1b. The sliding in example 7.1c varies considerably in speed and prominence, the slowest and heaviest sliding being reserved for the climactic intervals in bars 8–9. The Orchestra of the Berlin State Opera plays in a similar style at this period, though sometimes with a more casual approach to portamento, like British orchestras of the late 1920s. The Vienna Philharmonic Orchestra at this period uses prominent portamento more frequently than the Berlin orchestras, even in eighteenth-century music, as their recording of Haydn's Symphony No. 88 illustrates. The Vienna style comes fairly close to that of the Royal Albert Hall and Hallé Orchestras in the late 1920s, but the sliding of the Vienna Philharmonic Orchestra sounds more deliberately expressive, and less a matter of routine, than that of the British orchestras. This is partly because of the firmer dynamic shaping of the melodic line, partly because of the warmer and fuller string tone. This in turn may be related to the fact that the Vienna Philharmonic Orchestra was more regular in its membership, and more

Ex.7.8   Brahms, Symphony No. 3, third movement, bars 1–23. (a) Vienna PO, Krauss (dotted line); (b) Vienna PO, Walter (solid line).

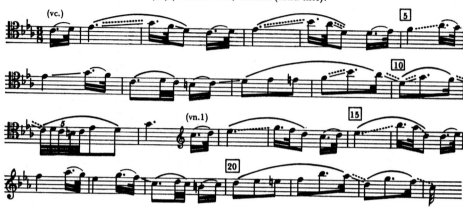

Ex.7.9   Tchaikovsky, Symphony No. 6, first movement, bars 86–90, Berlin PO, Furtwängler. (vn.1, vc. 8ve below)

frequently rehearsed, than the British orchestras at this date. Nevertheless, this performance provides strong evidence of a free approach to portamento even in the Vienna Philharmonic Orchestra. It includes instances where there are two, sometimes three successive portamentos. It is very unlikely that any one player would have played the phrases in this way, and it is probable that this results from different players shifting at different points. This is particularly likely in this movement, where violins and cellos play in unison, though it is not possible to distinguish the sliding of cellos from that of violins.

Brahms, Symphony No. 3, third movement (example 7.8)

Vienna Philharmonic Orchestra, cond. Krauss   (rec. c. 1931)
Vienna Philharmonic Orchestra, cond. Walter   (rec. 1936)

As in Britain, the frequency and prominence of portamentos decreased in Berlin and Vienna during the 1930s, although the Vienna Philharmonic Orchestra continued to use the portamento more frequently than the Berlin Philharmonic Orchestra. Example 7.8 shows a comparison between two performances of Brahms by the Vienna Philharmonic Orchestra, recorded five years apart. Krauss's recording (c. 1931) has quite warm, frequent sliding in both cellos and violins. Walter's version (1936) has the same number of slides in the cellos (bars 1–12), but they are generally faster and lighter than in 1931. The violins under Walter play with fewer portamentos than under Krauss, and in particular they avoid the conspicuous portamentos at bars 13–14 and 15–16.

However, freedom of fingering is still suggested by the consecutive portamentos in Walter's performance at bars 9–10 and 21–2.

Mozart, Serenade in G, K.525 ('Eine kleine Nachtmusik'), second movement

Vienna Philharmonic Orchestra, cond. Walter   (rec. 1936)

The general approach to sliding in the Vienna Philharmonic Orchestra in the late 1930s was similar to the approach of British orchestras at that date, but the distinction between the treatment of earlier and later periods of music, which is noticeable in recordings of the BBC and London Philharmonic Orchestras in the 1930s, is not encountered to the same extent in recordings of the Vienna Philharmonic Orchestra. The recording of Mozart's 'Eine kleine Nachtmusik' shows this orchestra playing quite conspicuous, though fairly fast, portamentos.

Tchaikovsky, Symphony No. 6, first movement (example 7.9)

Berlin Philharmonic Orchestra, cond. Furtwängler   (rec. 1938)

By comparison with the Vienna Philharmonic Orchestra, the Berlin Philharmonic Orchestra in the late 1930s had developed a string style which was rather more restrained in its use of portamento, even in late Romantic music. Example 7.9 shows some quite conspicuous portamentos in Tchaikovsky, but they are less frequent and generally less prominent than in the Vienna Philharmonic Orchestra's performances of late Romantic music at this date, as comparison with example 7.8b would suggest.

Schubert, Symphony No. 9, second movement

Vienna Philharmonic Orchestra, cond. Karajan   (rec. c. 1949)

As in Britain, the trend in Berlin and Vienna towards greater subtlety in the use of portamento continued into the post-war years. By the late 1940s, the Philharmonic Orchestras of Berlin and Vienna both played with only discreet portamento. In the slow movement of Schubert's Symphony No. 9, the portamento of the Vienna Philharmonic is very discreet, even at bars 93–102, where the cellos' slight portamentos would not be considered excessive even in a modern performance. Similar discretion is found in performances of the Berlin Philharmonic Orchestra in the late 1940s, and in melodic lines which do not have the wide intervals of Schubert's cello writing, there is often no noticeable portamento at all.

Ex.7.10   Stravinsky, *Petrushka*, fig. 92 (1911 ed.), Straram Orch., Stravinsky.

Ex.7.11   Debussy, *Prélude à l'après-midi d'un faune*, bars 63–74, Straram Orch., Straram.

RECORDINGS: FRANCE

French orchestras, like those of Britain, Austria and Germany, show a change in the use of portamento from the 1920s to the 1940s. But French orchestras adopted a generally discreet approach to portamento at an earlier date than orchestras in other European countries.

Debussy, Nocturnes, 'Nuages'

Paris Conservatoire Orchestra, cond. Gaubert   (rec. c. 1929)
Paris Conservatoire Orchestra, cond. Coppola   (rec. c. 1939)

Stravinsky, Petrushka (example 7.10)

[Straram Orchestra], cond. Stravinsky   (rec. 1928)

Debussy, *Prélude à l'après-midi d'un faune* (example 7.11)

Straram Orchestra, cond. Straram   (rec. c. 1931)

Recordings of Debussy's Nocturnes show a marked change of practice in the Paris Conservatoire Orchestra between the late 1920s and the late 1930s. The slow portamentos of Gaubert's performance are reminiscent of British playing in the late 1920s, whereas Coppola's version contains only very discreet portamentos. Examples 7.10 and 7.11 present an equally striking changes in recordings of the Straram Orchestra. Example 7.10 again contains slow portamentos reminiscent of the British at this date. This might seem surprising in a work conducted by Stravinsky, since he frequently objected to 'expressive' interpretation of his music. Example 7.11, recorded only three years later than example 7.10, shows a remarkably restrained use of portamento for its date compared with British, Austrian, and German examples, and considering the wide intervals of the melodic line. A few quite prominent portamentos are heard in this example, but they are infrequent and are all quite fast. This restraint even in late Romantic music had become general in French orchestras by the mid-1930s, at a time when most other European orchestras were still playing with fairly prominent and frequent portamentos. A similar approach is heard in recordings of the Colonne and Lamoureux Orchestras.

Fauré, Pavane

Paris Conservatoire Orchestra, cond. Munch   (rec. c. 1948)

The Paris Conservatoire Orchestra's recording of Fauré's Pavane is typical of French orchestral string-playing in the late 1940s. It contains occasional noticeable portamentos, but none which would be considered out of place in a modern performance of this music.

Ex.7.12   Tchaikovsky, Symphony No. 5, Concertgebouw Orch., Mengelberg. (a) first movement, bars 425–38. (b) second movement, bars 45–8;

RECORDINGS: THE NETHERLANDS

The orchestras of Britain, Austria, Germany, and France all showed a trend away from the heavy and frequent use of portamento during the 1930s. The Concertgebouw Orchestra of Amsterdam provides a striking contrast to this trend.

Tchaikovsky, Symphony No. 5 (a) first movement (b) second movement (example 7.12a and b)

Concertgebouw Orchestra, cond. Mengelberg   (rec. 1928)

J. C. Bach, Symphony in B flat, Op. 18 No. 2, second movement

Concertgebouw Orchestra, cond. Mengelberg   (rec. c. 1928)

Example 7.12 shows heavy and frequent portamentos, and seen on paper, they are reminiscent of the most extreme British examples of the 1920s. But the portamentos of the Concertgebouw Orchestra are fundamentally different from British examples. Unlike British orchestras of the 1920s, the Concertgebouw Orchestra was very thoroughly rehearsed, under a conductor renowned for his firm discipline.[9] Presumably, therefore, the orchestra's portamentos were not the result of routine sliding by unco-ordinated individual players, but were deliberately contrived. This impression is certainly confirmed when they are heard as well as seen. Example 7.12a shows Mengelberg using the element of surprise. Here the placing of the portamentos is quite unexpected. At bar 428, and again at bar 432, there is an upward portamento after a rest, an effect occasionally heard in solo playing but most unusual in orchestral playing. As the melody moves towards its climax at bars 434–5, Mengelberg avoids the obvious portamentos up a fourth (C sharp to F sharp, and D sharp to G sharp), but then inserts an unexpected slow portamento down a tone from the high G sharp in bar 435. At first sight example 7.12b seems more straightforward; the portamentos are very frequent (eight within four bars), and they include slides over all the large intervals in the passage. What is not visible on paper, but is obvious when heard, is the way Mengelberg chooses two portamentos for heavy emphasis. In bar 47 he lingers on the E, so as to emphasise the slow portamento down to the D, and in bar 48 he similarly lingers on the C sharp, emphasising another slow portamento down to B. One might expect such an effect to be reserved for the climax of a phrase or for the largest interval, but here they occur over small intervals which do not receive particular emphasis in most performances. Equally frequent and heavy portamento is heard in the recording of the slow movement of J. C. Bach's Symphony Op. 18, No. 2, with, at bar 19, another example of the slowest portamento being reserved for the interval *after* the climax of the phrase.

There can be no doubt that the Concertgebouw Orchestra's style of portamento was determined by its conductor, Mengelberg. The unusual, one might almost say perverse, placing of the portamentos in example 7.12 could only be a rehearsed effect. This still leaves open the question of how meticulously the string parts were actually fingered. In bar 48 of example 7.12b, there are three consecutive portamentos. With a less rehearsed orchestra, these could be attributed to unco-ordinated fingering. With Mengelberg's orchestra it is possible that these passages were deliberately fingered to produce these consecutive portamentos.

Certainly, this style of portamento was a speciality of the Concertgebouw Orchestra, and recordings made by Mengelberg with other orchestras do not show the same approach. In 1940, Mengelberg recorded Tchaikovsky's Symphony No. 5 with the Berlin Philharmonic Orchestra, which was generally quite restrained in its use of portamento by that date. This recording has few portamentos compared with the Concertgebouw Orchestra's performance. The passage shown in example 7.12b has only three portamentos in the Berlin performance, compared with the Concertgebouw's eight, and the passage shown in example 7.12a has only one slight portamento in the Berlin performance, avoiding the three strangely placed portamentos at bars 428, 432, and 435 in the Concertgebouw performance. This comparison does suggest that the unusual approach to portamento shown by the Concertgebouw Orchestra under Mengelberg was a stylistic feature which he developed with them over a long period of rehearsal, and that it was not a style which could be transferred to other orchestras when Mengelberg visited them. In the same way, Mengelberg's recordings with the Philharmonic Symphony Orchestra of New York in the late 1920s show an approach to portamento broadly similar to that of the orchestra's recordings under their principal conductor, Toscanini.

The Concertgebouw Orchestra continued to play with lavish use of portamento throughout the 1930s, at a time when all other European orchestras were refining the habit. After Mengelberg left the Concertgebouw Orchestra, and the orchestra made its first post-war recordings under Van Beinum in the late 1940s, its string style was quite different. The emphatic portamento of Mengelberg's period had been abandoned in favour of the restrained approach of other European orchestras.

RECORDINGS: OTHER EUROPEAN COUNTRIES

In general, the use of portamento elsewhere in Europe fell broadly within the trend shown by the major orchestras considered so far. The Budapest Philharmonic Orchestra and the Milan Symphony Orchestra, which both recorded in the late 1920s, showed the use of quite frequent slow portamentos, similar to those employed by British orchestras at that time. The Casals Orchestra of Barcelona at the same date was a little more restrained in its portamento, more comparable with the practice of the Berlin Philharmonic Orchestra. The Orchestra of the Accademia di Santa Cecilia, Rome, which recorded in the late 1940s, was as sparing in its use of portamento as the orchestras of Vienna, Berlin and Amsterdam by this date.

RECORDINGS: AMERICA

Over the period 1920–50 as a whole, the same trend towards the more sparing use of portamento is discernible in American as in European orchestras. In America, however, little change was heard until after 1940. This is principally because American orchestras had, by the late 1920s, already arrived at an approach to portamento which European orchestras did not, with the exception of some French orchestras, reach until the late 1930s. Several American orchestras in the late 1920s already played with a very restrained approach to portamento, and those that used it more frequently did so in a way which, as with Mengelberg's Concertgebouw Orchestra, sounds rehearsed and deliberate rather than casual and routine. Much of this difference between Europe and America must be attributable to the longer rehearsal time available to American orchestras in the 1920s and 1930s compared with the Europeans.

The most frequent and prominent portamento from the 1920s and 1930s is heard in recordings of the Philadelphia Orchestra under Stokowski.

Brahms, Symphony No. 2, second movement (example 7.1d)

Philadelphia Orchestra, cond. Stokowski   (rec. 1930)

J. S. Bach, arr. Stokowski, Prelude in E flat minor (48 Preludes and Fugues, book 1) (example 7.13)

Philadelphia Orchestra, cond. Stokowski   (rec. 1927)

Like the Concertgebouw Orchestra, the Philadelphia Orchestra owed much of its style to its conductor. The rich sonority of its unusually large string section, and the character of its portamentos, were unlike those of any other orchestra. Although Stokowski was opposed to standardised fingerings and bowings, it is clear from these two examples that the portamento is a carefully rehearsed

Ex.7.13   J. S. Bach, Prelude in E flat minor (48 Preludes and Fugues, I), arr. Stokowski, bars 1–7, Philadelphia Orch., Stokowski.

expressive ornament, even if, by the standards of the late twentieth century, it is greatly overused.[10] In example 7.1d there are twenty portamentos, almost as many as in example 7.1a (Royal Albert Hall Orchestra, 1925). But unlike the British portamentos, those of the Philadelphia Orchestra vary greatly in speed, prominence, and shaping, the most emphatic being reserved for the climactic rising sixths in bars 5, 8–9, and 11. Example 7.13 shows that Stokowski and his orchestra made little or no distinction between different periods of music in their use of portamento, which was as frequent in slow movements by Bach, Handel, and Mozart as in music by Brahms or Tchaikovsky.

Like Mengelberg and the Concertgebouw Orchestra, Stokowski and the Philadelphia Orchestra continued to play in the same style throughout the 1930s. But the Philadelphia and Concertgebouw portamentos are somewhat different in character. Whereas Mengelberg uses the portamento to create points of sudden emphasis, often with abrupt rallentandos and sometimes at unexpected moments (as in example 7.12), Stokowski's portamentos are generally more languorous than emphatic, and create a more continuous impression of an exaggeratedly legato line. Since Stokowski began his musical career in England at the turn of the century, it is possible to see his approach to the portamento as a refinement of the routine use of it by British orchestras during this period.

No other American orchestras used the portamento as frequently as the Philadelphia Orchestra, but conspicuous use of it was also made in the late 1920s and 1930s by the orchestras of Boston and Chicago. As in the Philadelphia Orchestra, little distinction was made between music of different periods. Koussevitsky's recordings with the Boston Symphony Orchestra include a movement of Handel's Concerto Grosso Op. 6, No. 12 (rec. c. 1937) played with a warm portamento, and Stock's recording of J. S. Bach's Suite No. 2 with the Chicago Symphony Orchestra (rec. c. 1929) contains some very casual-sounding portamento. The orchestras of New York – the Symphony Orchestra and the Philharmonic Orchestra until 1928, and thereafter the combined Philharmonic Symphony Orchestra of New York – were more restrained in their use of portamento.

Ex.7.14　Wagner, *Siegfried Idyll*, bars 1–23, New York PSO, Toscanini.

Brahms, Symphony No. 2, second movement (example 7.1e)

New York Symphony Orchestra, cond. Damrosch　(rec. c. 1928)

Haydn, Symphony No. 101, second movement (example 7.3b)

Philharmonic Symphony Orchestra of New York, cond. Toscanini　(rec. 1929)

Wagner, Siegfried Idyll (example 7.14)

Philharmonic Symphony Orchestra of New York, cond. Toscanini　(rec. 1936)

Examples 7.1e and 7.3b show the orchestras of New York in the late 1920s playing with more restraint in the use of portamento than any contemporary

European orchestras, except some of the French. The New York Symphony Orchestra in Brahms's Symphony No. 2 plays one fewer portamento than the Berlin Philharmonic Orchestra in 1931 (example 7.1c), and its sliding is even more discreet (except for one obtrusive slide where a cello overshoots). Examples 7.3b and 7.14 show that, under Toscanini, the Philharmonic Symphony Orchestra of New York made a clear distinction in the use of portamento between Classical and Romantic music, a distinction which has already been observed in Toscanini's recordings with the BBC Symphony Orchestra. Example 7.3b contains three quite unobtrusive portamentos in Haydn, which can be compared with the much more prominent portamentos of the Hallé Orchestra at almost the same date (example 7.3a). By contrast, example 7.14 shows the New York orchestra using much warmer and more frequent portamentos in Wagner.

In common with the European trend, American orchestras tended to play with fewer and subtler portamentos by the 1940s. The greatest change is found in the Philadelphia Orchestra, the least change in the Boston Symphony Orchestra.

Brahms, Piano Concerto no. 2, first movement (example 7.7b)

Philadelphia Orchestra, cond. Ormandy   (rec. c. 1946)

Mozart, Symphony No. 29, second movement

Boston Symphony Orchestra, cond. Koussevitsky   (rec. c. 1942)

Mahler, Symphony No. 4, third movement

Philharmonic Symphony Orchestra of New York, cond. Walter   (rec. 1946)

Example 7.7b shows how the Philadelphia Orchestra's approach to portamento changed when Ormandy replaced Stokowski as conductor in 1938. This passage contains three portamentos which are quite prominent but fairly fast. In performances of Brahms under Stokowski in the 1930s, the portamentos were slower and more numerous (as in example 7.1d). The Boston Symphony Orchestra, which was still conducted by Koussevitsky until 1949, continued to use quite marked portamentos even in Mozart. By contrast, the Philharmonic Symphony Orchestra of New York in the 1940s played with only discreet portamentos even in late Romantic works. Mahler's Symphony No. 4 includes passages where portamentos are indicated by Mahler in the score (for example at bar 221 of the slow movement). Even these specified portamentos are treated with discretion in Walter's performance, and the slow movement as a whole is as 'clean' as it would be in a modern performance.

Ex.7.15   Brahms, Symphony No. 1, NBC SO, Toscanini. (a) second movement, bars 12–16;
(b) third movement, bars 118–25.

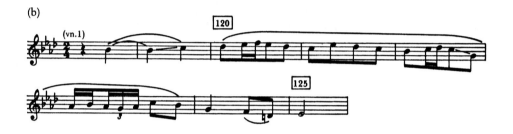

Haydn, Symphony No. 101, second movement (example 7.3c)

NBC Symphony Orchestra, cond. Toscanini   (rec. 1947)

Brahms, Symphony No. 1, (a) second movement (b) third movement (example 7.15 a and b)

NBC Symphony Orchestra, cond. Toscanini   (rec. 1941)

Finally, examples 7.3c and 7.15 show that Toscanini's NBC Symphony
Orchestra, like the Philharmonic Symphony Orchestra of New York and the
BBC Symphony Orchestra under the same conductor in the 1930s, made a
clear distinction between Classical and Romantic works in its use of portamento. The slight portamentos in example 7.3c (Haydn) are even less
conspicuous than in Toscanini's earlier recording with the Philharmonic Symphony Orchestra of New York (example 7.3b). By contrast, example 7.15
(Brahms) contains several quite prominent portamentos.

CONCLUSION

As with solo string-players, developments in orchestral portamento are
complex in detail but simple in overall trend. In the 1920s and 1930s there were
great differences between orchestras in different countries, and even between
orchestras within a single country. A few conductors exerted a strong influence.

Mengelberg in Amsterdam and Stokowski in Philadelphia encouraged the use of heavy portamentos throughout the 1930s, when most orchestras were becoming more sparing in its use. Henry Wood preferred restraint even in the 1920s. Toscanini seems to have encouraged a distinction between a warm style with some portamento in late Romantic music, and a clean style with little portamento in Classical music, a distinction which is also heard in other British recordings in the 1930s.

It is difficult enough in solo portamento to draw a line between convenient habit and expressive device. In orchestral playing there is the added complication that it is impossible to know how many players are sliding. When several different fingerings are in use simultaneously, even a deliberate expressive device becomes dissipated into a general effect, because the orchestra as a whole will play more portamentos than any one player.

There is little written evidence to clarify this, apart from some general information about the extent to which orchestras were rehearsed, a subject which was touched on in the introduction to this chapter. The recordings themselves give the strong impression that in British orchestras in the late 1920s (the earliest date from which there are recordings of full orchestras) there was little or no co-ordination of portamento; that, at the opposite extreme, the Concertgebouw and most American orchestras co-ordinated at least the most important portamentos; and that most continental orchestras (and British orchestras by the late 1930s) fell somewhere between these two extremes of laissez-faire and discipline. This broadly corresponds with the varying extent to which the different orchestras were rehearsed. That is not to say that uniform fingering is invariably the rule even in highly drilled modern orchestras. But most changes of position are far less audible than they used to be in the early part of the century, so that minor discrepancies in fingering are unnoticeable.

The difference between portamento as a habit and portamento as an expressive device is also to do with shaping. British portamento from the 1920s often sounds inexpressive and monotonous to late twentieth-century ears because it is generally unshaped and unvaried. By contrast, almost every portamento in recordings of the Philadelphia Orchestra conveys a sense of direction because of variations in speed and dynamic shaping. In this way too, many continental European examples fall between these two extremes, seeming sometimes positively expressive, at other times nearer to inexpressive routine.

By the 1940s these differences between orchestras were much smaller than in the 1920s, again partly because of rehearsal. In the 1920s orchestras varied from almost unrehearsed to highly disciplined, but by the 1940s even British orchestras received regular rehearsal. The casual attitude to portamento was becoming a thing of the past.

It is no coincidence that attitudes to portamento, both solo and orchestral, changed at the same time as the developments in vibrato, bowing styles, and general rhythm. The overall trend in string-playing was towards a neater, cleaner, more firmly projected, and expressively more homogeneous style. This modern style requires most notes to have a clearly defined beginning and end, so that the rhythm can be firm and accurately co-ordinated. Old-fashioned portamento in random places undermines this, and in ensembles it makes precise co-ordination impossible. Habitual portamento therefore contributes to the looser rhythmic style of the early twentieth century, which was discussed in the opening chapters of this book.

PART IV

IMPLICATIONS

8

Implications for the nineteenth century

INTRODUCTION

One of the reasons for writing this book is a belief that early twentieth-century recordings can shed new light on the performing styles of the nineteenth century. The most obvious link is that many of the musicians who performed on early recordings were brought up in the nineteenth century, and their playing must include remnants of nineteenth-century style. The fact, for example, that Ysaÿe studied under Vieuxtemps and Wieniawski, and that Joachim played under Mendelssohn and was associated with Brahms, gives particular importance to their recordings. But the recordings of the early twentieth century have a more general relevance to nineteenth-century practice. Stated at its simplest, it is that none of the aspects of early twentieth-century style described in this book can have arisen overnight.

In the use of vibrato and portamento, in flexibility of tempo, and in detailed rhythmic style, the performers of the early twentieth century can be heard moving towards what we now think of as modern style, and away from earlier practice – that is, the practice of the nineteenth century. This is no more than a statement of the obvious. In any period, performance is in a state of transition from the past to the future, and the early twentieth century is no exception. The difficult question, and the question of most interest to students of historical performance practice, is what aspects of early twentieth-century performance can be identified as surviving from the nineteenth century. A good starting point is to ask what stylistic traits clearly do *not* derive from the nineteenth century. One obvious answer is, any practices which can be heard beginning to develop on the recordings themselves. These include many aspects of modern style – the use of continuous vibrato on stringed and wind instruments, discretion in the use of portamento, restraint in flexibility of tempo (particularly acceleration), and the literal interpretation of rhythm, and consequent avoidance of rhythmic distortions such as overdotting, *notes inégales*, and the dislocation of melody and accompaniment. These are all stylistic features which developed during the first half of the twentieth century, and went on to form an important part of late twentieth-century style.

If these modern practices can be heard developing on twentieth-century recordings, the more old-fashioned practices from which they developed seem to have originated before the period of recordings. Restraint in the use of vibrato, the liberal use of portamento, great flexibility of tempo, the free application of overdotting, *notes inégales*, and the dislocation of melody and accompaniment are all habits which were already established by the early twentieth century, and were then gradually modified. So the stylistic features which sound most old-fashioned to modern ears are probably the ones which survived from the nineteenth century. This chapter examines this possibility by looking briefly at some of the evidence of the nineteenth century in the light of early twentieth-century recordings.

VIBRATO

The view of vibrato as a special effect for limited use was not new in the early twentieth century. Nineteenth-century writings suggest that the tradition was long-established. The oldest of the violinists who made recordings, Joachim, began his concert career in the 1840s, and Joachim and Moser's *Violinschule* (1905) bases its consideration of vibrato on a long quotation from Spohr's *Violinschule* (1832). Spohr classes the tremolo among the embellishments, and describes it as an imitation of

The singer's voice in passionate passages, or when he forces it to its most powerful pitch ... Avoid however its frequent use, or in improper places. In places where the *tremolo* is used by the singer, it may also advantageously be applied to the Violin. This *tremolo* is therefore properly used in passionate passages, and in strongly marking all the fz or >tones.[1]

Joachim and Moser describe these as 'lucid remarks'. From gramophone records we know that early twentieth-century calls for restraint, including Joachim and Moser's, indicate a very sparing use of vibrato by late twentieth-century standards. Spohr seems to be arguing for a similar approach, and he confirms this in extended musical examples, in which vibrato is indicated only on occasional notes (example 8.1).

The restrained approach to vibrato in the nineteenth century was not confined to the German school. Contemporary with Spohr's *Violinschule* was the method by Baillot (1834) who taught at the Paris Conservatoire. He distinguishes between two methods of producing vibrato. The first, which involves varying the pressure of the bow, was later described in the early twentieth century by Lucien Capet and others, though its role in twentieth-century violin-playing seems to have been very minor.[2] As to the more usual, left-hand vibrato, Baillot, like Spohr, likens the effect of 'undulation' to the sound of the voice 'when it is strongly touched with emotion'. Such a powerful effect makes the melody 'unnatural' if overused, and it must be 'rejected on a succession of notes. It gives a good effect only on long notes or when the same

Ex.8.1   Rode, Violin Concerto No. 7, second movement, bars 1–8, with fingering and vibrato indications by Spohr. *Violinschule*, 192.

note is repeated.'[3] Baillot includes music examples to illustrate how Viotti used the vibrato, and these show that, like Spohr, he restricted it to occasional notes.[4]

Baillot's successor at the Paris Conservatoire, Alard, makes no mention of the vibrato in his *Méthode* (1844), an indication in itself that, at most, vibrato can only have been of minor importance to him. Alard taught Sarasate who, in the recordings made in his last years, uses only a very shallow vibrato on sustained notes. Whether Alard used as much vibrato as this, or even less, must remain a subject for conjecture.

Alard was praised by Paganini, who was himself noted for his 'tremulous Adagio passages'.[5] The specific mention of adagio passages makes it very unlikely that Paganini's vibrato was continuous. Carl Guhr's book on Paganini (1829) makes no mention of vibrato.[6] Adela Fachiri mentions a copy of Paganini's *Caprices* with the composer's detailed markings: 'I frequently come across bars where he says, "Here use vibrato", giving us plainly to understand that where such a direction is absent vibrato is not wanted.'[7]

Charles de Bériot, a pupil of Baillot and the teacher of Vieuxtemps, allows only the limited use of vibrato in his *Méthode de violon* (1858), and cautions against its habitual use, by violinists and singers, even more strongly than Spohr and Baillot: 'We must ... employ vibrato only when the dramatic action compels it: but the artist should not become too fond of having this dangerous quality, which he must only use with the greatest moderation.'[8]

Nineteenth-century violinists therefore used the vibrato as an occasional ornament, applied only to certain notes which required expressive emphasis. Joachim, in quoting Spohr, shows that he was continuing a long-established tradition in this restrained, ornamental use of vibrato. Admittedly, the number of writers in the late nineteenth century who caution against excess suggests that vibrato was by then on the increase. But the evidence of recordings shows that, even so, it was not until the advent of Kreisler and his imitators that the modern continuous vibrato came into use. Even the 'excess' of the 1890s must have been, by modern standards, extremely restrained.

As with violin vibrato, the sparing use of vibrato by cellists in the early twentieth century represents the end of a long-established tradition. Van der Straeten's warning against 'the abuse of vibrato' (1898) occurs in a book which contains letters of approval from two of the most distinguished nineteenth-century cellists, Alfredo Piatti and David Popper. Hugo Becker, who studied with Piatti, remembers that he 'seldom used vibrato and then only in a very circumspect way ...'.[9] Piatti's own *Méthode de violoncelle* (1878) makes no mention of vibrato.

Other nineteenth-century writers on the cello, like violinists, make it clear that vibrato, when used at all, was only an occasional effect, not one of the basic ingredients of cello tone as in the late twentieth century. Kummer (1839) writes that 'a certain trembling [bebung]' produced by the hand can give occasional notes 'more expression and brightness'. But he warns the student 'that he should not make this style a permanent character of his playing by using it too frequently'.[10] Dotzauer (1832) emphasises that it is important to be able 'to sustain a beautiful, even note more strongly or more weakly according to the circumstances', without resort to such 'tricks' as vibrato.[11] Romberg (1840) writes that rapid trembling, 'if used infrequently, and with much strength of the bow', can lend the tone 'fire and life', but it should be used 'only at the beginning of the note, not for its whole duration'.[12] The most important French writer on cello playing in the early nineteenth century, Duport (c. 1810), makes no mention of vibrato.[13]

Clive Brown (1988) points to another source which confirms that the basic string sound throughout the nineteenth century was without vibrato, and that is the fingerings of the period. Brown quotes examples of fingerings by Spohr, David, Sterndale Bennett, and others, in which natural harmonics and open strings are included in cantabile passages. He rightly concludes that they 'would in most instances make no musical sense at all if the surrounding notes were to be played with vibrato'.[14]

The predominant nineteenth-century attitude to string vibrato, therefore, was restraint. The origin of the continuous vibrato, as first practised by Kreisler, is obscure, although Kreisler himself provides a clue to its origin when describing his studies at the Paris Conservatoire under Joseph Massart, the teacher of Wieniawski:

I believe Massart liked me because I played in the style of Wieniawski. You will recall that Wieniawski intensified the vibrato and brought it to heights never before achieved, so that it became known as the "French vibrato". Vieuxtemps also took it up, and after him Eugene Ysaÿe, who became its greatest exponent, and I. Joseph Joachim, for instance, disdained it.[15]

It is tempting to infer from this comment, which Kreisler made in the 1940s, that Wieniawski and Vieuxtemps developed the continuous vibrato. But Kreisler never heard either of them (both were dead by the time Kreisler was six), and there is no reason to suppose that Wieniawski's 'French vibrato' was continuous, even assuming it was unusually prominent for the period. Ysaÿe's vibrato was much less prominent than Kreisler's, and not continuous even in cantabile passages. Vieuxtemps was Ysaÿe's teacher, and the likelihood is, given the general trend during the late nineteenth century, that his vibrato was at least as restrained as Ysaÿe's, and probably more so.

One recurrent feature which links early twentieth-century vibrato with the sources of the nineteenth century is the frequent comparison between the violin and the voice, which implies that nineteenth-century singers and string-players shared a similarly cautious and selective attitude to vibrato. Writers on singing overwhelmingly support this implication, though their views on vibrato have to be treated with even greater caution than those of string-players. The mechanism of vocal vibrato cannot be seen, unlike that of string vibrato, and even into the early twentieth century there is some confusion about the subject, particularly about what exactly is meant by the terms *vibrato* and *tremolo*. Some writers use *tremolo* to mean a fluctuation in pitch and *vibrato* to mean a fluctuation in intensity, other writers use the two terms synonymously to mean a pitch fluctuation, and yet others use one or other term without defining it. But for nineteenth-century writers on singing, both vibrato and tremolo, however defined, are to be used, at most, sparingly at moments of particular emotional intensity. As H. C. Deacon puts it in *Grove I* (1879–89), 'The Vibrato and Tremolo are almost equally reprehensible as mannerisms',[16] and this was the predominant view of writers throughout the nineteenth century.

Manuel Garcia II, who together with his pupil Mathilde Marchesi taught many of the most famous singers of the late nineteenth and early twentieth centuries, discusses the *tremolo* at some length in his *Traité Complet de l'Art du Chant* (1847). According to Garcia, the origin of the tremolo lies in the natural effect of powerful emotions on the vocal organ: 'When ... agitation is caused by a grief so vivid that it completely dominates us, the organ experiences a kind of vacillation which is imparted to the voice. This vacillation is called *tremolo*.' In singing it must be used 'only to portray the feelings which, in real life, move us profoundly ...' In all other circumstances, 'it is necessary to guard against altering in any way the security of the sound', and the habitual use of the tremolo is either a vocal fault or a mannerism.[17]

Of writers on singing earlier in the nineteenth century, some, like Garcia, allow tremolo or vibrato as an occasional effect or ornament, many regard tremor of any kind as a fault, and many others make no mention of vibrato, tremolo, or any equivalent effect.[18] From the 1860s onwards, a number of writers on singing lament the recent growth of a habitual tremolo or vibrato, and such complaints of modern excess continue into the early part of the twentieth century.[19] However, as with string-playing, recordings of singers show that even in the early twentieth century, vocal vibrato was, by the standards of the late twentieth century, generally extremely delicate and unobtrusive. Will Crutchfield (1989) distinguishes between the 'very narrow, regular', and almost indetectable vibrato of English, Scandinavian, and German singers at the turn of the century, and the 'quick, intense, flickering' vibrato of

Spaniards and Italians. He points out that no recorded singer born before 1870 developed anything like the slower, wider type of modern vocal vibrato.[20] The recordings of Patti (b. 1843), one of the most admired of late nineteenth-century singers, reveal a vibrato of the utmost subtlety, which is often completely absent, and even her celebrated trill is no wider than many late twentieth-century singers' vibrato. To judge by the implications of writings, singers of the mid-nineteenth century must have sung with at least this degree of restraint in vibrato, and perhaps with a still 'purer' tone, reserving vibrato (tremolo) for occasional notes or phrases.

Vibrato on wind instruments was used only to a very limited extent even as late as the early twentieth century, and most nineteenth-century writers make no mention of it. *Grove I* (1879–89) writes that vibrato 'is sometimes heard on the flute and cornet'.[21] The 1865 revision of Koch's *Musikalisches Lexikon* writes, more enthusiastically, that 'on many wind instruments, such as the oboe and flute, vibrato is not only very possible, but also of very good effect', but, as on stringed instruments and the voice, it must be used 'with taste and at the right time'; used to excess, or as a habit, it is 'intolerable'.[22] Koch's 1802 original *Lexikon* makes no mention of wind vibrato, describing *bebung* as 'a fairly outdated manner of playing which is used on stringed instruments and the clavier' (that is, the clavichord).[23]

A number of writers mention 'vibration' on the flute, produced either with the breath or with a finger. It was particularly associated with the English flautist Charles Nicholson, who describes it in his *Complete Preceptor for the German Flute* [1815].[24] Though its effect is 'inconceivably delicate and sweet', it is no more than a 'Grace or Embellishment', to be used in much the same manner as a trill. The use of finger vibrato is also mentioned in bassoon tutors of the 1830s and 1840s, but again only as an occasional effect. Nineteenth-century oboe tutors do not discuss vibrato, and even flute 'vibration' is no longer mentioned in late nineteenth-century writings.[25]

On wind instruments, therefore, vibrato was even more restricted in its use in the nineteenth century than on stringed instruments and in singing. The great majority of writers on wind-playing have nothing to say about vibrato of any kind. If we add to this the evidence of early recordings, it seems clear that vibrato as an enhancer of tone, as opposed to an ornament, was unknown until its development by flautists of the Paris Conservatoire at the very end of the century.

PORTAMENTO

As with vibrato, so with portamento there is strong evidence that the practice of string-players in the early twentieth century derived from a long-established tradition. Joachim, whose recordings reveal frequent and prominent portamentos, was the violinist for whom Brahms wrote his violin concerto, and in the 1840s he had played Mendelssohn's concerto under the composer. Joachim's 1905 fingering of Mendelssohn's concerto includes the consecutive single-finger slides shown earlier (chapter 6, example 6.7). Although there is no direct evidence that Joachim played the passage in this way under Mendelssohn, or that Mendelssohn approved this fingering, it is reasonable to assume that Joachim's fingering of 1905 is closer to the fingering which Mendelssohn heard 60 years earlier than the 'cleaner' fingerings of the late twentieth century. Joachim and Moser's *Violinschule* bases its discussion of the portamento on instructions from Spohr (1831) which were quoted earlier.[26] Spohr insists on the B-portamento for large intervals, rejects the L-portamento except to a harmonic, and is anxious to avoid 'unpleasant howling' or an audible intermediate note. This does not mean that he rejects audible portamento. Among the requirements for 'a fine style or delivery', Spohr lists in second place, after variety of bowing, 'The artificial shifts which are not used merely on account of any easier mode of playing, but for expression and tone, to which belongs also, the gliding from one note to another . . .'[27] Specific instructions for gliding are given in the annotated concertos which Spohr includes in his book. One example occurs at the beginning of the second movement of Rode's Concerto No. 7 (see example 8.1). Spohr writes, 'the soft gliding from one note to another, must not only be upwards, as in the first bar from G to E, but also downwards as in the same from C to the open E, and in the following one from G to B.'[28] In the first three bars, therefore, Spohr recommends four glides: the three which he mentions in the commentary, and a single-finger portamento in the third bar. He asks for 'soft gliding' in this example, and elsewhere he sometimes recommends a diminuendo and a softening of the tone during the slide. This sounds as if Spohr is not asking for quite the heaviness of portamento which was common in the early twentieth century. But early twentieth-century writers also called for taste and discretion, so it cannot be assumed that we know quite what Spohr meant. As to the frequency of Spohr's portamento, William Honeyman (c. 1891) writes, 'Spohr himself was too elevated and rigid in his taste to indulge much in this impassioned vocalising effect, as anyone who heard him play may remember . . .'[29] Again, it is tempting to judge such a statement by the standards of the late twentieth century. But it was written by someone accustomed to the frequent, heavy portamento of Joachim and his contemporaries. It cannot be taken to mean that Spohr's use of portamento was sparing by the standards of the late twentieth century.

As with objections to vibrato, nineteenth-century recommendations of portamento are not confined to the German school. Bériot (1858), the teacher of Vieuxtemps, describes three distinct styles of portamento for use in different musical circumstances: the 'light and rapid' portamento for fast passages, the 'gentle' portamento for passages of a tender character, and the 'dragged' portamento for sorrowful passages. He uses three shapes of wedge to illustrate

Ex.8.2 Bériot's 'dragged' portamento in Mozart's String Quintet in G minor.

these three different types. He gives as one of his examples what would now seem a surprisingly insistent use of the 'dragged' portamento in Mozart's String Quintet in G minor (example 8.2).[30] Alard (1844), Sarasate's teacher at the Paris Conservatoire, recommends the single-finger slide or the B-portamento, as also recommended by Spohr. Alard gives two exceptions which allow a slide with the second of the two fingers: a slide to a harmonic, which Spohr also allows to be taken with the second finger, but also 'when the second finger is separated from the first by one or more strings'. This is an L-portamento after a change of string, which Dunn (1898) identifies as characteristic of the French school. It perhaps also accounts for the use of the L-portamento by Alard's pupil Sarasate. As to the shading of the portamento, Alard writes 'in the Allegro, it must be played directly and precipitately. In the Adagio, while it must be played less quickly, one must avoid making the intermediate notes audible. Equally, one must be careful to increase the power when ascending to a higher note, and conversely to diminish it when one descends to a lower note.'[31]

Alard's predecessor at the Paris Conservatoire, Baillot, recommends 'dragged notes' in *L'Art du Violon* (1834). But he warns, '*Expressive fingerings*, like all kinds of effects, should be employed with discretion and delicacy. One should therefore avoid using them too often and also sliding the finger either in too forceful a manner or with the slightest affectation ...'[32] Baillot's discussion is not without ambiguities. As well as the usual problem in defining 'discretion', it is not clear what he means by sliding the finger in 'too forceful' a manner. Does he mean 'too fast', or does he mean 'in a manner which makes the slide too prominent', a fault which would be as much to do with the bow as with the sliding finger? Certainly he makes it clear that a single-finger portamento, whatever its exact manner of execution, is a desirable expressive effect.

Elsewhere, Baillot writes that, of earlier violinists, Viotti 'remained almost always in the same position, that is to say he avoided shifting his hand, which compelled him to change from one string to another', a habit which would tend to minimise the use of portamento. By contrast Kreutzer favoured frequent changes of position, and Rode in particular 'changed position on the same strings, a style which favours the *portamento* in graceful melodies ...'[33]

As to the general practice of the early nineteenth and late eighteenth centuries, Stowell (1985) writes, 'Whether or not *portamenti* generally accompanied shifts is a controversial point about which available evidence is conflicting.' Burney (1776–89) recommends the 'beautiful expressions and effects' of single-finger slides, but quotes Geminiani against them. Reichardt (1776) approves them if used tastefully by a soloist, and Stowell cites other examples of portamento from Leopold Mozart (1756), L'Abbé le fils (1761), Cambini (c. 1790), Woldemar (c. 1800), Lolli (c. 1800) and Habenek (c. 1840). The works of Paganini contain many examples of portamento, some for spectacular effect and others for a smooth legato.[34]

Further evidence for the general use of portamento on the violin in the early nineteenth century is to be found in flute methods. Nicholson was noted for his 'gliding' on the flute, and he writes (1815), 'This Expression is much practised and with sweet effect by the generality of Performers on the Violin.'[35] The glide is mentioned in several other nineteenth-century flute tutors.[36]

Of German cellists in the early nineteenth century, Dotzauer (1832) provides the most detailed discussion of portamento. He devotes a section of his book to 'Dragging from one note to another'. This is an effect of practical use, since it makes it easier for the singer and instrumentalist 'in some cases to hit the next note with greater certainty'. Sliding takes place in a manner 'which does not descend to howling', but gives 'a very pleasing effect'.[37] Kummer (1839) allows the 'gradual drawing up or down of the finger from one note to another', but he warns against using it too frequently, 'since both hearing and emotion run the risk of being so badly distorted by it that, by degrees, even the greatest excess in this manner of playing seems tasteful'.[38] Romberg (1840) writes of 'carrying the voice (portamento di voce)', in which 'the most strongly stressed note of the song is drawn together with the previous note', thus giving the melody 'more grace'.[39]

Portamento was therefore an accepted practice on the cello in Germany in the early nineteenth century, though, as with later writers, it is impossible to deduce from the writings alone how frequently or how prominently portamento was usually played.

The French cellist Duport (c. 1810), is regarded as important for his ideas on fingering, which included fingering scales in such a way as to avoid single-finger portamentos. Duport writes,

It will perhaps be thought extraordinary that, in these scales, I have taken the greatest care to avoid playing two notes with the same finger, which has been done in all the instruction books hitherto published. My opinion is that it is a vicious method and produces a bad effect ... for if the bow do not act on the string at the instant when the finger is slid, a very disagreeable sound will be heard.[40]

As with Spohr's warning against 'unpleasant howling', it is easy to be misled into thinking that this indicates a general dislike of portamento. Admittedly Duport recommends that 'if a passage can be played, either wholly or in part, in the same position, we should not quit it, unless the bowing requires it, or some particular expression is sought to be given'.[41] But he also indicates in what circumstances the 'particular expression' of a portamento is appropriate:

It is true that, in a rather slow time, two notes may be taken with the same finger; and even an interval of a third, a fourth, or a fifth &c. may be thus played by a forcible sliding of the finger, which produces a very good effect, and is called the *portamento* ... but, in a quick movement, where neatness forms the greatest merit, two notes played with the same finger are, in my opinion, indefensible, as being wholly opposed to such neatness.[42]

How frequently Duport used the portamento in slow music, and how prominently, must of course remain a matter of conjecture.

As with vibrato, a number of nineteenth-century writers make it clear that string-players' use of the portamento largely derives from the example of singers. Nineteenth-century writers on singing confirm that the portamento was a valued effect used as much by singers as by string-players. As with vibrato, there is room for some confusion, because the term *portamento* changed its meaning from the eighteenth to the nineteenth centuries. Originally a term to describe the general deportment of the voice as it moves from one note to another (which might or might not include a slide), it came, by the mid-nineteenth century, to signify an audible slide, as in the modern meaning of the word. Even the English term 'glide', which is much used in nineteenth-century sources, is not without ambiguities, because it is sometimes used in mid-nineteenth-century writings to translate the French word 'liaison' or the Italian 'passare', neither of which necessarily implies a slide.[43]

Despite these problems, there is a mass of unambiguous evidence that the portamento, in the sense of a slide, was used as an essential part of vocal practice, as of string practice, throughout the nineteenth century.[44] Manuel Garcia II (1847) makes the nature of the portamento absolutely clear:

Gliding or Slurring (Con Portamento)

To slur is to conduct the voice from one note to another through all intermediate sounds. The time occupied by a slur should be taken from the last portion of the note quitted; and its rapidity will depend on the kind of expression required by any passage in which it occurs. This dragging of notes will assist in equalising the registers, timbres and power of the voice ... the slur ... is indicated by the following sign: ☞.

Were it possible to give a representation of the different modes of executing a passage we should do it thus:

       Slurred sounds [Portamento]   Smooth sounds [legato]

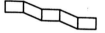

45

Garcia includes examples of how to use the portamento, including several as sung by his father and by Pasta, indicating that the portamento is not a new fashion of his own generation. Earlier nineteenth-century writers on singing, despite ambiguities, similarly make it clear that portamento, in the sense of a slide, was a necessary part of the singer's equipment.[46]

Even eighteenth-century sources on singing, despite the earlier meaning of portamento, sometimes strongly imply the use of portamento in the modern sense. Tosi (1723) writes about 'slurs' or 'gliding notes', which are 'Like several Notes in one Stroke of the Bow on the Violin'. This might seem like straightforward legato, until one reads, 'The use of the *Slur* is pretty much limited in Singing, and is confined within such few Notes ascending or descending, that it cannot go beyond a fourth without displeasing.'[47] Is it conceivable that Tosi means this limitation to apply to mere legato? It seems much more likely that he is cautioning against too long a portamento in the modern sense, with the consequent implication that it was much used by violinists when playing several notes 'in one Stroke of the Bow', even as early as the 1720s.[48] This conjecture takes us far beyond the scope of this book. But it is another illustration of the point that, once one begins to lose reliance on modern taste in the interpretation of earlier documents, there are surprising implications to be found, which often relate more closely to the practice of the early twentieth century than to that of the late twentieth century.

FLEXIBILITY OF TEMPO

As in the early twentieth century, writers in the nineteenth century recommend or imply tempo fluctuations, though without recordings there is usually no way of knowing what degree of flexibility is meant.

The problems raised by nineteenth-century sources are well illustrated by trying to assess Bülow's interpretative style. Oscar Bie (1898) compares Bülow with Rubinstein:

The impressionist Rubinstein and the draughtsman Bülow had each the technique which suited him. The one rushed and raved, and a slight want of polish was the natural result of his impressionist temperament; the other drew carefully the threads from the keys ... while every tone and every tempo stood in ironbound firmness, and every line was there before it was drawn.[49]

But if 'every tempo stood in ironbound firmness' when Bülow played the piano, how do we reconcile this with Weingartner's attack on followers of Bülow as 'tempo-rubato conductors?' Dannreuther writes of Bülow's 'passionate intellectuality', explaining that 'all details were thought out and mastered down to the minutest detail; all effects were analysed and calculated with the utmost subtlety, and yet the whole left an impression of warm spontaneity'.[50] Does this suggest that 'ironbound firmness' of tempo really means tempos which were carefully calculated, but not necessarily constant? This seems to be a way of reconciling Bie and Weingartner, with the help of Dannreuther, but without recordings we are left to guess at the real answer to the question. Bülow's edition of Beethoven's piano sonatas certainly advocates some flexibility, but how freely he played in actual practice is a matter for conjecture. However, one thing which is clear about nineteenth-century sources is that, as in the early twentieth century, very many writers, like Bülow, argue in favour of tempo fluctuation to some degree. Writing about Bülow's fluctuations of tempo, Hanslick writes (1884), 'Metronomic evenness of tempo has, in any case, been disavowed by all modern conductors.'[51]

Wagner regarded fluctuations in tempo as essential for the proper characterisation of extended pieces of music.[52] Brahms, though he did not publish aesthetic theories on the subject as Wagner did, makes it clear in a letter to Sir George Henschel that tempo in his music can not be constant, nor can a 'correct' tempo be established:

I am of the opinion that metronome marks go for nothing. As far as I know, all composers have as yet retracted their metronome marks in later years. Those figures which can be found before some of my compositions – good friends have talked them into me; for myself I have never believed that my blood and a mechanical instrument go very well together.[53]

Hubay, who gave the first performances of Brahms's violin sonatas with the composer, told Szigeti of the importance which Brahms attached to the tempo changes which he marked in the score, 'how he would insist that the *poco a poco più sostenuto* in the development section of the first movement of the G major sonata should be really *più sostenuto* until the recapitulation which is in the (faster) *tempo primo*'.[54] According to a member of the Joachim Quartet, Brahms's favourite violinist had a spontaneous and unpredictable approach to tempo: 'To play with him is damned difficult. Always different tempi, different accents ...'[55] Liszt writes (1870) that 'A metronomical performance is certainly tiresome and nonsensical; time and rhythm must be adapted to and identified with the melody, the harmony, the accent and the poetry ... But how indicate all this? I shudder at the thought of it.'[56]

These opinions of composers and performers are backed up by a number of late nineteenth-century theorists who emphasise the importance of the accelerando and rallentando for expressive performance, among them Adolph Kullak (1861), Mathis Lussy (1874, a writer who impressed Liszt and Riemann), and Adolph Christiani (1885).[57] Writing in favour of fluctuating tempo is also common in the early part of the nineteenth century.

Spohr (1831) lists among the requirements of a correct style or delivery 'a strict observance of time', but he did not mean by this a constant tempo, because his requirements for a *fine* style or delivery include 'the increasing of time in furious, impetious [sic], and passionate passages, as well as the retarding of such as have a tender, doleful, or melancholly character'.[58] Weber (1824) writes about the metronome markings in *Euryanthe*,

The beat should not be a tyrannical restriction or the driving of a mill hammer. On the contrary, it should be to the music what the pulse-beat is to the life of man. There is no slow tempo in which passages which demand a faster movement do not occur, and thereby prevent the feeling of dragging. Conversely, there is no *presto*, which does not call for the slower execution of certain passages, so that the expression will not be marred by overzealousness.[59]

Domenico Corri (1810, a student of Porpora) writes that a performance may be improved 'by the singer delivering some phrases or passages in quicker or slower time than he began with, in order to give emphasis, energy, or pathos, to particular words . . .'[60]

Accounts of Beethoven's playing and conducting are sometimes contradictory, but several suggest some freedom of tempo. Beethoven made use of Maelzel's metronome for a time, but his reservations about it are shown by his heading to the song, 'Nord oder Süd' (WoO 148): '100 according to Maelzel; but this must be held applicable to only the first measures, for feeling also has its tempo and this cannot entirely be expressed in this figure'.[61] The most extravagant claims for Beethoven's flexibility are given by Schindler in the first edition of his biography of Beethoven (1840). He describes 'the manner in which Beethoven himself used to play' the two Piano Sonatas Op. 14, with many detailed changes of tempo. However, he was persuaded to remove this section from the third edition of the biography (1860), in which he observes more generally that Beethoven's playing 'was free of all constraint in respect to the beat, for the spirit of his music required freedom.'[62] Two other pupils of Beethoven who, unlike Schindler, knew him before his piano-playing declined suggest that Beethoven's flexibility was more limited. Ferdinand Ries reports that he 'remained for the most part strictly in tempo, pushing the tempo only on rare occasions. Now and then he would hold the tempo back during a crescendo, creating a crescendo with ritardando, which had a very beautiful and most striking effect.'[63] Carl Czerny writes in detail on the 'Proper Performance' of Beethoven's piano works, occasionally recommending an increase or decrease in tempo, but most frequently advising against 'dragging'.[64] Indirect evidence that Beethoven may have approved of fluctuating tempo comes from Mendelssohn, who in 1831 heard the pianist Dorothea von Ertmann, a favourite pupil of Beethoven to whom he dedicated his Sonata Op. 101. Mendelssohn writes, 'She sometimes rather exaggerates the expression dwelling too long on one passage and then hurrying the next.'[65] This begs the question of what Mendelssohn regarded as exaggeration, but there can be little doubt that Ertmann played with noticeable fluctuations of tempo.

Several writers from the first half of the nineteenth century, while recommending tempo fluctuations, stress that they must be used selectively. Manuel

Garcia II writes (1847), 'The compositions of Haydn, Mozart, Cimarosa, Rossini, etc., require a complete exactness in the rhythmic movement. Every change made in the values must, without altering the movement of the measure, result from the use of *tempo rubato*.' By contrast, 'The music of Donizetti and especially that of Bellini includes a great number of passages which, without carrying the indication of the rallentando or the accelerando, call for the use of them.'[66] Hummel (1828) also complains about excessive tempo fluctuation, and advises 'In his performance, the Player ought not to let it be for a moment doubtful, even to the uninitiated, whether he is playing an adagio or an allegro.' But Hummel then adds, 'I do not by any means intend to say, that we may not occasionally retard the time in an allegro, or that we ought not to introduce embellishments into an adagio; but this must be done with moderation and in the proper place.'[67] Rode, Baillot, and Kreutzer, in an instruction book for violinists (1823) discuss at length the question of tempo fluctuation, and the delicate balance between correctness and feeling. They conclude: 'The true art of a performer, then, would seem to be, in keeping an equilibrium between the feelings that hurry him away, and a rigid attention to time.'[68] One can imagine musicians from the eighteenth to the late twentieth centuries nodding their heads in agreement with this carefully worded advice, without having the least idea how much tempo fluctuation the authors really had in mind.

Finally, the strictest approach to tempo in early nineteenth-century sources is to be found in Sonnenleither's description of Schubert's accompanying: 'I heard him accompany and rehearse his songs more than a hundred times. Above all he always keeps the most strict and even time, except in the few cases where he expressly indicated in writing a ritardando, morendo, accelerando etc ...'[69] This, at least, is unambiguous, whether or not it is believable.

The great majority of writers throughout the nineteenth century admit the need for flexibility of tempo, some with caution, others without any calls for restraint. Without metronome marks it is impossible to pin these sources down to a particular range of flexibility. Nevertheless, given that a wide tempo range was usual in the early twentieth century, and that the modern kind of restraint only became widespread from the 1940s onwards, it seems very possible that most writers in the nineteenth century were recommending a much greater fluctuation of tempo than we are accustomed to in the late twentieth century. The further back in time one goes, the more hazardous such an assumption becomes, of course. Even so, if one wished to argue that early nineteenth-century tempo fluctuation was narrower than in the early twentieth century, one would need to find evidence that the acceptable tempo range increased at some time between the early nineteenth and the early twentieth centuries.

TEMPO RUBATO

Nineteenth-century descriptions of tempo rubato suggest strong links with the styles of rubato heard on early twentieth-century recordings. Like twentieth-century sources, nineteenth-century writers show some confusion about the meaning of the term tempo rubato, and disagreement about what kind of flexibility is desirable.

Oscar Bie's contrast between the rhythmic freedom of Rubinstein and Bülow, which was quoted in the preceding section, strongly suggests that Rubinstein's rubato would have used greater tempo fluctuation than Bülow's. Hugo Leichtentritt (1924) writes, more ambiguously, of the 'elasticity and precision of [Busoni's] rhythms'.[70]

Several writers from the second half of the nineteenth century recommend detailed tempo fluctuation rather than other kinds of rubato, including Kullak (1861), Lussy (1874), and Engel (1853).[71] Engel warns pianists against excessive flexibility, which he calls tempo rubato, and specifically condemns 'dragging the melody after the accompaniment', and 'the want of precision in striking octaves or chords'. But it was precisely this sort of rhythmic dislocation which lay at the root of a traditional kind of tempo rubato which many nineteenth-century writers describe, and echoes of which survived into the early years of recording. Adolf Christiani (1885) has already been quoted in Chapter 2 as a proponent of melodic freedom over a strict bass. He defines the real rubato not as accelerando and ritardando, but as 'That capricious and disorderly mode of performance by which some notes are protracted beyond their proper duration and others curtailed, without, however, changing the aggregate duration of each measure ...' This kind of rubato, which he calls 'the *rubato* of Chopin', is best executed while the accompanying hand keeps strict time. 'Chopin's often reiterated counsel to his pupils was substantially this: "Let your accompanying hand be your conductor, and let it keep time, even while your other hand plays *rubato*."'[72] Christiani's description of Chopin's rubato is confirmed by several other writers, including Chopin's pupil Carl Mikuli: 'While the singing hand, either irresolutely lingering, or as in passionate speech eagerly anticipating with a certain impatient vehemence, freed the truth of the musical expression from all rhythmical fetters, the other, the accompanying hand, continued to play strictly in time.'[73]

The idea of, literally, strict time in the pianist's left hand presents the same problem here as in early twentieth-century sources. But if we take this to mean that the accompaniment preserves the sense of pulse, with the melody deviating from it, then we have a style of rubato which has much in common with rubato as actually practised in the early twentieth century. Christiani's description of Chopin's accompanying hand as the 'conductor' is very significant. Melodic rubato was not just for pianists, and it must surely have originated in music in which solo and accompaniment are performed by different musicians.

Just as Chopin's melodic style owes much to the opera of his day, so his style of rubato was probably modelled partly on that of singers. Melodic rubato is certainly described by many singers and string-players throughout the nineteenth century.

Manuel Garcia II (1847) writes, 'In order to make the effect of the tempo rubato perceptible in singing, it is necessary to sustain the tempo of the accompaniment with precision. The singer, free on this condition to increase and decrease alternately the partial values, will be able to set off certain phrases in a new way.'[74] According to Garcia, his father and Paganini both excelled in the use of tempo rubato. Baillot, in *L'Art du Violon* (1834), writes that rubato 'tends to express trouble and agitation', and is usually improvised according to the inspiration of the moment. The performer 'must only make use of it in spite of himself, as it were, when, carried away by the expression, it apparently forces him to lose all sense of pulse . . .' But he must 'preserve a sort of steadiness that will keep him within the limits of the harmony of the passage and make him return at the right moment to the exact pulse of the beat.'[75] Spohr (1831) discusses how tempo rubato and changes of pace affect the accompaniment: 'The solo performer must neither be hurried nor retarded by the accompaniment; he should be instantly followed wherever he deviates a little from the time. This latter deviation, however, does not apply to the *Tempo Rubato* of the solo performer; the accompaniment continuing its quiet, regular movement.'[76]

Detailed discussion of earlier periods is beyond the scope of this book, but there is no shortage of eighteenth-century descriptions of tempo rubato in which individual notes are lengthened and shortened, and the accompaniment keeps strict time. Mozart writes to his father in 1777, 'What these people cannot grasp is that in tempo rubato in an Adagio, the left hand should go on playing in strict time. With them the left hand always follows suit.'[77] Leopold Mozart, the recipient of that letter, writes in his *Violinschule* (1756),

Many, who have no idea of taste, never retain the evenness of tempo in the accompanying of a concerto part, but endeavour always to follow the solo-part. These are accompanists for dilletanti and not for masters ... But when a true virtuoso who is worthy of the title is to be accompanied, then one must not allow oneself to be beguiled by the postponing or anticipating of the notes, which he knows how to shape so adroitly and touchingly, into hesitating or hurrying, but must continue to play throughout in the same manner; else the effect which the performer desired to build up would be demolished by the accompaniment.'[78]

This sounds remarkably like Ysaÿe's advice to his accompanist a century and a half later (see pp. 43–4 above).

Finally, an interesting early eighteenth-century example of what amounts to tempo rubato is the 'Suspension' in François Couperin's *Pièces de Clavecin* (1713) (example 8.3). Arnold Dolmetsch (1916) writes that 'The *tempo rubato* effect it produces is very characteristic and charming.'[79] Oscar Bie (1896) is similarly

Ex.8.3 Couperin's *suspension*, as quoted by Dolmetsch.

Signe.

Effet.

enthusiastic about it: 'the short pause, like the white mounting of a picture, raises the important note, giving to it its meaning, and with the meaning the due expression'.[80] It is clear from the evidence of recordings, that the reason that Dolmetsch and Bie were able to write so enthusiastically about Couperin's suspension was that they were able to relate it to a familiar expressive device of their own time. Similarly, the descriptions of tempo rubato in eighteenth- and nineteenth-century sources, which bear almost no resemblance to late twentieth-century notions of rubato, would have presented little problem to readers of the early twentieth century. In particular, the idea of rhythmic adjustment of individual notes, rather than just tempo fluctuation, and the insistence that a rubato phrase should proceed quite independently of the accompaniment, are found very frequently in eighteenth-, nineteenth-, and early twentieth-century sources, and have only ceased to be an accepted part of rhythmic flexibility in very recent years.[81] Of course, saying that descriptions of rubato retained similar elements over hundreds of years is not to say that the practice of rubato remained unchanged. Dolmetsch had no doubt that early twentieth-century tempo rubato derived from a long tradition: 'This device is as old as music itself . . . If there are people who think that the old music does not require the *tempo rubato*, it is because they do not perceive its meaning; and are, moreover, ignorant of the fact that it was as common formerly as it is now.'[82] It is questionable whether the relationship between the past and the present is ever quite as simple as Dolmetsch implies. But as with portamento and vibrato, early twentieth-century styles of rubato at least give us important clues to the possible meaning of earlier descriptions of rubato, and however tenuously, they provide a link to a continuing tradition of rhythmic flexibility, separate from flexibility of pulse, a link which has been broken only in the later twentieth century.

LONG AND SHORT NOTES

Early twentieth-century sources provide little written evidence for the treatment of short notes and dotted rhythms which is heard in recordings of the period. There is just as little written evidence about this aspect of rhythm in the nineteenth century, though, as in the early twentieth century, there are some indications from the notation of the period.

As was mentioned in Chapter 3, some writers in recent years have turned

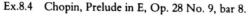

Ex.8.4   Chopin, Prelude in E, Op. 28 No. 9, bar 8.

their attention to the interpretation of dotted rhythms where they occur with triplets in nineteenth-century music. In some instances the notation suggests that the dotted rhythm is meant to be adjusted to fit the triplets. One example which seems unambiguous is Chopin's Polonaise-Fantaisie, Op. 61,[83] in which the conjunction of dotted rhythm and triplet occurs frequently, sometimes with a triplet quaver and duplet semiquaver joined by a tail. The autograph of Chopin's Prelude No. 9 in E similarly contains many examples of alignment of dotted rhythms and triplets, often with the tail of the semiquaver being joined to the final triplet quaver. However, the editors of the Chopin Institute Edition take the view that this example is not as simple as it seems. They point out that Chopin aligned a duplet and a triplet on the first beat of bar 8 (example 8.4). On the basis of that alignment they argue that Chopin meant the dotted rhythms elsewhere to be played literally. Even in the Polonaise Fantaisie, they argue that the dotted rhythm should only be adjusted to match the triplets when it is impossible to play it literally. Paderewski was originally a member of this editorial team, and in view of his own freedom in the treatment of dotted rhythms it is unlikely that he would have taken so rigid a stance. These notes were the work of his two co-editors, written after Paderewski's death. Cortot, in his edition of Chopin's Polonaises, takes a view more characteristic of early twentieth-century practice, arguing that the dotted rhythm in the Polonaise-Fantaisie is used in a traditional way to indicate triplet rhythms.[84]

Other examples which very strongly suggest adjustment of dotted rhythms include Brahms's Piano Concerto No. 2 (bar 11 of the first movement), Schumann's Fantasiestücke, Op. 111 (No. 2, bars 34–40), and Schubert's Piano Sonata in B flat, D.960 (second movement, bar 52 and similar bars). There are very many instances from nineteenth-century music of more ambiguous examples which, on the evidence of the notation alone, may or may not have been intended to be synchronised. These range from Chopin's Ballade in F minor (bar 223) to Beethoven's 'Moonlight' Sonata (first movement). However, suggestive though such evidence may be, it does not, on its own, provide proof of a general habit of flexible treatment of dotted rhythms, any more than do the early twentieth-century examples given in Chapter 3.

Ex.8.5   Schubert, Impromptu in C minor, D. 899 No. 1, bar 105.

Another nineteenth-century source relating to this topic is the composers' alignment of rhythms in their autographs. Examples of Chopin's alignment of duplet semiquavers with triplet quavers have already been mentioned. In an article about this rhythmic problem in Schubert, Franz Eibner states that in many cases in which Schubert writes  the semiquaver is consistently and exactly aligned with the final triplet quaver. He gives as an example the Impromptu in C minor, D. 899 No. 1, bar 105 (example 8.5). Here, Eibner writes, all the short notes are exactly aligned in the autograph, and several other writers have made similar observations about Schubert's autographs.[85] However, even a superficial glance at the few Schubert manuscripts published in facsimile reveals examples where Schubert is anything but consistent. There is, for instance, the song 'Frühlingsglaube', D. 686. Schubert wrote three versions, two in which duplet against triplet rhythms are dominant, the other in which the duplet rhythms are dotted. The autograph of this dotted version shows that the placing of the demisemiquaver of the dotted rhythm is quite random, sometimes directly above the triplet semiquaver, at other times before or after it.[86] The main message of the autograph seems to be that Schubert expected the reader to know how to play the rhythm without pedantic placing by the composer.

Inconsistencies in published editions give the most general indication of a relaxed attitude to dotted rhythms in the nineteenth century. For instance, the upbeat first note of Beethoven's Symphony no. 2, according to Beethoven and the most authoritative editions, is a demisemiquaver. However, at least three nineteenth-century publications of the symphony print this first note as a semiquaver: the arrangements by Hummel (chamber group, [1825–35]), Watts (piano duet, c. 1830), and Winkler (piano duet, c. 1860). Schott's edition of the full score (1867) prints the note in the score correctly as a demisemiquaver, but the same note in the incipit as a quaver.

There are similar inconsistencies in the notation of Beethoven's Symphony No. 3 ('Eroica'), second movement, bar 5. Here, the double-bass line is notated by Beethoven as in example 8.6. Arrangements by Hummel (1825–35), Winkler (c. 1860), and Montgomery (piano [1853]) halve the value of the demisemiquavers. It seems most unlikely that these inconsistencies reveal

Ex.8.6   Beethoven, Symphony No. 3, second movement, bar 5.

different views as to how long the notes should be played. Rather, they suggest that, in the pattern of dotted rhythms, short notes would in any case be played short, whatever their precise note value.

Comment about the treatment of dotted rhythms is sparse throughout the nineteenth century. Hummel (1827) writes about the articulation of dotted rhythms, depending on whether they are slurred or not, but says nothing about overdotting even though his editions of Beethoven's Symphonies are among those which imply a flexible attitude. Molineux (1831) writes: 'the duration of the longer notes, in passages where the notes are unequal, is of great importance. The effect is much improved by allowing the voice to linger, beyond the exact time, on the longer, the dotted, and the double-dotted notes'.[87]

The cellist Romberg (1840) gives advice about the length of upbeats: 'In an Adagio or in any slow tempo the upbeat, if it consists of a single note, must be played longer than written, so that it blends more, as it were, with the main beat. On the other hand, in an Allegro it must be shorter than written, to give the note on the main beat more strength.'[88] By contrast, Engel (1853) writing on the Funeral March in Beethoven's Piano Sonata in A flat, Op. 26, advises against overdotting: 'Bar 1 . . . take care to hold the dotted quaver exactly its value, as also the semiquaver, thus: ♩.♪'.[89]

Research may bring to light many more examples of writers either recommending or cautioning against overdotting. But the majority of nineteenth-century writers, like their successors in the early twentieth century, largely ignored the treatment of dotted rhythms. This may seem strange, given that the evidence from nineteenth-century notation very strongly suggests a degree of flexibility in the interpretation of dotted rhythms. But it is no stranger than the situation in the early twentieth century. Here, as we saw in Chapter 3, the notation of the period often suggests overdotting, and yet comment on the subject by contemporary writers is sparse and contradictory. The evidence of recordings shows that, despite the shortage of comment, players in the early twentieth century very often overdotted rhythms. Recording only began at the very end of the nineteenth century, and so for most of the century we are left with the notation and little else to guide us. But given our knowledge of overdotting in the eighteenth and twentieth centuries, it seems extremely unlikely that the literal interpretation of dotted rhythms was the rule throughout the nineteenth. Until evidence is presented to the contrary, we must assume that the overdotting heard on early twentieth-century recordings represents the end of a tradition stretching back through the nineteenth century. Early twentieth-century overdotting was clearly only a distant echo of eighteenth-century practice, and already in the nineteenth century we must be dealing with a very vague and variable habit, rather than anything approaching an acknowledged worked-out rule. Nevertheless the implication of nineteenth-century notation, that some flexibility in the interpretation of dotted rhythms was practised throughout the century, is transformed by the evidence of early twentieth-century recordings into a very strong likelihood. One of the consequences of this is the equal likelihood that late twentieth-century insistence on the literal interpretation of rhythm is an entirely new development, not a return to 'Classical' values after the excesses of late Romanticism.

CONCLUSION

This survey of nineteenth-century sources has inevitably been brief and sketchy. An increasing number of scholars are working on specialist areas within the nineteenth century, and this chapter does not pretend to have summarised their work. Nevertheless, it is worth looking even superficially at some of the most obvious documents, so as to show how strikingly some of them seem to anticipate features of early twentieth-century performance. Of course, there is a natural tendency, when examining the evidence of the past, to find what one is looking for, and there is always more than one possible interpretation of any document. But the starting point for this chapter, the supposition that many of the practices of the early twentieth century derive from the nineteenth century, is really no more than common sense, and nineteenth-century documents seem to confirm it,

A late twentieth-century musician, who finds the habits of 70 or 80 years ago merely old-fashioned, may have some difficulty accepting that they might represent the end of a long tradition, stretching back to periods which we now think of as historical rather than old-fashioned. And it would certainly be naïve to imagine that musicians performed in the 1820s as they did in the 1920s, just because the documents suggest some similarities. Comparison between documents and recordings in the early twentieth century has already shown some of the problems of reconciling writings with actual practice. But in attitudes to vibrato, portamento, tempo fluctuation, rubato, and the interpretation of note values, nineteenth-century documents time and again suggest a strong link with the habits of the early twentieth century.

So it does seem that early recordings, which are, after all, as close as we can really get to the nineteenth century, provide a vital key to the performance practice of the more distant past. Performers on period instruments, who are currently working their way forward through the nineteenth-century repertoire, have so far paid almost no attention to early recordings. Unintentionally, period performances do sometimes produce results which have something in common with early twentieth-century style, though in very limited ways – restraint in vibrato, and fast (though rarely flexible) tempos. Other characteristics of the early twentieth century which have an equal claim to have survived from the nineteenth century – melodic rubato, portamento, flexibility of tempo – are an embarrassment to modern musicians, and are therefore ignored.

By the time this book is published, the period performers will probably have reached Elgar, and then there will be a collision between authentic Elgar, as recorded by the composer, and 'authentic' Elgar, as reconstructed. It will be a collision between two worlds, a real world which no longer exists, and a reconstructed world which never wholly existed except in the imagination of the late twentieth century. This conflict highlights the fact that recordings are a mixed blessing. They enable us to step back in time, and hear how a previous generation played, but in doing so they present us with the whole truth, not just what we want to know. The problems which this raises are discussed in the final chapter of this book.

9

Implications for the future

The most obvious trends in performing style over the first half of the twentieth century are easily summarised. Broadly speaking, early twentieth-century playing was characterised by the following habits: the sparing use of vibrato by string-players, its discreet use by singers, and the general avoidance of vibrato on woodwind instruments by most players except those of the French school; the frequent use of prominent, often slow, portamento by string-players and singers; the use of substantial tempo changes to signal changes of mood or tension, and the adoption of fast maximum tempos; varieties of tempo rubato which included not only detailed flexibility of tempo, but also accentuation by lengthening and shortening individual notes, and the dislocation of melody and accompaniment; and a tendency, in patterns of long and short notes, to shorten the short notes, and to overdot dotted rhythms. Instruments were also different from their modern equivalents in some ways – gut strings (used to a decreasing extent after World War I), wooden flutes (widely used except by the French school), French bassoons (not in Germany and Austria), and, though they have not been discussed in this book, the continued use of narrow-bore brass instruments.

By the 1930s there were clear trends away from these early twentieth-century characteristics: the spread of continuous vibrato on stringed instruments, its increasing prominence among singers, and its adoption by many woodwind-players, including a move towards slower vibrato than the fast tremor sometimes heard earlier in the century; the decreasing prominence and frequency of portamento on both strings and voice; a trend towards stricter control of tempo and slower maximum speeds; more emphatic clarity of rhythmic detail, more literal interpretation of note values, and the avoidance of rhythmic irregularity and dislocation; the adoption of steel on the upper strings of stringed instruments, the increasing use of the metal flute, the German bassoon, and wider-bore brass instruments.

It is possible to summarise all these elements as a trend towards greater power, firmness, clarity, control, literalness, and evenness of expression, and away from informality, looseness, and unpredictability. It is more difficult to draw neat conclusions from them. The problem arises from the very completeness of the evidence. Recordings show in detail how performing styles developed from the early years of the twentieth century up to the present time. This makes it possible to compare our own styles with those of almost a century ago, a comparison which was impossible in previous periods. Enthusiasts for 'authentic' performance may regard this as an opportunity to begin creating reconstructions of early twentieth-century performances. But access to the truth about developing style faces us with some fundamental questions, about the nature of modern style and taste, about the ways in which they have developed, and about the extent to which it is desirable, or even possible, to recreate the performance practices of an earlier period.

The early twentieth century is the earliest period for which the primary source material of performance practice – the performance itself – has been preserved. It lies at the transition between two musical worlds, the old world in which performers were heard only in actual performance, and each performance occurred only once, and the modern world in which a performance (which may not even have been a complete performance) can be heard simply by playing a recording. The recorded performance is available to anyone, including the musician who performed it, and can be repeated any number of times. The recordings of the early twentieth century are themselves transitional in character. They are of the new world, in that they are available and repeatable, but the performances which they preserve are largely of the old world, survivals of a style evolved for unique performance to an audience.

The changes in performance practice over the century have been greatly influenced by this shift of emphasis. Recorded performances from the early part of the century give a vivid impression of being projected as if to an audience. They have a sense of being 'put across', so that the precision and clarity of each note is less important than the shape and progress of the music as a whole. They are intended to convey what *happens* in the music, to characterise it. The accurate reproduction of the musical text is merely a means to this end.

In the late twentieth century the balance has shifted significantly. The accurate and clear performance of the musical text has become the first priority, and the characterisation of the music and its progress is assumed to be able to take care of itself. Of course, this is a crude generalisation. The most admired late twentieth-century performers convey the progress of the music very vividly, and there are some dull and pedantic performances on early recordings. But the general change in emphasis has nevertheless been from the characterisation of musical events to the reproduction of a text. This is particularly true in the recording studio, which has had such a strong influence, good and bad, on performance. Musicians are now used to performing routinely without an audience, and the atmosphere in a recording studio is not like that of a concert-hall. Musicians know that movements and sections can be repeated, and that a finished performance can be assembled from the best parts of different takes. The overwhelming priority is to get each section *right* at least once. One of the most familiar remarks of a recording producer at the end of a session is, 'I think we've got it all somewhere.' There is no need for a complete performance at all.

Recording before the war, and right up to the advent of editable tape in the 1950s, was a very different matter. Rachmaninoff expressed a widespread view of the recording studio:

> I get very nervous when I am making records, and all whom I have asked say they get nervous too. When the test records are made, I know that I can hear them played back at me, and then everything is all right. But when the stage is set for the final recording and I realise that this will remain for good, I get nervous and my hands get tense.[1]

Musicians knew that they had to play at their very best, and that any mistakes would be preserved for ever, unless a side was repeated. Sides were indeed repeated, many times on occasions, but it comes as a surprise to a modern musician to find how many 78 rpm recordings consist of first or second takes. For example, of the nine sides of Rachmaninoff's recording of his third concerto, seven are first takes. Admittedly the division of a long movement into several sides made it impossible to play right through the movement; but in many other ways the atmosphere of recording in the pre-tape period was much closer to that of a live performance than modern recording sessions.

The changes in recording and the recording studio have in turn fed back into the concert-hall. If pre-war recordings are remarkably like live performances, many late twentieth-century live performances are remarkably like recordings. Detailed clarity and control have become the priority in modern performance, in the concert-hall as well as in the studio. No doubt this is partly because musicians have become accustomed to playing in this way, but it is also because audiences, themselves trained by recordings, have come to expect it. Clarity and accuracy are required in modern recordings, because any inaccuracies will be repeated every time the record is played. This has led to a standard which is, in a limited sense, incredibly high. The price is that many modern performances place accuracy and clarity above all other considerations.

Rehearsal is an important element in this development, and it has been mentioned from time to time in this book. By modern standards many performances of the early twentieth century, particularly orchestral concerts, were seriously under-rehearsed. When Barbirolli joined the Queen's Hall Orchestra as a cellist in 1916, the orchestra played the entire season of Promenade Concerts, six nights a week for six weeks, with three rehearsals for each week of concerts. As Barbirolli remembered, 'We had to sight-read half the stuff when the time came. But old Henry J. was a master at keeping us on the rails.'[2] When Mahler made his debut at the Vienna Opera in 1897, there were no orchestral rehearsals for operas which were already in the repertoire. He conducted Wagner's *Ring* under these conditions.[3] Puccini recounts similar horror stories in Italian opera houses.[4] There were exceptions to this lack of rehearsal, such as important premières, but regular multiple orchestral rehearsals were the exception rather than the rule. Lamoureux in Paris, Mahler in Vienna, Nikisch in Leipzig, Mengelberg in Amsterdam, and Toscanini in Milan were among the conductors who pioneered the habit of regular rehearsal around the turn of the century, but it was not until the 1930s that the habit became general.

But despite the complaints of Mahler, Puccini, and others, it cannot therefore be assumed that the orchestras of the early years of the century, with their shortage of rehearsal, were generally regarded as being of a low standard at the time. Many writers at the turn of the century convey an acceptance of short rehearsal time and the need for musicians to think on their feet. The leader of the Covent Garden orchestra in the 1890s advises violinists, 'The rehearsals are very trying, especially of the old operas known by heart by myself and others. They are, however, made necessary in consequence of the periodical advent of new conductors, soloists or fresh members of the orchestra.'[5] The implication of this is that an orchestra of regular membership with a familiar conductor and soloists would not need to rehearse operas already in the repertoire at all. Tetrazzini (1923) takes a similar attitude to rehearsals in her advice to aspiring opera singers:

Rehearsals are a necessary evil and the sensible artist will try to make the best of them. Undoubtedly they are very tedious and trying, but they are quite unavoidable unless you happen to have attained sufficient eminence to be dispensed attendance at them. Even then it is not always wise to avoid them if you wish to procure the best results.[6]

Such writing reveals a musical world very different from that of the late twentieth century, and the difference is as much one of expectations as of practical results. To say that orchestral performances at the turn of the century were generally under-rehearsed, and therefore of a low standard, is to judge them from a late twentieth-century point of view. To be sure, Mahler and others fought to change things, but they were fighting against the general performance practice of the time, to which the mass of musicians and audiences were accustomed. In any case, as the chapters on rhythm have demonstrated, it is impossible to draw a clear distinction between competence and style. A rhythm which now sounds unclear or slapdash would be judged incompetent or under-rehearsed by a modern listener, but would not necessarily have seemed so to an early twentieth-century audience. And the casual rhythmic style of the early twentieth century is found not only in under-rehearsed orchestras but also in the most highly rehearsed chamber ensembles. Adolfo Betti, the leader of the Flonzaley Quartet, writes (1923), 'thirty or thirty-five are the usual number [of rehearsals] required to master an important modern quartet (our organization, the Flonzaley Quartet, needed fifty-five to produce Schoenberg's Op. 7)'.[7] And yet the Flonzaley now sounds as old-fashioned in its treatment of rhythmic detail as the under-rehearsed orchestras of the 1920s.

Nor was there unanimous praise for the new standards being achieved by the

1930s. The Vienna correspondent of the *Musical Times* in 1930 preferred the Vienna Philharmonic Orchestra to Toscanini's visiting New York Orchestra: 'Toscanini's watchword is unconditional subordination of his men: the Vienna men are given the liberty to "sing" to their heart's content, to be co-ordinate, not subordinate to their leader.'[8] It would also be a mistake to suppose that there is always a simple relationship between the amount of rehearsal and the standard of performance. When Toscanini first conducted the Vienna Philharmonic in 1933, he declared himself satisfied after the second rehearsal and cancelled the remaining three. It was the intensity and concentration of his conducting which achieved results, rather than sheer time.[9] By contrast, Casals's orchestra in Barcelona in the early 1920s rehearsed for about twenty hours for each concert.[10] And yet recordings reveal that, at least around 1930, its standards of rhythmic clarity and tuning were, from a late twentieth-century viewpoint, very low.

Many of the changes in performance practice over the century can be seen in the context of the increasing demand for precision and clarity. Even the developments in instruments, which have been little discussed in this book, are to some extent related to this change. Wide-bore German and American horns, for example, are a great deal easier to play than the old narrow-bore French horns. First introduced in the late nineteenth century, they met resistance, particularly in France, right up to World War II, on the grounds that their tone was inferior to that of the French horn. Their final general acceptance was brought about by the need for accuracy and reliability in the late twentieth century. Similar reasons apply, with some qualifications, to the general rejection of the French bassoon, even in France in recent years. The adoption of steel strings, which were widespread by the 1930s, has everything to do with reliability and power, and little to do with tone quality.

Of course the demand for reliability resulted not just from the pressures of the recording studio, but also from the character of new music which musicians were beginning to play during this period. The extreme difficulty of much new music, from Strauss and Schoenberg onwards, encouraged the adoption of instruments which were more reliable and easier to play. In music which broke radically from conventional nineteenth-century structures and expression, conventional expressive devices began to become irrelevant. The breakdown of traditional harmonic and melodic tensions encouraged the evening out of traditional expressive nuances. The accurate rendering of the text became all-important.

The requirement of clarity and accuracy has also influenced detailed performing habits. The literal interpretation of note-values is the most obvious example. Even though some flexibility is still allowed, many performances on early recordings now seem slapdash and casual in this respect. The dislocation of melody and accompaniment in tempo rubato has a similar effect on a modern listener. It disturbs our expectation of regularity in the rhythmic progress of a melody and of synchrony between treble and bass. In modern performance, only the subtlest dislocation is allowed to disturb the clear placing of the beat (except in jazz playing, which has become the last refuge of old-fashioned melodic rubato).

These changes in rhythmic style are related to the changes in approach to tempo. Every modern music student is familiar with the principle that a tempo must be chosen so that the shortest note-values can be played accurately and clearly. The very fast maximum tempos of many pre-war recordings were possible because the modern degree of clarity and precision was not part of the general performance practice of the time. The predominantly slower maximum tempos of modern performances are an inevitable result of the emphasis on rhythmic clarity. Few modern conductors would dream of taking the fastest of the Enigma Variations as fast as Elgar himself did; and if they were to, it would be with a virtuoso orchestra capable of delivering them with exceptional precision as a kind of athletic feat. The panache of Elgar's day is no longer the priority. The flexibility of pre-war tempos also goes against modern notions of control and orderliness. Again, every modern music student is accustomed to being told not to rush the loud passages; hurrying is regarded as lack of control. But speeding up in the exciting passages was one of the most characteristic habits of pre-war performance practice. Conveying the shape of the movement, and characterising its contrasts, were more important than 'control'.

In a less obvious way, the old-fashioned use of the portamento offends against modern ideas of rhythmic clarity and precision. The sliding of many performances of the 1920s and earlier gives the impression of a somewhat improvised, at times random, placing of portamentos, in such a way as to create unpredictable rhythmic emphases. Like dislocation by rubato, portamento has a vertical as well as a horizontal effect. A performance of a string quartet in the 1920s will have frequent portamento in all the parts, which can create contrapuntal strands even in a succession of apparently simple chords. This produces a curiously three-dimensional effect. Modern performance requires that a portamento, if used at all, should be placed so as to underline a particularly emphatic move in the melodic line. The more casual old-fashioned placing of portamentos is, by comparison, rhythmically disorderly and imprecise.

Even the vibrato has some link with notions of control. The old-fashioned use of the vibrato as an ornament, or at most as a way of intensifying a climax, is, like the portamento, a means of emphasis. The modern vibrato is a continuous colour, producing uniformity.

The performances of the early twentieth century, therefore, are volatile, energetic, flexible, vigorously projected in broad outline but rhythmically informal in detail. Modern performances are, by comparison, accurate, orderly, restrained, deliberate, and even in emphasis. When we describe early twentieth-century performance in this way, we are describing the performances of, among others, Elgar, Vaughan Williams, Rachmaninoff, Richard Strauss, Bartók, Stravinsky and Poulenc. Given the clear links between the performance practice on early recordings and the descriptions of the late nineteenth century, we can also be sure that early recordings take us quite close to the practice of Mahler, Brahms, Debussy, Wagner, and Tchaikovsky. Late twentieth-century musicians, with their interest in constructing the performance practice of the past, are bound to ask what one should do with this information.

Early twentieth-century recordings and documents demonstrate that any literal reconstruction of the past is impossible. It is not as if players simply had 'rules' which they applied, and which we could decide to apply too. In order to use portamento as string players of the early twentieth century did, a modern player might be tempted simply to note where the slides occur in Elgar's recordings and mark them in the part. But this would be to use portamento in a modern way, even if to excess. To slide like a string player of Elgar's day, one would have to abandon the modern notion that 'clean' playing is tasteful playing, and relearn the habit of sliding audibly at most changes of position.

Rhythmic style presents even greater difficulties. Trying to unlearn modern ideas of clarity and precision would involve redefining the borderline between competence and style. On the whole, modern musicians who try to reconstruct the styles of the past adhere quite closely to modern notions of clarity and control, however much they may apply certain rhythmic rules of particular periods. A player of today would have the greatest difficulty learning to play with the casual and flexible approach to short notes with which early twentieth-century players were brought up, and the same would be true of old-fashioned rubato with its dislocation of melody and accompaniment.

Even vibrato, which is at least a current topic of debate, is not a simple matter. We have become accustomed to restraint in the use of vibrato by players in the early music field, but few players go beyond what sounds 'tasteful' in phrasing and vibrato to modern ears. Of course even modern taste does not remain static, but the fact is that much woodwind-playing of the early twentieth century, particularly British, sounds flat and unmusical to modern ears because of its lack of vibrato and dynamic nuances. String-playing of the period can similarly seem bald and expressionless. Modern taste would not be able to cope with such a style.

If an attempt to reconstruct early twentieth-century performance practice is doomed to failure, imagine how much worse the situation would be if there were no recordings from the period, but we had to rely on written sources as we do for earlier periods. We would admittedly pick up clues about several areas of performance practice. We would know that vibrato was a controversial subject in the early years of the century, and that portamento was widely used by singers and string players. We would know that many writers encouraged flexibility of tempo, and that some sort of tempo rubato was

frequently employed by pianists, though we would also find that some writers
used the term to mean detailed fluctuations of tempo, and others used it to
mean rhythmic adjustment of the melodic line. We might also pick up clues
about the overdotting of dotted rhythms from the notation of the period,
though we would search in vain for anything which would reveal the general
rhythmic style of the period. In fact with all of these practices, even the most
widely described, we would be left to guess how they were really applied in
performance, and we would certainly guess wrong.

We would be unable to establish, to take only a few obvious examples, the
degree of flexibility of Elgar's tempos, the prominence of Joachim's portamento, the lightness of rhythm of Bartók's piano playing, the reedy tone of
French bassoons and clarinets in Stravinsky's Paris recordings, or the nature of
Rachmaninoff's rubato. Our only sure area of knowledge would be a field
which has been discussed very little in this book, the physical nature of the
instruments themselves: violins with gut strings, narrow-bore French horns,
French bassoons, wooden flutes, and so on. But one thing which the recordings
of the early twentieth century teach us is that changes in tone quality over the
century pale into insignificance compared with other changes in performance
practice.

Even when we know as much as we do about the performances of Elgar,
Bartók, Rachmaninoff, and Stravinsky, there is a danger of taking too simplis-
tic a view of their recordings as 'authentic'. Composers' relationship with the
changing string style, for example, is complicated. Elgar wrote his violin
concerto for Kreisler, recorded it with Marie Hall and Yehudi Menuhin, and
often performed it with Albert Sammons. Kreisler, Menuhin, and Sammons
were of the modern school of violin-playing, with continuous vibrato and
selective portamento, but Hall was of the old school, with much prominent
portamento and restrained vibrato. Elgar approved of all of them in turn.
Delius dedicated his second violin sonata to Sammons, but his first to Arthur
Catterall, a much more old-fashioned player. Arnold Rosé, who premièred a
number of Schoenberg's chamber works in the early years of the century, was
described by Flesch as playing in the style of the 1870s, 'with no concession to
modern tendencies in our art'.[11] Schoenberg wrote an article in about 1940
deploring the 'goat-like bleating' of the modern continuous vibrato.[12] And yet
the violinist with whom he was most closely associated between the wars,
Rudolf Kolisch, whom Schoenberg described as leading 'the best string quartet
in the world', played with a prominent, continuous vibrato in the modern
manner. Of Stravinsky's violinists, Dushkin was a much more old-fashioned
player than Szigeti. Hindemith (himself a viola player in the modern manner)
played with the violinists Amar and Goldberg, who were similarly contrasted
in style.

The problem is not restricted to string-playing. The London Symphony
Orchestra was described by Elgar in the early years of the century as 'a jolly fine

orchestra', and he thought the new BBC Symphony Orchestra thirty years later 'marvellous'. But the two orchestras were very different, in string-playing, wind-playing, rhythmic style, and degree of rehearsal. Elgar spent most of his life apparently accepting oboists with little or no vibrato, and yet when he recorded with the London Philharmonic Orchestra in 1933 he wrote, 'Leon G[oosens]'s oboe passages in *Froissart* are divine – what an artist!'[13] In his *Autobiography* of 1936, Stravinsky singles out for praise the instrumental soloists of Paris with whom he worked in concerts and recordings, including the flautist Marcel Moyse.[14] Two years later, he recorded *Jeu de Cartes* with the Berlin Philharmonic Orchestra, which he described as 'magnificent'.[15] The woodwind of Paris and Berlin played in utterly different styles in the 1930s. It is impossible that a composer as demanding as Stravinsky did not notice the stylistic differences between the musicians with whom he worked. But no composer, not even Stravinsky, has an unchanging idea of the 'right' way to perform his music. Recordings demonstrate, more conclusively than indirect evidence can, that composers' views evolve as performance practice evolves.

Students of performance practice in earlier periods surely have something to learn from all of this. Performers on period instruments have sometimes spoken of their work as being like stripping the varnish off an old painting to reveal the original colours. But the earliest period to which this analogy could possibly apply is the early twentieth century, because it is the earliest period from which the 'paintings' (that is, the works as originally performed) still exist. For earlier periods we have no such paintings, but only an inadequate set of instructions describing what the painting is supposed to look like, written by people who had no prophetic knowledge of late twentieth-century taste, and couched in terms comprehensible only to contemporaries.

One of the reasons that reconstruction of earlier playing styles is so difficult is precisely the fact that we start from the viewpoint of late twentieth-century taste and habits, and use them as the basis for comparison. And one of the most valuable aspects of early recordings is that they reveal just what modern taste and habits consist of, and how they have developed. They reveal, as will be obvious from the preceding chapters, that modern performers use more vibrato and less portamento than was used earlier in the century, that they are more concerned with clarity of detail and exact note-values, that they change tempo less frequently and to a lesser degree, and that their maximum tempos are generally slower.

What is most striking about these fundamental changes in general performance practice is that they have occurred so recently. And that being so, we have to be very cautious of using them as a basis for investigating earlier playing styles. As an illustration of this, it is instructive to read the documents of, say, the early nineteenth century through the eyes of the early twentieth century instead of our own time. Consider, for example, the following three quotations:

The beat should not be a tyrannical restriction or the driving of a mill hammer. On the contrary, it should be to the music what the pulse-beat is to the life of man.

(Weber 1824)[16]

Undulation, when discreetly introduced, gives to the sound of the instrument a great similarity to the voice when it is strongly touched with emotion. This means of expression is very powerful, but if employed too often it would soon lose its moving quality ...   (Baillot 1834)[17]

The Glide is the same mode of ascending or descending to a higher or lower note with the voice, as that which is produced by sliding the finger to a higher or lower place on the string of a violin ... It is introduced to qualify the effect of two notes, whether neighbouring or distant, and it is always expressive of tenderness. (Molineux 1831)[18]

The late twentieth-century scholar is, of course, aware of the danger of generalising from a single source. These three quotations come from, respectively, Germany, France, and England, and no reputable modern musi-cologist would make the mistake of assuming that any of them represented views outside the writer's immediate circle, without further evidence. But the dangers of our own prejudice are less widely recognised. The modern reader may well prefer to think that Weber had only subtle changes of tempo in mind, that Baillot might have used a slight vibrato most of the time, and that Molineux's 'glides' were probably discreet. But such preferences are based on modern taste, and nothing more. A reader of the early twentieth century would have quite different assumptions: that Weber's tempo changes were substantial, that Baillot played for much of the time with no vibrato at all, and that in Molineux's England singers and violinists used the portamento as unashamedly as they did in the early twentieth century. There is no reason to assume that our taste is a better guide to such matters than that of the early twentieth century. On the contrary, since we know from the evidence of recordings that many aspects of modern taste are of recent development, we can be sure that our taste is a very poor guide to the interpretation of nineteenth-century documents.

It is possible to go further, and to say that, since changes in performance practice during the twentieth century have been conditioned and accelerated to a significant extent by the influence of recordings, which did not exist in earlier periods, the style of the early twentieth century represents the end of a long tradition of performance practice which, though it certainly changed over the years, probably changed much more slowly than it has later in the twentieth century. In this case, examining early recordings is, one might say, rather like sending a telescope outside the earth's atmosphere; it is possible to see more clearly into the past, because of the absence of local interference. It may strike the modern reader as eccentric to suggest that performances on early recordings represent some sort of unpolluted pre-industrial purity. But it is a great deal more plausible than the notion that what sounds tasteful now probably sounded tasteful in earlier periods, which is an assumption behind many modern reconstructions of earlier performance practices and much writing on the subject. For this reason period performances ignore a great deal of evidence which goes against modern taste. The combined evidence of early recordings and nineteenth-century documents suggest two particularly embarrassing examples – portamento and rubato. It is very likely that string-players and singers throughout the nineteenth century used portamento in a manner uncomfortably close to that of the early twentieth century. It is virtually certain that musicians of all kinds, as far back as Mozart and beyond, used a kind of rubato in which the melody becomes rhythmically free of its accompaniment. But the period instrument performers have so far ignored old-fashioned portamento and rubato, and it will be a bold musician who dares to affront modern taste by taking them seriously.

Writers are sometimes seduced by modern taste into the most wishful interpretations of documentary evidence. Eigeldinger, for example, in his book on Chopin, quotes Saint-Saëns on the difficulty of playing tempo rubato while maintaining the rhythm in the accompaniment:

This way of playing is very difficult since it requires complete independence of the two hands; and those lacking this give both themselves and others the illusion of it by playing the melody in time and dislocating the accompaniment so that it falls beside the beat; or else – worst of all – content themselves with simply playing one hand after the other.

Eigeldinger leaps on this as an opportunity to discredit the kind of dislocation heard on early recordings, specifically condemning Leschetizky, Pugno, Pachmann, Friedman, Paderewski, and Rosenthal.[19] The possibility that something as old-fashioned as early twentieth-century dislocation might be *really* old-fashioned, and represent the end of a nineteenth-century tradition, is unthinkable. In a similar way, Donington finds it impossible to accept that nineteenth-century violinists could ever have played without a continuous vibrato, despite the strong implications of their writings and the evidence of early recordings. In this, as Clive Brown rightly states, Donington 'is clearly mistaken'.[20]

Early recordings expose the anachronism in this sort of judgement for what it is, and thereby open the way to a clearer understanding of earlier performance practices. But they also reveal how complex changes in practice really are, and how much is left out in written descriptions of performance. The result is rather disturbing. On the one hand, recordings reveal that modern taste is a recent development, and is therefore not to be trusted as a basis for assessing earlier documents. On the other hand, they also reveal that any attempt to reconstruct the past accurately, even the recent past, is impossibly complicated, and that even if we were to succeed, the result would be no more than a contrivance.

The way out of this dilemma is surely through a better understanding of that overworked word 'authentic'. Elgar's performances on record are authentic not just in the limited sense that they reproduce what he did. They are also authentic in a deeper sense: they show a composer working with musicians whose style and habits, abilities and limitations, were an integral part of his own musical world. They are authentic because, quite simply, they are the real thing.

The problem for anyone aiming at 'authentic' Elgar, or Bartòk, or Rachmaninoff, is that the real thing is no longer available. Time, taste, habits, and every aspect of performance practice have moved on. And authenticity does not consist in reconstructing a dead style, whether a hundred or three hundred years old. The belief that we can do so is an illusion, as recordings vividly demonstrate. The only authenticity available to us consists in creating performances which work *now*, not performances which supposedly worked for the composer. This is not to say that we should throw out all the old recordings and the even older documents, and do as we like with the music. Most of the major revelations in musical performance over recent years have come out of the study of performance practice in earlier centuries, which has profoundly affected our perceptions of the music of all periods. The value of such work is not in question. We do, however, need constantly to remind ourselves what we are doing. A modern performance of *Messiah* on period instruments with a small choir is not a performance of the 1740s but a performance of today. However carefully we choose the instruments and read the documents, we have really very little idea what a performance of the 1740s would have sounded like. To judge by the way things have changed over only the last hundred years, it might have been almost incomprehensible to us.

In the end, therefore, it does all come down to a question of taste and judgement. Modern taste, which is so unreliable a guide to the interpretation of old documents, is nevertheless the only taste we have. This is as true in the 1990s as it was in the 1890s and the 1790s, and it is a mistake to think that it could be otherwise. Because, if early recordings teach us anything, it is that no musicians can ever escape the taste and judgement of their own time.

NOTES

1 FLEXIBILITY OF TEMPO

1 *Musik-Lexicon* (Leipzig, 1882; English translation London, 1897), 226.
2 *The Singing of the Future* (London, 1906), 162–3.
3 *The Interpretation of the Music of the XVII and XVIII Centuries* (London, 1916), 284. For similar remarks, see C. W. Pearce, *The Art of the Piano-Teacher* (London [1920]), paragraph 646, J. Lhevinne, *Basic Principles in Pianoforte Playing* (Philadelphia, 1924; reprinted 1972), 6, and H. T. Finck, *Success in Music and How it is Won* (New York, 1909), 429.
4 *The Art of Teaching Pianoforte Playing* (London [1910]), 113–14.
5 *A Practical Guide to Violin-Playing* (London, 1913), 112. See also A. Broadley, *Chats to 'Cello Students* (London, 1899), 98.
6 *Perfection in Singing* (London, 1906), 133.
7 M. Sterling Mackinlay, *The Singing Voice and its Training* (London, 1910), 156.
8 *Über das Dirigieren*, (Leipzig, 1869; English translation 1887, 4th edn 1940, reprinted 1972), 43. This book contains a number of illustrations of tempo modification in specific works.
9 N. Bauer-Lechner, *Erinnerungen an Gustav Mahler* (Vienna, 1923; English translation London, 1980), 46.
10 *Ibid.*, 112.
11 Letter, 14 July 1892, in K. Martner (ed.), *Selected Letters of Gustav Mahler* (London, 1979), 143.
12 C. Ambrust in *Hamburgisches Fremdenblatt* (31 March 1891), quoted in H.-L. de la Grange, *Mahler* (London, 1974), I, 235.
13 De la Grange, *Mahler*, 489–90.
14 *Ibid.*, 195.
15 In 1887 – *ibid.*, 169.
16 Bauer-Lechner, *Erinnerungen an Gustav Mahler*, 95.
17 G. E. Kaplan, 'How Mahler performed his Second Symphony', *Musical Times* (hereafter *MT*) 127 (May 1986), 267.
18 'Richard Strauss as an Opera Conductor', *Music & Letters* (hereafter *M&L*) 45 (1964), 8.
19 *Ibid.*, 10–11.
20 I. Newton, *At the Piano* (London, 1966), 186.
21 Letter, 1 July 1903, in P. M. Young, *Letters to Nimrod from Edward Elgar* (London, 1965), 192.
22 *Sunday Times*, 25 October 1933, quoted in E. O. Turner, 'Tempo Variation: With examples from Elgar', *M&L* 19 (1938), 320.
23 See D. Cherniavsky, 'Sibelius's Tempo Corrections', *M&L* 31 (1950), 53–5.
24 Sir A. Boult, 'Interpreting "The Planets"', *MT* 111 (1970), 263–4.

25 *Au Piano avec Gabriel Fauré* (Paris, 1963; English translation London, 1980), 66.
26 *Ibid.*, 72.
27 *Ibid.*, 84.
28 *Ibid.*, 94.
29 *Au Piano avec Maurice Ravel* (Paris, 1971; English translation London, 1973), 16.
30 *Ibid.*, 84.
31 Quoted in H. Milne, *Bartók his Life and Times* (Tunbridge Wells, 1982), 67.
32 B. Suchoff (ed.), *Béla Bartók Essays* (London, 1976), 465.
33 A. Schoenberg, *Style and Idea*, ed. Leonard Stein (London, 1975, revised 2nd edn 1985), 342.
34 *Ibid.*, 320.
35 E. F. Kornstein, 'How to Practise a String Quartet', *M&L* 3 (1922), 330.
36 'Of Quartet-Playing', *M&L* 4 (1923), 2–3.
37 I. Stravinsky, *An Autobiography* (New York 1936; reprinted 1962), 34.
38 See R. Craft (ed.), *Stravinsky: Selected Correspondence* (London, 1982), I, 223, 296–7, 392, 397, II, 169.
39 F. Weingartner, *Über das Dirigieren* (Leipzig, 1895, revised 3rd edn 1905; English translation 1906), 27–9.
40 Quoted in H. Schonberg, *The Great Conductors* (London, 1968), 252.
41 *MT* 41 (1900), 34.
42 E. Blom, *Beethoven's Piano Sonatas Discussed* (London, 1938), 122.
43 F. Weingartner, *Die Symphonie nach Beethoven* (Leipzig, 1897; English translation 1907), 41–3.
44 See note 21.
45 See note 20.
46 P. M. Young, *Letters of Edward Elgar* (London, 1956), 99–100.
47 At the Elgar Birthplace, Broadheath, near Worcester.
48 Percy M. Young (ed.), *Letters to Nimrod from Edward Elgar* (London, 1965), 211.
49 See note 15.
50 See note 19.
51 Note for HMV record No. HLM 7014.
52 Misprinted in original edition as ♩ = 84. See Robert Craft (ed.), *Stravinsky: Selected Correspondence*, I (London, 1982), 393.
53 Stravinsky, *Autobiography*, 150–1.
54 Letter to Walter Legge, 13 June 1933, reprinted with the reissue of this recording, Kajanus's recording of the Fifth Symphony, and others, on World Records SH 173–4. This reissue also includes notes on the recordings by Robert Layton.
55 Stravinsky, *Autobiography*, 150–1.
56 At the Elgar Birthplace, Broadheath, near Worcester.

2 TEMPO RUBATO

1 *Basic Principles in Pianoforte Playing* (Philadelphia, 1924; reprinted 1972), 45.
2 *The Violin and its Technique* (London, 1921), 44.
3 *MT* 67 (1926), 550.
4 *The Times* (27 April 1926), 14.
5 *The Times* (March 1929), quoted in J. Northrop Moore, *Edward Elgar, A Creative Life* (Oxford, 1984), 779.

6 J. B. Förster quoted in de la Grange, *Mahler*, I, 316.

7 M. Krause in *Leipziger Tageblatt* (10 August 1886), quoted in *ibid.*, 150.

8 *Erinnerungen an Gustav Mahler*, 109.

9 E. F. Kravitt, 'Tempo as an Expressive Element in the Late Romantic Lied', *Musical Quarterly* (hereafter *MQ*) 59 (1973), 507.

10 *Ibid.*, 507.

11 M. Long, *Au Piano avec Gabriel Fauré*, (Paris, 1963; English translation London, 1980), 72.

12 *Au Piano avec Claude Debussy*, (Paris, 1960; English translation London, 1972), 19.

13 V. Perlemuter and H. Jourdan-Morhange, *Ravel d'après Ravel* (5th edn Lausanne, 1970), 18.

14 Quoted in H. Milne, *Bartók his Life and Times*, 67.

15 In Bratislawa in 1920. B. Suchoff (ed.), *Béla Bartók Essays*, 465.

16 Revised edition by Sir J. Stainer (London, 1898), 439.

17 *Musik-Lexicon*, 673.

18 'Paderewski on Tempo Rubato', in H. Finck, *Success in Music and How it is Won*, 459.

19 D. Restout (ed.), *Landowska on Music* (London, 1965), 383–4; W. Gieseking and K. Leiner, *The Shortest Way to Pianistic Perfection* (1932), reprinted in *Piano Technique* (New York, 1972), 43–4.

20 *Technique and Expression in Pianoforte Playing* (London, 1897), 73.

21 H. Wessely, *A Practical Guide to Violin Playing* (London, 1913), 112–13.

22 (London, 1893), 65.

23 *The Singing of the Future* (London, 1906), 163.

24 *The Voice: Its Downfall, its Training, and its Use* (London, 1904), 55.

25 *Perfection in Singing* (London, 1906), 133.

26 *Musical Interpretation* (London, 1913), 70–1.

27 *Ibid.*, 63.

28 *Grove I*, III, 188.

29 *Grove III*, IV, 465.

30 *Piano Questions Answered* (London, 1909), reprinted with *Piano Playing* (New York, 1976), 100.

31 'Paderewski on Tempo Rubato', in H. T. Finck, *Success in Music and How it is Won*, 459.

32 D. Restout (ed.), *Landowska on Music*, 383.

33 'Tempo Rubato from the Aesthetic Point of View', *Monthly Musical Record* (hereafter *MMR*) 43 (1913), 116.

34 J. A. Johnstone, *Essentials in Pianoforte Playing and Other Musical Studies* (London, 1914), 45, 52.

35 'How Leschetizky taught', *M&L* 35 (1954), 220–6.

36 R. Dunstan, *A Cyclopaedic Dictionary of Music* (London, 1908), 347.

37 A. Greenish, *Dictionary of Musical Terms* (London, 1917), 77.

38 *Musik-Lexicon*, 13.

39 *Katechismus des Klavierspiels* (Leipzig, 1888); 8th edn as *Handbuch des Klavierspiels* (Berlin, 1922).

40 *Essentials in Pianoforte Playing and Other Musical Studies*, 45.

41 J. A. Fuller Maitland, *Joseph Joachim* (London and New York, 1905), 29–30.

42 'How Leschetizky taught', 224.

43 Finck, *Success in Music and How it is Won*, 316.

44 *Ibid.*, 300.

45 *The Singing Voice and its Training* (London, 1910), 156–7.

46 *The Voice in Song and Speech* (London [1917]), 129.

47 *Vocalism: Its Structure and Culture from an English Standpoint* (London, 1904), 108.

48 *Piano Questions Answered* (London, 1909), reprinted with *Piano Playing* (New York, 1976), 100.

49 J. F. Cooke, *Great Pianists on Piano Playing* (Philadelphia, 1913; reprinted 1976), 201–2.

50 *Technique and Expression in Pianoforte Playing* (London, 1897), 73.

51 'Tempo Rubato from the Aesthetic Point of View', *MMR* 43 (1913), 29.

52 A. F. Christiani, *The Principles of Expression in Pianoforte Playing*, 300.

53 *Memoirs* (London, 1957), 79, quoted in L. Ginsburg, *Ysaÿe* (Moscow, 1959, English translation Neptune City, N.J., 1980), 301.

54 *My Life of Music* (London, 1938), 128, quoted in *ibid.*, 271.

55 'Eugène Ysaÿe: Quelques notes et souvenirs', *La Revue Musicale* 188 (1939), 30–1.

56 *Au Piano avec Claude Debussy*, 19.

57 *Au Piano avec Gabriel Fauré*, 68.

58 J. B. McEwen, *Tempo Rubato or Time-Variation in Musical Performance* (London, 1928).

59 *Ibid.*, pp. 13–14. The quotations which McEwen gives in these questions are taken from Franklin Taylor's definition of rubato quoted earlier in this chapter.

60 *Ibid.*, pp. 14–15.

61 *Ibid.*, p. 15.

62 *Essentials in Pianoforte Playing*, 52.

63 See note 19.

3 LONG AND SHORT NOTES

1 *Vocalism: Its Structure and Culture from an English Standpoint*, 108.

2 *A Modern School for the Violin* (London, 1898–1908), No. 15 (notes on Handel's Overture to *Sampson*).

3 *Technique and Interpretation in Violin-Playing* (London, 1920), 97.

4 *The Interpretation of the Music of the XVII and XVIII Centuries*, 53.

5 *Au Piano avec Maurice Ravel*, 94.

6 V. Perlemuter and H. Jourdan-Morhange, *Ravel d'après Ravel*, 66.

7 *Ibid.*, 24.

8 F. Weingartner, *Über das Dirigieren*, 14.

9 *An Encyclopaedia of the Violin* (London, 1925), 259.

10 A. C. Boult, 'Casals as Conductor', *M&L* 4 (1923), 150.

11 *John Barbirolli* (London, 1971), 55.

12 D. Restout (ed.), *Landowska on Music*, 386–7.

13 G. Beechey, 'Rhythmic Interpretation: Mozart, Beethoven, Schubert and Schumann', *Music Review* (hereafter *MR*) 33 (1972), 233–48; H. Ferguson, *Keyboard Interpretation from the 14th to the 19th Century* (London, 1975), 97; D. Shawe Taylor; 'Schubert as Written and Performed', *MT* 104 (1963), 626; F. Eibner, 'The Dotted Quaver and Semiquaver Figure with Triplet Accompaniment in the Works of Schubert', *MR* 23 (1962), 281–4.

14 'Rhythmic Interpretation', 248.

15 *Au Piano avec Gabriel Fauré*, 86.

16 J. Northrop Moore, *Elgar on Record* (London, 1974), 195.

17 E. W. Atkins, *The Elgar-Atkins Friendship* (Newton Abbot, 1984), 457.

18 Elgar Birthplace, Broadheath, Volume No. 1481. See R. Philip, 'The Recordings of Edward Elgar (1857–1934)', *Early Music* 12 (1984), 481–9.

19 See M. Long, *Au Piano avec Claude Debussy*, 56n.

20 See A. Betti (leader of Flonzaley Quartet), 'Of Quartet-Playing', *M&L* 4 (1923), 2.

21 Flesch states that Joachim's fingers in his last years 'had become gouty and stiff'. *Memoirs* (London, 1957), 30.

4 STRING VIBRATO

1 C. Flesch, *Memoirs* (London, 1957), 144, and *Die Kunst des Violinspiels* (2 vols., Berlin, 1923–8); tr. F. H. Martens as *The Art of Violin Playing* (New York, 1924–30), I, 11.

2 S. Eberhardt, *Wiederaufstieg oder Untergang der Kunst des Geigens (Die kunstfeidliche Stahlseite)* [Recovery or Ruin of the Art of Violin Playing (The Steel String, Enemy of Art)] (Amsterdam 1938), quoted in Werner Hauck, *Vibrato on the Violin* (Cologne, 1971, English translation London, 1975), 30.

3 J. Corredor, *Conversations with Casals* (London, 1956), 24; A. Piatti, *Méthode de Violoncelle* (London 1878), 3.

4 J. Joachim and A. Moser, *Violinschule* (Berlin, 1905), I, 13–14.

5 *Conversations with Casals*, 24.

6 *The Art of Violin Playing*, I, 52.

7 C. Brown, 'Bowing Styles, Vibrato and Portamento in Nineteenth-Century Violin Playing', *Journal of the Royal Musical Association* (hereafter *JRMA*) 113 (1988), 97–128.

8 *The Art of Violin Playing*, I, 40.

9 *Violinschule*, II, 94.

10 J. MacLeod, *The Sisters d'Aranyi* (London, 1969), 48.

11 *Memoirs*, 79.

12 J. Szigeti, *Szigeti on the Violin* (London, 1969), 174.

13 L. Auer, *Violin Playing as I Teach it* (New York, 1921), 22–3. Similar points are made by many minor writers, for example J. Dunn, *Violin Playing* (London, 1898), 66; H. Chabert, *Le Violon* (Lyon, 1900), 36; J. Winram, *Violin Playing and Violin Adjustment* (Edinburgh, 1908), 34.

14 IV, 260.

15 II, 50.

16 V, 494. See also articles in *The Strad* quoted in C. Brown, 'Bowing Styles', 116.

17 *La Technique Supérieure de l'Archet* (Paris, 1927), quoted in Hauck, *Vibrato on the Violin*, 22. See also A. Rivarde, *The Violin and its Technique* (London, 1921), 28.

18 Quoted in Hauck, *Vibrato on the Violin*, 39.

19 *A Practical Guide to Violin-Playing* (London, 1913), 90.

20 *Modern Violin-Playing* (New York, 1920).

21 'Beauty of Tone in String Playing' (1938), reprinted in *My Viola and I* (London, 1974), 147–8. See also G. Stratton and A. Frank, *The Playing of Chamber Music* (London, 1935), 11.

22 C. Schroeder, *Handbook of Violoncello Playing* (Hamburg, 1889; English translation 1893), 167.

23 E. Van der Straeten, *Technics of Violoncello Playing* (London, 1894; 4th edn 1923), 135.

24 A. Broadley, *Chats to 'Cello Students*, 70 and 75.

25 D. Alexanian, *The Technique of Violoncello Playing* (Paris, 1922), 96–7.

26 G. Suggia, 'Violoncello Playing', *M&L* 2 (1921), 130–4.

27 H. Becker and D. Rynar, *Mechanik und Ästhetik des Violoncellspiels* (Vienna, 1929 reprinted 1971), 199–202.

28 J. Stutschewsky, *Das Violoncellspiel/ The Art of Playing the Violoncello* (Mainz, 1932–7), III, 1–3.

29 For example, W. C. Honeyman, *The Secrets of Violin Playing* (c. 1892), 55; J. Dunn, *Violin Playing*, 66; Joachim and Moser, *Violinschule*, II, 94; L. Auer, *Violin Playing as I Teach it*, 22–3; C. Schroeder, *Handbook*, 67; E. Van der Straeten, *Technics*, 135.

30 *A Modern School for the Violin* (London, 1899–1908), IIIA, viii.

31 *The Art of Violin Playing*, I, 36–9. A similar description of vibrato technique is given in A. Rivardè, *The Violin and its Technique* (London, 1921), 29.

32 See note 28.

33 *The Secrets of Violin Playing*, 55.

34 IV, 260.

35 *Violin Playing*, 22.

36 See note 25.

37 See note 27.

38 J. H. Allen, *The Technique of Modern Singing* (London, 1935), 64.

39 *Memoirs*, 30, 40.

40 A. Ysaÿe and B. Radcliffe, *Ysaÿe: His Life, Work and Influence* (London, 1947), 118.

41 J. MacLeod, *The Sisters d'Aranyi*, 42. See also A. Fachiri, letter in *M&L* 31 (1950), 283; C. Courvoisier, *The Technics of Violin Playing* (London, 1908, with preface by Joachim dated 1894), 107.

42 *Violin Playing*, 24.

43 *Memoirs*, 153–4.

44 See note 8.

5 WOODWIND VIBRATO

1 T. Boehm, *Die Flöte und das Flötenspiel* (Munich, 1871; English translation 1908), 30.

2 H. Berlioz, revised R. Strauss, *Instrumentationslehre* (Leipzig, 1904; English translation 1948), 227.

3 For example H. E. Atkins, *Boosey and Co's Complete Modern Tutor for Flute and Piccolo* (London, 1927); O. Langey, *Practical Tutor for the Flute* (revised edn London, 1934).

4 *Nicholson's Complete Preceptor for the German Flute* [1815], 22.

5 Article by H. C. Deacon, IV, 260.

6 Article by H. C. Colles, V, 494.

7 See, for example, C. Forsyth, *Orchestration* (2nd edn, London, 1935), 494; F. G. Rendall, 'English and Foreign Wood-Wind Players and Makers', *M&L* 12 (1931), 149.

8 N. Toff, *The Flute Book* (London, 1985), 101.

9 L. Taylor, 'The Englishmen's Wooden Flutes', *The Instrumentalist* (1951), reprinted in *Brass Anthology* (Evanston, Ill., 1974), 8.

10 H. M. Fitzgibbon, *The Story of the Flute* (London, 1914), 217–18.

11 P. Taffanel and L. Fleury, 'Flûte', in A. Lavignac (ed.), *Encyclopédie de la musique et dictionnaire du Conservatoire* (Paris, 1921–31), 2ème Partie, III, 1523.

12 A. Hennebains, quoted in M. Moyse, 'The Unsolvable Problem: Considerations on Flute Vibrato', *Woodwind Magazine* 7 (1950), 4, quoted in N. Toff, *The Flute Book*, 111.

13 P. Taffanel and P. Gaubert, *Méthode complète de la flûte* (Paris, 1923), 186, quoted in N. Toff, *The Flute Book*, 111.

14 'Expression Unconfined', *MQ* 30 (1944), 193, quoted in N. Toff, *The Flute Book*, 112–13.

15 *How I Stayed in Shape* (West Brattleboro, Vt., 1974), 5, quoted in N. Toff, *The Flute Book*, 107.

16 P. Bate, 'Oboe', *The New Grove Dictionary of Music and Musicians* (London, 1980) XIII, 469–71.

17 J. Sellner, *Theroretische-praktische Oboeschule* (Vienna, 1825, revised 2nd edn 1901).

18 A. Eaglefield-Hull (ed.), *A Dictionary of Modern Music and Musicians* (London, 1924), 356.

19 *Orchestral Wind Instruments* (London, 1920), 43.

20 Berlioz/Strauss, *Instrumentationslehre*, 183.

21 *The Orchestra and How to Write for it* (London, 1895), 39.

22 B. Wynne, *Music in the Wind* (London, 1967), 64.

23 A. Lavignac (ed.), *Encyclopédie*, 2ème Partie, III, 1542.

24 A. Eaglefield-Hull (ed.), *A Dictionary of Modern Music*, 364.

25 L. Goossens and E. Roxburgh, *Oboe* (London, 1977), 87; see also B. Wynne, *Music in the Wind*, 64–5.

26 A. Baines, *Woodwind Instruments and their History* (London, 1957; 3rd edn 1967), 121–3.

27 A. Gigliotti, 'The American Clarinet Sound', *The Instrumentalist* (1968), reprinted in *Woodwind Anthology* (Evanston, Ill., 1972), 341–2.

28 'English and Foreign Wood-Wind Players and Makers', 149.

29 *Les Instruments à vent* (Paris, 1948), 46.

30 *The Clarinet and Clarinet Playing* (New York, 1949), 246.

31 J. Weissenborn, *Praktische Fagott-Schule* (Leipzig, 1887).

32 M. Letellier and E. Flament, 'Le Basson', in A. Lavignac (ed.), *Encyclopédie*, 2ème Partie, III, 1595.

33 *Les Instruments à vent*, 58.

34 F. Corder, *The Orchestra and How to Write for it*, 44.

35 U. Daubeny, *Orchestral Wind Instruments*, 51–2.

36 M. Kennedy, *The Hallé Tradition* (Manchester, 1960), 222.

37 A. Baines, *Woodwind Instruments and their History*, 153.

38 W. Waterhouse, 'Bassoon', *The New Grove* II, 277.

6 SOLO PORTAMENTO

1 III, 18.

2 IV, 482.

3 *Violinschule*, II, 92.

4 *Violin Playing*, 24.

5 E. Van der Straeten, *Technics . . .*, 137–8.

6 H. Riemann, *Musik-Lexikon*, 611; Joachim and Moser, *Violinschule*, 93; J. Winram, *Violin Playing and Violin Adjustment*, 45; W. Ritchie, *Chats with Violinists or How to Overcome Difficulties* (London, c. 1916), 107; F. Thistleton, *The Art of Violin Playing* (London, 1924), 127–8.

7 *The Art of Violin Playing*, I, 30.

8 *Violinschule*, II, 92.

9 See note 5.

10 C. Courvoisier, *The Technics of Violin Playing*, 41, and H. Wessely, *A Practical Guide to Violin Playing*, 84.

11 *The Violin: How to Master It* (Newport, Fife, 5th edn 1892), 12.
12 *Violin Fingering, its Theory and Practice*, tr. B. Schwarz (London, 1966, but written before 1944), 365.
13 See note 5.
14 *Violin Playing* (London, 1898), 31.
15 *Violin Fingering, its Theory and Practice*, 365–6.
16 *Memoirs*, 336.
17 *A Practical Guide to Violin Playing*, 85–6.
18 I. M. Yampolsky, *Osnovi Skripichnoy Applikaturi* (*The Principles of Violin Fingering*) (Moscow, 1933; revised 3rd edn 1955, English translation 1967), 123.
19 *The Art of Violin Playing*, I, 30.
20 *A Practical Guide to Violin Playing*, 88.
21 E. Feuermann, ''Cello Playing: A Contemporary Revolution', *Violoncello Society Newsletter* (Spring 1972), 2, quoted in E. Cowling, *The Cello* (London, 1975), 172.
22 *Conversations with Casals*, 199.
23 D. Alexanian, *The Technique of Violoncello Playing*, 158–61.
24 *Ibid.*, 65–6.
25 See, for example, Lillian Littlehales, *Pablo Casals* (London, 1929), 189; Juliette Alvin, 'The Logic of Casals's Technique', *MT* 71 (1930), 1078–9; Flesch, *Memoirs*, 235–6.
26 H. Becker and D. Rynar, *Mechanik und Ästhetik des Violoncellspiels*, 193–5, and 114n.
27 J. Stutschewsky, *Das Violoncellspiel*, III, 114–15.
28 *Ibid.*, III, 117.
29 *Violinschule*, II, 92.
30 *Violin Fingering, its Theory and Practice*, 338.
31 *Memoirs*, 250.
32 A. Bachmann, *An Encyclopedia of the Violin* (New York, 1925), 209.
33 *Violin Playing*, 31.
34 *The Bel Canto with Particular Reference to the Singing of Mozart* (London, 1923), 30.
35 *Violin Playing as I Teach it*, 24.
36 *Memoirs*, 50.
37 See note 4.
38 *Grove II*, IV, 482–3.

7 ORCHESTRAL PORTAMENTO

1 A. Broadley, *Chats to 'Cello Students*, 43.
2 O. Cremer, *How to Become a Professional Violinist* (London, 1924), 62.
3 A. C. Boult, 'Casals as Conductor', *M&L* 4 (1923), 150.
4 J. Dunn, *Violin Playing*, 24.
5 J. F. Russell, 'Hamilton Harty', *M&L* 22 (1941), 218.
6 H. Welsh, 'Orchestral Reform', *M&L* 12 (1931), 23.
7 H. J. Wood, *The Gentle Art of Singing* (London, 1927), 87.
8 On the London Philharmonic's rehearsals, see A. Jefferson, *Sir Thomas Beecham*, (London 1979), 88; on the BBC Symphony Orchestra's rehearsals, see A. C. Boult, *My Own Trumpet* (London, 1973), 98–9 and elsewhere.
9 Carl Flesch writes of Mengelberg's 'unlimited rehearsals' in *Memoirs*, 228–9.

10 On Stokowski's objections to standardisation, see L. Stokowski, *Music for All of Us* (New York, 1943), 195, quoted in O. Daniel, *Stokowski: A Counterpoint of View* (New York, 1982), 291.

8 IMPLICATIONS FOR THE NINETEENTH CENTURY

Vibrato

1 L. Spohr, *Violinschule ... mit erlaeuternden Kupfertafeln* (Vienna [1832]); tr. C. Rudolphus as *Louis Spohr's Grand Violin School* (London [1833]), 1612.
2 L. Capet, *La Technique supérieure de l'archet* (Paris, 1927), 22.
3 P. M. F. de Sales Baillot, *L'Art du violon: nouvelle méthode* (Paris, 1834), quoted in Stowell, *Violin Technique and Performance Practice in the Late Eighteenth and Early Nineteenth Centuries* (Cambridge, 1985), 208.
4 Stowell, *Violin Technique*, 208–10. Stowell also discusses technical aspects of vibrato, and gives further examples from Spohr.
5 Hauck, *Vibrato on the Violin*, 17.
6 *Über Paganini's Kunst die Violine zu Spielen ...* (Mainz, 1839); English edition revised by C. E. Lowe [1915].
7 Letter in *M&L*, 31 (1950), 283.
8 C. de Bériot, *Méthode de violon* (Mainz [1858]), 242, quoted, with musical example, in C. Brown, 'Bowing Styles, Vibrato and Portamento in Nineteenth-Century Violin Playing', *JRMA* 113 (1988), 114–15. Brown also argues convincingly that the selective use of vibrato was widely implied in the nineteenth century by the short crescendo–diminuendo < > over a single note. As he says, 'this indication becomes virtually meaningless if every possible note has a vibrato'. *Ibid.*, 119.
9 H. Becker and D. Rynar, *Mechanik und Asthetik des Violoncellspiels*, 199–202.
10 F. A. Kummer, *Violoncellschule* Op. 60 (Leipzig, 1839), 30, quoted in J. Eckhardt, *Die Violoncellschulen von J. J. F. Dotzauer, F. A. Kummer und B. Romberg* (Regensburg, 1968), 122.
11 J. J. F. Dotzauer, *Violoncellschule* Op. 165 (Mainz, 1832), 47, *ibid.*, 122–3.
12 B. Romberg, *Méthode de violoncelle* (Berlin, 1840), 85, *ibid.*, 122–3.
13 J. L. Duport, *Essai sur le doigté du violoncelle et sur la conduite de l'archet* (Paris, c. 1810; tr. J. Bishop, London, 1853). A number of writers imply that vibrato used to be more fashionable in the late eighteenth century, for example, B. Romberg, *ibid.*, 85, quoted in E. Van der Straeten, *Technics*, 135; C. J. Smyth, *Six Letters on Singing, from a Father to his Son* (Norwich, 1817), 4; H. C. Koch, *Musikalisches Lexikon* (Frankfurt-am-Main, 1802), 'Bebung'.
14 C. Brown, 'Bowing Styles', 117–18.
15 L. P. Lochner, *Fritz Kreisler* (London, 1951), 19.
16 *Grove I*, IV, 167.
17 II, English translation collated with 1872 edition (New York, 1972), 149–51.
18 'Tremulousness' is criticised in S. Novello, 'Voice and Vocal Art', *MT* 9 (1859), 23, D. Crivelli, *L'Arte del Canto* (London [1841]), 7, and A. Costa, *Analytical Considerations on the Art of Singing* (London, 1838), 29. The occasional use of the effect is admitted by, among others, J. Molineux in *The Singer's Systematic Guide to the Science of Music* (London, 1831), 21–2, and observed in singers by Spohr in *Violinschule* (Vienna 1831), English translation, 161.

19 See, for example, H. Chorley, *Thirty Years' Musical Recollections* (London, 1862 reprinted 1972), 21; W. H. Daniell, *The Voice and How to Use it* (Boston, 1873), 53; C. Lunn, *The Philosophy of Voice* (10th edn London, 1906, based on articles published in 1873), 51, 170; C. Morell, *Modern Theoretical and Practical Singing Method* (London, 1910), 14.
20 H. M. Brown and S. Sadie (eds.), *Performance Practice: Music after 1600* (London, 1989), 453.
21 IV, 260.
22 H. C. Koch, rev. A. von Dommer, *Musikalisches Lexikon* (Heidelberg, 1865), 'Bebung'.
23 *Ibid.*
24 *Nicholson's Complete Preceptor for the German Flute* [1815], 22.
25 D. Charlton in H. M. Brown and S. Sadie (eds.), *Performance Practice* . . ., 253–5, 259, 410–11, 416–17.

Portamento
26 Spohr, *Violinschule*, 106.
27 *Ibid.*, 179.
28 *Ibid.*, 193.
29 *The Violin: How to Master It*, 12.
30 C. de Bériot, *Méthode de violon*, quoted, with further examples, in Clive Brown, 'Bowing Styles', 127.
31 *Méthode de violon*, 56.
32 Stowell, *Violin Technique*, 115.
33 *Ibid.*, 94–5.
34 *Ibid.*, 98–101.
35 *Nicholson's Complete Preceptor for the German Flute*, 21.
36 See Brown and Sadie (eds.), *Performance Practice* . . ., 253.
37 *Violoncellschule* Op. 165, quoted in J. Eckhardt, *Die Violoncellschulen*, 132.
38 *Violoncellschule*, 30, ibid., 132.
39 B. Romberg, *Méthode de violoncelle*, 85, ibid., 132.
40 J. L. Duport, *Essai sur le doigté*, 17–18.
41 *Ibid.*, 114.
42 *Ibid.*, 17–18.
43 See, for example, P. Pergetti, *A Treatise on Singing* (London [1850?]), 28; P. S. Agnelli, *New Method of Solfeggio and Singing* (London [c. 1855]), 11.
44 See W. Crutchfield in Brown and Sadie (eds.), *Performance Practice*, 295, 301.
45 *Garcia's Treatise on the Art of Singing* (London, 1857), 10.
46 See, for example, J. Molineux, *The Singer's Systematic Guide to the Science of Music*, para 244; L. Lablache, *A Complete Method of Singing* (London [1840]), 22; A. Panzeron, *Méthode complète de vocalisation pour mezzo-soprano* (Paris [1855]; English translation [1872]), 22–5; D. Corri, *The Singer's Preceptor* (London, 1810), 63.
47 P. F. Tosi, *Observations on the Florid Song* (Bologna, 1723; English translation by Galliard, London, 1743, reprinted 1905), 29.
48 E. T. Harris discusses the subject of slurs in the Baroque era, including this quotation from Tosi, but does not suggest that portamento might be implied. See Brown and Sadie (eds.), *Performance Practice*, 106–7.

Flexibility of tempo
49 O. Bie, *Das Klavier und seine Meister* (Munich, 1898), English translation *A History of the Pianoforte and Pianoforte Players* (London, 1899, reprinted 1966), 295–6.

50 Bülow, Hans von, in *The New Grove*, III, 452.

51 Review of Bülow's concerts in Vienna, December 1884, in E. Hanslick, *Music Criticisms 1846–99*, ed. H. Pleasants (revised edn London, 1963), 235.

52 *Über das Dirigieren* (Leipzig, 1869; English translation 1887, 4th edn 1940, revised 1972).

53 Quoted in *MT* 41 (1900), 158.

54 J. Szigeti, *A Violinist's Handbook* (London, 1964), 152.

55 J. Levin in *Die Musik* (1926), quoted in Joseph Szigeti, *Szigeti on the Violin* (London, 1969), 176.

56 Letter of 10 January 1870, quoted in William S. Newman, 'Freedom of Tempo in Schubert's Instrumental Music', *MQ* 61 (1975), 528.

57 A. Kullak, *The Aesthetics of Pianoforte-Playing* (Berlin, 1861; English translation New York, 1893, revised 1972), 280–94; M. Lussy, *Traité de l'expression musicale* (Paris, 1874; English translation London, 1885), 162–96; A. F. Christiani, *The Principles of Expression in Pianoforte Playing* (New York, 1885; revised 1974), 264–96.

58 L. Spohr, *Violinschule*, 179.

59 G. Kaiser (ed.), *Carl Maria von Weber, Sämmtliche Schriften* (Berlin, 1908), quoted in S. Morgenstern (ed.), *Composers on Music* (London, 1958), 100–1.

60 *The Singer's Preceptor* (London, 1810), 6.

61 E. Forbes (ed.), *Thayer's Life of Beethoven* (Princeton, 1967), 687–8, quoted in J. L. Stokes, 'Beethoven's Endorsements of Maelzel's Metronome', *Studies in Music* (London, Ontario), I (1976), 23–30.

62 A. Schindler, *Biographie von Ludwig van Beethoven* (3rd edn 1860), ed. D. W. McArdle as *Beethoven as I Knew Him* (London, 1966), 412.

63 Quoted in P. Badura-Skoda (ed.), Carl Czerny, *On the Proper Performance of all Beethoven's Works for the Piano* (Vienna, 1970), 3. See also W. S. Newman, *Performance Practice in Beethoven's Piano Sonatas* (London, 1972), 53–5.

64 Czerny, *ibid.*

65 Letter to his family, 14 July 1831, quoted in W. S. Newman, 'Freedom of Tempo in Schubert's Instrumental Music', *MQ* 61 (1975), 528.

66 *Traité complet de l'art du chant*, II (Paris, 1847; English translation New York, 1972), 71–3.

67 J. N. Hummel, *Ausführlich Theoretisch-Practische Anweisung zum Piano-forte Spiel* (Vienna, 1828), III, 40–1.

68 *Rode, Baillot & Kreutzer's Method of Instruction for the Violin* (English translation London, 1823), 21.

69 In O. Deutsch, *Schubert: Memoirs by his Friends*, quoted in W. S. Newman, 'Freedom of Tempo in Schubert's Instrumental Music', 528.

Tempo rubato

70 A. Eaglefield-Hull (ed.), *A Dictionary of Modern Music and Musicians*, 72.

71 A. Kullak, *The Aesthetics of Pianoforte-playing*, 280–94; M. Lussy, *Traité d'expression musicale*, 162–96; C. Engel, *The Pianist's Handbook* (London, 1853), 7, 64.

72 *The Principles of Expression in Pianoforte Playing*, 299–303.

73 Foreword to *Chopins Pianoforte-Werke*, ed. Mikuli (Leipzig [1880]), 3, quoted in F. Niecks, 'Tempo Rubato from the Aesthetic Point of View', 58. For other descriptions of Chopin's rubato, see J.-J. Eigeldinger, *Chopin vu par ses élèves* (Neuchâtel, 1970), English translation *Chopin: Pianist and Teacher as Seen by his Pupils* (Cambridge, 1988), 49–51.

74 M. Garcia, *Traité complet de l'art du chant*, II, 75–8. See also J. Jousse, *Introduction to the Art of Sol-fa-ing and Singing* (London [1815?]), 37; G. G. Ferrari, *A Concise Treatise on Italian Singing* (London, 1818), 20; and D. Corri, *The Singer's Preceptor*.

75 Baillot, *L'Art du violon: nouvelle méthode*, 136–7, quoted in R. Stowell, *Violin Technique*, 274.

76 Spohr, *Violinschule*, 183, 232.

77 Emily Anderson (ed.), *The Letters of Mozart and his Family* (London, 1938, 2nd edn 1966), I, 340.

78 L. Mozart, *Versuch einer Gründlichen Violinschule* (Augsburg, 1756, English translation, 2nd edn), 223–4.

79 *The Interpretation of the Music of the XVII and XVIII Centuries*, 277.

80 *Das Klavier und seine Meister*, 58.

81 With the obvious exception of jazz performance, which surely has valuable clues for students of historical rubato.

82 *The Interpretation of the Music of the XVII and XVIII Centuries*, 284.

Long and short notes

83 For comment on this and other examples, see G. Beechey, *Rhythmic Interpretation*, 247; F. Dawes in 'Schubert as Written and Performed: A Symposium', *MT* 104 (1963), 627.

84 See F. Chopin, *Complete Works*, ed. I. Paderewski, L. Bronarski, and J. Turczynski (Warsaw, 1949), I, 76, and VIII, 150.

85 F. Eibner, 'The Dotted-Quaver-and-Semiquaver Figure with Triplet Accompaniment in the Works of Schubert', *MR* 23 (1962), 281–8. See also 'Schubert as Written and Performed: A Symposium', 626–8; H. Ferguson, *Keyboard Interpretation from the 14th to the 19th century*, 97.

86 Facsimile of first page given in Franz Schubert, *Neue Ausgabe sämtlicher Werke*, (Kassel, 1970), Lieder, Ia, xxxiii.

87 J. Molineux, *The Singer's Systematic Guide to the Science of Music*, 236.

88 B. Romberg, *Méthode de Violoncelle*, 127, quoted in J. Eckhardt, *Die Violoncellschulen von J. J. F. Dotzauer, F. A. Kummer und B. Romberg*, 128.

89 Engel, *The Pianist's Handbook*, 150.

9 IMPLICATIONS FOR THE FUTURE

1 A. J. and K. Swan, 'Rachmaninoff: Personal Reminiscences', *MQ* 30 (1944), 11.

2 C. Reid, *John Barbirolli*, 24.

3 N. Bauer-Lechner, *Erinnerungen an Gustav Mahler*, 99.

4 *Corriere della Sera*, 27 December 1922, quoted in G. R. Marek, *Toscanini* (London, 1976), 129.

5 J. T. Carrodus, *How to Study the Violin* (London, 1895), 41.

6 L. Tetrazzini, *How to Sing* (London, 1923), 115.

7 A. Betti, 'Of Quartet-Playing', *M&L* 4 (1923), 2.

8 *MT* 71 (1930), 750.

9 Hugo Burghauser, chairman of the Vienna Philharmonic, interviewed in B. H. Haggin, *The Toscanini Musicians Knew* (2nd edn, New York, 1980), 154.

10 A. C. Boult, 'Casals as Conductor', 149–52.

11 *Memoirs*, 50–1.

12 *Style and Idea*, 345–7.
13 J. N. Moore, *Elgar on Record*, 194.
14 *Autobiography*, 157.
15 R. Craft (ed.), *Stravinsky: Selected Correspondence*, III, 258.
16 G. Kaiser (ed.), *Carl Maria von Weber, Sämtliche Schriften*, quoted in S. Morgenstern, *Composers on Music*, 100–1.
17 Stowell, *Violin Technique*, 208.
18 J. Molineux, *The Singer's Systematic Guide to the Science of Music*, 21–2.
19 J. J. Eigeldinger, *Chopin: Pianist and Teacher as seen by his Pupils*, 49.
20 See C. Brown, 'Bowing Styles', 117.

DISCOGRAPHY

――――――――― · ―――――――――

NOTE: This discography gives details and page references of all recordings mentioned in the text. The record numbers are those of the original 78 rpm records, except where LP or CD is specified. Where approximate dates are given, these are in most cases based on the date of the first review in *The Gramophone*.

Adam, *Giselle* (extracts)
Royal Opera House Orch., Lambert (rec. c. 1946) Col.   DX1270–1   124, 130

Albéniz, *Iberia*, 'El Corpus en Sevilla' (orch. Arbós)
Lamoureux Orch., Branco (rec. c. 1950) HMV   DB9462–5   134

J. C. Bach, Symphony in B flat, Op. 18 No. 2
Concertgebouw Orch., Mengelberg (rec. c. 1928, 1st and 2nd movts.) Col.   L2047
  127, 196

J. S. Bach, Mass in B minor
London Symphony Orch., Coates (rec. c. 1929) HMV   C1710–26   185

J. S. Bach, Brandenburg Concerto No. 1
Busch Chamber Players (rec. 1935) Col.   LX436–8   124, 189–90

J. S. Bach, Brandenburg Concerto No. 4
Berlin Philharmonic Orch., Melichar (rec. c. 1933) Decca   LY6069–71   117

J. S. Bach, Concerto in D minor for 2 Violins
Kreisler, Zimbalist, String Quartet (rec. 1915) HMV   DB587–8   106–7, 160–3
A. and A. Rosé (rec. c. 1930) HMV   D2014–6   160–3
Busch, Magnes, Busch Chamber Players (rec. 1945) Col.   71674–5D   160–3

J. S. Bach, Suite No. 2 in B minor
Chicago Symphony Orch., Stock (rec. c. 1929) HMV   D1673–4   85, 114, 199
Busch Chamber Players (rec. 1936) HMV   DB3015–7   85

J. S. Bach, Fantasia in C minor BWV 537 (arr. Elgar)
Royal Albert Hall Orch., Elgar (rec. 1926) HMV   HLM7107 (LP)   123

J. S. Bach, Italian Concerto
Gordon-Woodhouse (rec. c. 1927) HMV   D1281–2   60–1
Landowska (rec. 1935–6) HMV   DB5007–8   60–1

J. S. Bach, Partita No. 1 in B minor for Unaccompanied Violin, Sarabande
Huberman (rec. 1936) Col.   LX513   65

J. S. Bach, Partita No. 3 in E for Unaccompanied Violin, Gavotte
Burmester (rec. 1909) Pearl GEMMCD 9436 (CD)   65

J. S. Bach, Prelude in E flat minor (48 Preludes and Fugues, I, arr. Stokowski)
Philadelphia Orch., Stokowski (rec. 1927) HMV   D1464   198–9

J. S. Bach, Sonata No. 1 in G minor for Unaccompanied Violin, Adagio
Joachim (rec. 1903) HMV   047903   63–5, 88, 104, 158
Kreisler (rec. 1926) HMV   DB995   63–5, 158
Rosé (rec. c. 1931) HMV   D2016   63–5

J. S. Bach, Suite No. 6 in D for Unaccompanied Cello
Casals (rec. 1936–7) HMV   DB3674–7   65

Balakirev, Symphony No. 1
Philharmonia Orch., Karajan (rec. 1949) Col.   LX1323–8   130

Bartók, Concerto for Orchestra
Concertgebouw Orch., Van Beinum (rec. c. 1949) Decca   AK2042–6   127, 132, 136

Bartók, Suite Op. 14
Bartók (rec. 1929) HMV   AN468 (LP)   92

Beethoven, Piano Concerto No. 4
Backhaus, London Symphony Orch., Ronald (rec. c. 1930) HMV   DB1425–8   25
Schnabel, Chicago Symphony Orch., Stock (rec. 1942) Victor   11–8416–9   122–129
Backhaus, Vienna Philharmonic Orch., Schmidt-Isserstedt (rec. c. 1958)
    Decca   SXL2010 (LP)   25

Beethoven, *Ruins of Athens*, Overture
Casals Orch. of Barcelona, Casals (rec. 1932) HMV   D1728   136

Beethoven, Symphony No. 1
Philharmonic Symphony Orch. of New York, Mengelberg (rec. c. 1931)
    HMV   D1867–70   134

Beethoven, Symphony No. 3 ('Eroica')
Symphony Orch., Coates (rec. 1926) HMV   D1158–63   78–9
Vienna Philharmonic Orch., Weingartner (rec. 1936) Col.   LX532–7   23, 78–9, 126
NBC Symphony Orch., Toscanini (rec. 1939) HMV   DB5946–52   78–9
Boston Symphony Orch., Koussevitsky (rec. 1945) Victor   11–9796–801   78–9

Beethoven, Symphony No. 4
Hallé Orch., Harty (rec. c. 1927) Col.   L1875–9   130
Casals Orch. of Barcelona, Casals (rec. 1932) HMV   D1725–8   79–80, 132
BBC Symphony Orch., Toscanini (rec. 1939) HMV   DB3896–9   115, 130, 188–9

Beethoven, Symphony No. 5
Berlin Philharmonic Orch., Nikisch (rec. 1913) HMV   D89–92   30
Royal Albert Hall Orch., Ronald (rec. c. 1923) HMV   D665–8   135
Royal Philharmonic Orch., Weingartner (rec. 1927) Col.   L1880–3   123
Berlin State Opera Orch., Strauss (rec. 1928) Pol.   66814–7   30, 83
Hallé Orch., Barbirolli (rec. 1947) HMV   C3716–9   135

Beethoven, Symphony No. 6

BBC Symphony Orch., Toscanini (rec. 1937) HMV   DB3333–7   135

Colonne Orch., Paray (rec. c. 1935) Col.   DX655–9   114, 128, 134

Accademia di Santa Cecilia, Rome, De Sabata (rec. c. 1947) HMV   DB6473–7   117, 127, 132, 136

Vienna Philharmonic Orch., Furtwängler (rec. 1952) HMV ALP 1041 (LP)   136

Beethoven, Symphony No. 7

Philharmonic Symphony Orch. of New York, Toscanini (rec. 1936)
    HMV   DB2986–90   122, 129

Berlin Philharmonic Orch., Furtwängler (rec. 1943) DG   427775–2 (CD)   117

Philharmonia Orch., Galliera (rec. c. 1950) Col.   DX1697–701   115

Beethoven, Symphony No. 8

Vienna Philharmonic Orch., Schalk (rec. c. 1928) HMV   D1481–3   79

Vienna Philharmonic Orch., Weingartner (rec. 1936) Col.   LX563–5   79

Beethoven, Violin Concerto

Kreisler, Berlin State Opera Orch., L. Blech (rec. 1926) HMV   DB990–5   16–17, 132, 136

Szigeti, Symphony Orch., Walter (rec. 1932) Col.   LX174–8   16–17

Huberman, Vienna Philharmonic Orch., Szell (rec. 1936) LX509–13   16–17, 132, 136

Kreisler, London Philharmonic Orch., Barbirolli (rec. 1936) DB2927–32S   16–17, 130

Kulenkampff, Berlin Philharmonic Orch., Schmidt-Isserstedt (rec. 1936)
    Telef. E2016–21   16–17

Heifetz, NBC Symphony Orch., Toscanini (rec. 1940) DB5724–8S   16–17, 129, 134

Menuhin, New Philharmonia Orch., Klemperer (rec. 1966) HMV   ASD2285 (LP)   16–17

I. Oistrakh, Vienna Symphony Orch., D. Oistrakh (rec. c. 1971) RCA   GL25005 (LP)   16–17

Szeryng, Concertgebouw Orch., Haitink (rec. 1973) Phil.   6500 531 (LP)   16–17

Grumiaux, Concertgebouw Orch., C. Davis (rec. 1974) Phil.   6500 775 (LP)   16–17

Zukerman, Chicago Symphony Orch., Barenboim (rec. c. 1977) DG   2530 903 (LP)   16–17

Beethoven, Quintet for Piano and Wind

Wolff, Members of Berlin Philharmonic Orch. (rec. c. 1933) Decca   LY6072–4   132, 136

Beethoven, String Quartet in F minor, Op. 95

Busch Quartet (rec. 1932) HMV   DB1799–80   87

Beethoven, String Quartet in C sharp minor, Op. 131

Busch Quartet (rec. 1936) HMV   DB2810–4   169–71

Beethoven, Violin Sonata in A, Op. 47 ('Kreutzer')

Sammons, Murdoch (rec. 1927) Col.   9352–6   18

Thibaud, Cortot (rec. 1929) HMV   DB1328–31   18

Huberman, Friedman (rec. c. 1930) Col.   LX72–5   18

Kulenkampff, Kempff (rec. 1934) Decca   CA8207–10   18

Y. and H. Menuhin (rec. c. 1935) HMV   DB2409–12   18

Kreisler, Rupp (rec. 1936) HMV   DB3071–4   18

Szigeti, Bartók (rec. 1940) Philips AL3524 (LP)   18

Busch, Serkin (rec. 1941) Col.   71344–7D   18

Szigeti, Arrau (rec. 1944) SRV302 (LP) 18
Heifetz, Smith (rec. 1960) RCA RB1627 (LP) 18
Menuhin, Kempff (rec. 1970) DG 2530 135 (LP) 18
Perlman, Ashkenazy (rec. 1973) Decca SXL6632 (LP) 18

Beethoven, Violin Sonata in G, Op. 96
Fachiri, Tovey (rec. c. 1928) NGS114–7 62, 88

Beethoven, Piano Sonata in C minor, Op. 13 ('Pathétique')
Lamond (rec. 1926) HMV DB2955–60 61–2

Beethoven, Piano Sonata in B flat, Op. 106 ('Hammerklavier')
Schnabel (rec. 1935) HMV DB2955–60 90–1

Berlioz, *Harold in Italy*
Primrose, Boston Symphony Orch., Koussevitsky (rec. 1944) HMV DB6261–5 122

Berlioz, *Romeo and Juliet* (extracts)
Colonne Orch., Pierné (rec. c. 1930) Odeon 123526–7 121

Berlioz, Symphonie Fantastique
Hallé Orch., Barbirolli (rec. c. 1947) Col. C3563–7 115, 124, 130

Bizet, *Carmen*, Act IV, Prelude ('Aragonaise')
Orch. of La Scala, Milan, Toscanini (rec. 1921) Victor 839 127

Bizet, Symphony in C
London Philharmonic Orch., Goehr (rec. c. 1938) HMV C2986–9 124, 125
London Philharmonic Orch., Munch (rec. c. 1948) Decca AK1781–4 124

Borodin, *In the Steppes of Central Asia*
Paris Conservatoire Orch., Gaubert (rec. c. 1929) Col. L2219 128

Brahms, Academic Festival Overture
Concertgebouw Orch., Mengelberg (rec. 1930) Col. LX58–9 84

Brahms, Piano Concerto No. 2
Serkin, Philadelphia Orch., Ormandy (rec. c. 1946) Col. LX1276–81 190, 201–2
Solomon, Philharmonia Orch., Dobrowen (rec. 1947) HMV C3610–5 190–1

Brahms, Symphony No. 1
London Symphony Orch., Weingartner (rec. 1924) Col. L1596–1600 123
Berlin State Opera Orch., Klemperer (rec. 1928) Parl. E10807–12 24
Philadelphia Orch., Stokowski (rec. c. 1928) HMV DB2874–8 24, 121
London Symphony Orch., Weingartner (rec. 1939) Col. LX883–7 115, 124
NBC Symphony Orch., Toscanini (rec. 1941) HMV DB6124–8 114, 122, 202
Vienna Philharmonic Orch., Furtwängler (rec. 1947) HMV DB6634–9 117, 132
Philharmonia Orch., Klemperer (rec. c. 1958) HMV SAX2262 (LP) 24
London Symphony Orch., Stokowski (rec. 1972) Decca PFS4305 (LP) 24

Brahms, Symphony No. 2
Royal Albert Hall Orch., Ronald (rec. c. 1925) HMV D871–4 181–3
Philadelphia Orch., Stokowski (rec. 1930) HMV D1877–82 182, 198–9
New York Symphony Orch., Damrosch (rec. 1928) Col. L2151–5 182, 200–1

Berlin Philharmonic Orch., M. Fiedler (rec. 1931) Decca   CA8004–8   23, 182, 191
London Philharmonic Orch., Beecham (rec. 1936) Col.   LX515–9   23, 182, 187
London Philharmonic Orch., Weingartner (rec. 1940) Col.   LX899–903   23
Royal Philharmonic Orch., Beecham (rec. 1956–9) HMV   HQS1143 (LP)   23
Vienna Philharmonic Orch., Kertesz (rec. 1964) Decca   SXL6172 (LP)   23
Cleveland Orch., Maazel (rec. 1976) Decca   D39D4 (LP)   23

Brahms, Symphony No. 3
Philadelphia Orch., Stokowski (rec. 1928) HMV   D1769–73   129
Vienna Philharmonic Orch., Krauss (rec. c. 1931) HMV   C2026–9   117, 192–3
Vienna Philharmonic Orch., Walter (rec. 1936) HMV   DB2933–6   192–3
Berlin Philharmonic Orch., Furtwängler (rec. 1949) Unicorn   WFS4 (LP)   117, 126, 132

Brahms, Symphony No. 4
London Symphony Orch., Abendroth (rec. c. 1927) HMV   D1265–70   130
BBC Symphony Orch., Walter (rec. 1934) HMV   DB2253–7   115
Berlin Philharmonic Orch., De Sabata (rec. 1939) Decca   LY6171–6   84

Brahms, Tragic Overture
BBC Symphony Orch., Toscanini (rec. 1937) HMV   DB3349–50   22, 188–9
NBC Symphony Orch., Toscanini (rec. 1953) RCA   LM7026–1 (LP)   22

Brahms, Variations on a Theme by Haydn
Philharmonic Symphony Orch. of New York, Toscanini (rec. 1936)
   HMV   DB3031–2   22–3, 85
NBC Symphony Orch., Toscanini (rec. 1952) RCA   RB16092 (LP)   22–3

Brahms, Violin Concerto
Szigeti, Hallé Orch., Harty (rec. 1928) Col.   L2265–9   123
Menuhin, BBC Symphony Orch., Boult (rec. 1943) BBC Recording   124
Heifetz, Boston Symphony Orch., Koussevitsky (rec. 1939) HMV   DB5738–42S   129
Neveu, Philharmonia Orch., Dobrowen (rec. 1946) HMV   DB6415–9   124

Brahms, Clarinet Quintet
Kell, Busch Quartet (rec. 1937) HMV   DB3383–6   130

Brahms, Hungarian Dance No. 1 in G minor, arr. violin and piano
Joachim (rec. 1903) HMV   O47907   87–8, 104
Auer (rec. 1920) Pearl GEMMCD   9436 (CD)   87–8

Brahms, Violin Sonata in A, Op. 100
Busch, Serkin (rec. 1932) HMV   DB1805–6   88–9

Bruckner, Symphony No. 4
Dresden State Opera Orch., Böhm (rec. 1936) HMV   DB4450–7   24
Vienna Philharmonic Orch., Böhm (rec. 1972) Decca   6BB171–2 (LP)   24

Chopin, Piano Concerto No. 2
Rubinstein, London Symphony Orch., Barbirolli (rec. 1931) HMV   DB1494–7   135

Chopin, Barcarolle
Rubinstein (rec. 1928) HMV   DB1161   25
Rubinstein (rec. 1962) RCA   RB6683   25

Chopin, Etude in C minor Op. 10 No. 12 ('Revolutionary')
Cortot (rec. 1933) HMV   DB2029   91

Chopin, Mazurka in C sharp minor, Op. 63 No. 3
Rachmaninoff (rec. 1923) RCA   AVM3-0260 (LP)   51–4
Pachmann (rec. c. 1928) HMV   DB1106   51–4
Paderewski (rec. 1930) HMV   DB1763   51–4

Chopin, Nocturne in E flat, Op. 9 No. 2
Paderewski (rec. 1930) HMV   DB1763   55–7
Drdla (rec. 1903, arr. violin and piano) HMV   47929   155–6
Sarasate (rec. 1904, arr. violin and piano) Opal   804 (LP)   104, 155–6
Weist Hill (rec. c. 1915, arr. cello and piano) Pearl   GEM105 (LP)   165–8
Casals (rec. 1926, arr. cello and piano) HMV   DB966   165–8
Feuermann (rec. c. 1938) Col.   LX719   165–8

Chopin, Nocturne in F sharp, Op. 15 No. 2
d'Albert (rec. c. 1916) Grammophon   65562   56–7
Gaubert (rec. 1918–19, arr. flute and piano) Pearl   GEMM302 (LP)   113

Chopin, Nocturne in D flat, Op. 27 No. 2
Pachmann (rec. c. 1925) HMV   DB860   55–7

Chopin, Polonaise in A flat, Op. 53
Rubinstein (rec. 1935) HMV   DB2497   25–6
Rubinstein (rec. 1964) RCA   SB6640 (LP)   25–6

Chopin, Piano Sonata No. 3 in B minor
Grainger (rec. 1925) Col.   L1695–7   19–20, 57–9
Cortot (rec. 1933) HMV   DA1333–6   19–20, 57–9
Rosenthal (rec. 1939) RCA VIC   1209 (LP)   57–9
Lipatti (rec. 1947) Col.   LX994–6   19–20
Kempff (rec. c. 1959) Decca   SXL2025 (LP)   19–20
Rubinstein (rec. 1959/1961) RCA   SB2151 (LP)   19–20
Perahia (rec. c. 1974) CBS   76242 (LP)   19–20
Barenboim (rec. c. 1975) HMV   ASD3064 (LP)   19–20
Ax (rec. c. 1975) RCA   ARL1 1030 (LP)   19–20

Chopin, Waltz in A flat, Op. 42
Rachmaninoff (rec. 1919) Edison   82202   91–2

Cimarosa, *Matrimonio Segreto*, Overture
Milan Symphony Orch., Molajoli (rec. c. 1929) Col.   9695   117

Debussy, Nocturnes
Royal Albert Hall Orch., Ronald (rec. c. 1925, No. 2) HMV   D1000   135
Berlin State Opera Orch., Klemperer (rec. 1926) Pol.   66565   84
Philadelphia Orch., Stokowski (rec. c. 1928, No. 2) HMV   E507   84
Colonne Orch., Pierné (rec. c. 1928) Odeon   123642–3 and 123668   84
Paris Conservatoire Orch., Gaubert (rec. c. 1929, Nos. 1 and 2) Col.   9656–7   84, 114, 121, 134, 194–5
Paris Conservatoire Orch., Coppola (rec. c. 1939) HMV   DB5066–8   84, 114, 134, 194–5

Elgar, Overture, 'In the South'
London Symphony Orch., Elgar (rec. 1930) HMV   DB1665–7   82, 84

Elgar, Symphony No. 1
London Symphony Orch., Elgar (rec. 1930) HMV   DB4225–30   26–7
Philharmonia Orch., Barbirolli (rec. 1963) HMV   ASD540 (LP)   26–7
London Philharmonic Orch., Boult (rec. 1967) Lyrita   SRCS39 (LP)   26–7
London Philharmonic Orch., Solti (rec. c. 1972) Decca   SXL6569 (LP)   26–7
London Philharmonic Orch., Barenboim (rec. c. 1974) CBS   76247 (LP)   26–7

Elgar, Variations on an Original Theme ('Enigma')
Royal Albert Hall Orch., Elgar (rec. 1926) HMV   D1154–7   28, 36, 81–2, 130, 183–4
Hallé Orch., Harty (rec. 1932) Col.   DX322–5   81–2, 183–4
BBC Symphony Orch., Boult (rec. 1936) HMV   DB2800–2   81–2, 183, 187
Hallé Orch., Barbirolli (rec. 1947) HMV   C3692–5   81–2, 183, 190

Elgar, Violin Concerto
Hall, Symphony Orch., Elgar (rec. 1916, cut) HMV   D79–80   163–4
Sammons, New Queen's Hall Orch., Wood (rec. 1929) Col.   L2346–51   163–4, 186–7
Menuhin, London Symphony Orch., Elgar (rec. 1932) HMV   DB1751–6   163–4, 186–7

Fauré, Pavane
Paris Conservatoire Orch., Munch (rec. c. 1948) Decca   K1644   134, 194–5

Franck, *Psyché*
Lamoureux Orch., Wolff (rec. c. 1935) Decca   CA8192–3   121, 128

Franck, Symphony in D minor
New Queen's Hall Orch., Wood (rec. c. 1924) Col.   L1569–72   123

Gluck, *Orphée et Eurydice*, 'Dance of the Blessed Spirits'
Barrère (rec. c. 1916) Pearl   GEMM284 (LP)   113
Paris Symphony Orch., Cohen (rec. 1929) Col.   DX60   114
Philharmonic Symphony Orch. of New York, Toscanini (rec. c. 1930) HMV   D1784   113

Grieg, *Peer Gynt*, Suite No. 1
Vienna Symphony Orch., Kerby (rec. c. 1934) Col.   DB1268–9   117

Handel, Concerto Grosso, Op. 6 No. 12
Boston Symphony Orch., Koussevitsky (rec. c. 1937, 2nd movt.) HMV   DB3010   199

Haydn, Symphony No. 39
Vienna Symphony Orch., Sternberg (rec. c. 1952) Parl.   SW8145–6   126

Haydn, Symphony No. 88
Vienna Philharmonic Orch., Krauss (rec. c. 1931) HMV   E539–41   191–2

Haydn, Symphony No. 101 ('The Clock')
Hallé Orch., Harty (rec. c. 1928) Col.   L2088–91   185
Philharmonic Symphony Orch. of New York, Toscanini (rec. 1929)
  HMV   D1668–71   185, 200–1
NBC Symphony Orch., Toscanini (rec. 1946–7) Victor   12–1130–3   185, 202

Holst, *The Planets* ('Mars')
London Symphony Orch., Holst (rec. 1926) Col.   L1528   31, 82
BBC Symphony Orch., Boult (rec. 1945) HMV   DB6227   31

D'Indy, Symphonie sur un chant montagnard
Darré, Lamoureux Orch., Wolff (rec. c. 1932) Decca   CA 8123–5   121
M. Long, Colonne Orch., Paray (rec. c. 1935) Col.   LX362–4   121

Joachim, Romance in C   •
Joachim (rec. 1903) HMV   047906   104, 157

Mahler, *Das Lied von der Erde*
Vienna Philharmonic Orch., Walter (rec. 1936) Col.   ROX165–701   117

Mahler, Symphony No. 4
Philharmonic Symphony Orch. of New York, Walter (rec. 1946) Col.   LX949–54   201–2

Mendelssohn, Overture 'Hebrides'
BBC Symphony Orch., Boult (rec. c. 1934) HMV   DB2100   25
BBC Symphony Orch., Boult (rec. c. 1960) BBC Recording   25

Mozart, Bassoon Concerto
Camden, Hallé Orch., Harty (rec. c. 1927) Col.   L1824–6   135

Mozart, Divertimento in D, K. 251, 3rd movement
Hallé Orch., Turner (rec c. 1943) Col.   DX1128   124

Mozart, *Magic Flute*, Overture
Royal Philharmonic Orch., Beecham (rec. c. 1950) HMV   DB21023   135

Mozart, Piano Concerto in G, K. 453
Dohnányi, Budapest Philharmonic Orch. (rec. c. 1928) Col.   L2215–8   117, 127, 136
E. Fischer and his Chamber Orch. (rec. 1937) HMV   DB3362–4   91

Mozart, Serenade in G, K. 525 ('Eine kleine Nachtmusik')
Barbirolli's Chamber Orch., Barbirolli (rec. c. 1929) HMV   C1655–6   80
Vienna Philharmonic Orch., Walter (rec. 1936) HMV   DB3075–6   192–3

Mozart, Sinfonia Concertante, K. 297b
Berlin Philharmonic Orch., Konoye (rec. c. 1937) Col.   LX661–4S   126

Mozart, Symphony No. 29 in A
Boston Symphony Orch., Koussevitsky (rec. c. 1942) HMV   DB5957–8   201–2

Mozart, Symphony No. 35 in D ('Haffner')
Philharmonic Symphony Orch. of New York, Toscanini (rec. 1929) HMV   D1782–4   22
NBC Symphony Orch., Toscanini (rec. 1946) Victor   11–9901–3   22

Mozart, Symphony No. 40 in G minor
Berlin State Opera Orch., Strauss (rec. c. 1926) Pol.   95442–5   20–1
Royal Opera House Orch., Sargent (rec. c. 1928) HMV   C1347–9   20–1
Berlin State Opera Orch., Walter (rec. c. 1930) Col.   DX31–3   20–1
London Philharmonic Orch., Koussevitsky (rec. c. 1935) HMV   DB2343–5   20–1
London Philharmonic Orch., Beecham (rec. 1937) Col.   LX656–8   20–1

London Philharmonic Orch., Kleiber (rec. c. 1950) Decca LX3022 (LP)   20–1
London Symphony Orch., Krips (rec. c. 1953) Decca ACL128 (LP)   20–1
London Symphony Orch., C. Davis (rec. 1961) Philips 835113AY (LP)   20–1
Columbia Symphony Orch., Walter (rec. c. 1963) CBS SBRG72138 (LP)   20–1
English Chamber Orch., Britten (rec. 1968) HMV ASD2424 (LP)   20–1
Berlin Philharmonic Orch., Karajan (rec. 1971) HMV ASD2732 (LP)   20–1
Vienna Philharmonic Orch., Böhm (rec. 1977) DG 2530780 (LP)   20–1

Mozart, Clarinet Quintet
C. Draper, Lener Quartet (rec. 1928) Col. L2252–5   130

Mozart, Flute Quartet in D, K. 285
Le Roy, International Trio (rec. c. 1928) NGS 112–3   113

Mozart, String Quartet in G, K. 387
Lener Quartet (rec. c. 1930) Col. LX24–7   113, 171

Mozart, String Quartet in D minor, K. 421
Lener Quartet (rec. c. 1927) Col. L1965–7   67–9, 86
Flonzaley Quartet (rec. c. 1928) HMV DB1357–8   67–9, 86

Mozart, String Quartet in E flat, K. 428
Pro Arte Quartet (rec. c. 1937) HMV DB2820–2   87

Mozart, Violin Sonata in A, K. 526
Catterall, Harty (rec. c. 1924) Col. L1494–6   88
Y. and H. Menuhin (rec. 1933) HMV DB2057–8   88

Mozart, Piano Sonata in D, K. 576
K. Long (rec. c. 1929) NGS 129–30   21
E. Joyce (rec. c. 1941) Col. DX1011–2   21

Mozart, Rondo in A minor, K. 511
Schnabel (rec. 1946) HMV DB6298   90

Poulenc, Caprice in C ('D'après le final du bal masqué')
Poulenc (rec. c. 1932) Col. LFX266   92

Rachmaninoff, Piano Concerto No. 2 in C minor
Rachmaninoff, Philadelphia Orch., Stokowski (rec. 1929) HMV DB1333–7
  28–9, 54, 134

Rachmaninoff, Rhapsody on a Theme of Paganini
Rachmaninoff, Philadelphia Orch., Stokowski (rec. 1934) HMV DB2426–8   54, 92

Rachmaninoff, Prelude in G minor, Op. 23 No. 5
Rachmaninoff (rec. 1920) HMV DB410   90
Lhevinne (rec. 1921) International Piano Archive IPA117   90

Ravel, *Boléro*
Concertgebouw Orch., Mengelberg (rec. c. 1930) Col. LX48–9   117, 132
Lamoureux Orch., Ravel (rec. 1932) Pol. 66947–8   114, 134

Ravel, *Ma mère l'oye*
New York Symphony Orch., Damrosch (rec. c. 1928) Col.   9516–8   134

Respighi, *Pines of Rome*
Milan Symphony Orch., Molajoli (rec. c. 1929) Col.   5310–3   132

Rossini, *William Tell*, Overture
Berlin State Opera Orch., Melichar (rec. c. 1933) Pol.   24155–6   126

Rossini, *Tancredi*, Overture
Royal Opera House Orch., Bellezza (rec. c. 1930) HMV   C1998   115, 123

Rossini, *William Tell*, 'Ah! Mathilde' (arr. oboe and piano)
G. Gillet (rec. 1905) Odeon   36252   121

Roussel, *Petite Suite*
Paris Conservatoire Orch., Munch (rec. c. 1948) Decca   K1643–4   128

Schubert, Symphony No. 8 ('Unfinished')
New Queen's Hall Orch., Wood (rec. c. 1927) Col.   L1791–3   115, 130

Schubert, Symphony No. 9
London Symphony Orch., L. Blech (rec. c. 1928) HMV   D1390–5   78
Hallé Orch., Harty (rec. c. 1928) Col.   L2079–85   78
BBC Symphony Orch., Boult (rec. c. 1935) HMV   D2415–20   78, 124
London Symphony Orch., Walter (rec. c. 1938) HMV   DB3607–12   78
Philadelphia Orch., Toscanini (rec. 1941) RCA   RB6549 (LP)   78, 129
Vienna Philharmonic Orch., Karajan (rec. c. 1949) Col.   LX1138–43   78, 193

Schubert, *Ave Maria*
McCormack, Kreisler (rec. 1914) HMV   02543   176–8
Schumann (rec. 1934) HMV   DB2291   176–8
Gigli (rec. 1947) HMV   DB6619   176–8
Heifetz (rec. 1926, arr. Wilhelmj) HMV   DB1047   176–8
Menges (rec. c. 1927, arr. Wilhelmj) HMV   D1313   176–8
Huberman (rec. c. 1929, arr. Wilhelmj) Col   LX155   176–8
Zimbalist (rec. c. 1931, arr. Wilhelmj) Col.   9671   176–8

Schubert, Impromptu in A flat, D. 935 No. 2
Paderewski (rec. 1926) HMV   DB1037   89–90
Pouishnoff (rec. c. 1928) Col.   9400   89–90
E. Fischer (rec. 1938) HMV   DB3483–6   89–90
Schnabel (rec. 1950) HMV   DB21500   89–90

Schubert, Impromptu in B flat, D. 935 No. 3
Paderewski (rec. 1924) HMV   DB833   49–51, 89–90
E. Fischer (rec. 1938) HMV   DB3483–6   49–51, 89–90
Schnabel (rec. 1950) HMV   DB21611   49–51, 89–90

Sibelius, *Swan of Tuonela*
Philadelphia Orch., Stokowski (rec. 1929) HMV   D1997   122
Philadelphia Orch., Ormandy (rec. c. 1941) HMV   DB5832   122

Sibelius, Symphony No. 2
Boston Symphony Orch., Koussevitsky (rec. 1935) HMV   DB2599–604   121, 134
Boston Symphony Orch., Koussevitsky (rec. 1950) RCA   VIC1186 (LP)   134

Sibelius, Symphony No. 5
London Symphony Orch., Kajanus (rec. 1932) HMV   DB1739–42   33–4

Sibelius, Symphony No. 7
BBC Symphony Orch., Koussevitsky (rec. 1933) HMV   DB1984–6   34–5

Smetana, String Quartet No. 1 in E minor
Bohemian Quartet (rec. 1928) Pol.   95076–9   168–9

Spohr, Violin Concerto No. 9 in D minor, second movement
Soldat-Roeger (rec. c. 1920) Masters of the Bow   MB1019 (LP)   157–8

R. Strauss, *Don Juan*
Royal Philharmonic Orch., Walter (rec. c. 1928) Col.   L2067–8   135
Berlin State Opera Orch., Strauss (rec. 1929) Decca   CA8126–7   30–1, 83, 117, 126
Dresden State Opera Orch., Böhm (rec. 1938) HMV   DB4625–6   30–1, 117, 126, 132, 136

Stravinsky, *Firebird*, Suite
[Straram Orch.], Stravinsky (rec. 1928) Col.   L2279–82   82–3
London Philharmonic Orch., Ansermet (rec. c. 1947) Decca   K1574–7   130, 135

Stravinsky, *Petrushka*
[Straram Orch.], Stravinsky (rec. 1928) Col.   L2173–5   31–3, 36, 83, 194–5
London Symphony Orch., Coates (rec. 1927–8) HMV   D1521–4   31–3
Danish Radio Orch., Malko (extracts, rec. 1933) Danacord   DACO135 (LP)   31–3
Philadelphia Orch., Stokowski (rec. 1937) HMV   DB3511–4   31–3, 134
Columbia Symphony Orch., Stravinsky (rec. 1960) CBS   78307 (LP) 31–3

Stravinsky, *Rite of Spring*
[Straram Orch.], Stravinsky (rec. 1929) Col.   LX119–23   36, 134

Tchaikovsky, *Romeo and Juliet*
Concertgebouw Orch., Mengelberg (rec. 1930) Col.   LX55–6   127
Boston Symphony Orch., Koussevitsky (rec. 1936) HMV   DB3165–7   122

Tchaikovsky, *Sleeping Beauty* (extracts)
Royal Opera House Orch., Lambert (rec. c. 1946) Col.   DX1281–2   115

Tchaikovsky, *Swan Lake* (extracts)
Royal Opera House Orch., Rignold (rec. c. 1949) HMV   C3822–3   135

Tchaikovsky, Symphony No. 5
Concertgebouw Orch., Mengelberg (rec. 1928) Col.   L2176–82   136, 195–6
Philharmonia Orch., Kletzki (rec. c. 1946) Col.   LX969–74   135

Tchaikovsky, Symphony No. 6
New Queen's Hall Orch., Wood (rec. c. 1924) Col.   L1489–90   135
Boston Symphony Orch., Koussevitsky (rec. c. 1931) HMV   D1923–7   114, 129, 134
Berlin Philharmonic Orch., Furtwängler (rec. 1938) HMV   DB4609–14   193
Philharmonic Symphony Orch. of New York, Rodzinski (rec. 1944)
    Col.   DX1205–9   129, 134

INDEX

———————— · ————————

Printed in the United States
24074LVS00001B/193-198